The New Strong-Willed Child

THE NEW STRONG-WILLED CHILD

Birth Through Adolescence

DR. JAMES DOBSON

TYNDALE HOUSE PUBLISHERS, INC.
WHEATON, ILLINOIS

Visit Tyndale's exciting Web site at www.tyndale.com

Designed by Zandrah Maguigad

This book is a completely revised edition of *The Strong-Willed Child,* first published in 1978 by Tyndale House Publishers, Inc.

Library of Congress Cataloging-in-Publication Data

Dobson, James C., date.
  The new strong-willed child : birth through adolescence / James C. Dobson.
    p. cm.
  Rev. ed. of: The strong-willed child, 1978.
  Includes bibliographical references.
  ISBN: 0-8423-3622-2 (hc)
  1. Child rearing.   2. Discipline of children.   3. Child psychology.   I. Dobson, James C., date. Strong-willed child.
II. Title
  HQ772.D58 2004
  649′.1—dc22   2004005986

ISBN: 1-4143-0281-9 (International Edition)

THIS BOOK IS AFFECTIONATELY DEDICATED TO MY OWN LATE MOTHER, *who was blessed with a brilliant understanding of children. She intuitively grasped the meaning of discipline and taught me many of the principles I've described on the following pages. And, of course, she did an incredible job raising me, as everyone can plainly see today. But I've always been puzzled by one troubling question: Why did my fearless mother become such a permissive pushover the moment we made her a grandmother?*

CONTENTS

FOREWORD

IN 1978, when the first edition of *The Strong-Willed Child* was published, I had recently made a dramatic career move. I had resigned from the faculty of the University of Southern California School of Medicine where I had been an associate clinical professor of pediatrics for a number of years. My decision to leave this rewarding position resulted from an increasing awareness that the institution of the family was rapidly deteriorating—and that I needed to do what I could to help. Thus, I left my secure nest to create a humble little nonprofit outfit called Focus on the Family and began a radio program heard initially on thirty-four stations. Frankly, I wondered if the phone would ever ring.

More than twenty-five years later, the radio program and its derivatives are heard by 220 million people each day on 7,300 radio stations located in 122 countries around the world. The staff consists of 1,400 members, who are also committed to the preservation of the family. Upwards of 200,000 listeners and readers call or write to us each month, many of whom are asking questions about how to raise healthy, well-adjusted kids. Today, when I meet these moms and dads whose lives we have touched through the years, some of them smile and tell me stories about their children, some hug me, and some get teary eyed. Many will say, "Thank you for helping me raise my kids." Being able to assist these special folks through the child-rearing years has provided one of the greatest satisfactions of my life, both personally and professionally.

One of the first writing projects I tackled after leaving academia in 1977 was the original version of the book you hold. As the title indicates, it focused on the basic temperaments of boys and girls and what influences them to do what they do. Of particular interest to me is a characteristic I call "the strength of the will." Some kids seem to be born with an easygoing, compliant nature that makes them a joy to raise. As infants they don't cry very often; they sleep through the night from the second week; they goo at their grandparents; they smile while being diapered; and they are very patient when dinner is overdue. And, of course, they never spit up on the way to church. During later childhood, they love to keep their room clean and they especially like doing their homework. There aren't many of these supercompliant children, I'm afraid, but they are known to exist in some households (though they didn't in ours).

Just as surely as some children are naturally compliant, others seem to be defiant upon exit from the womb. They come into the world smoking a cigar and yelling about the temperature in the delivery room and the incompetence of the nursing staff and the way the doctors are running things. Long before their children are born, mothers of strong-willed children know there is something different going on inside, because their babies have been trying to carve their initials on the walls. In infancy, these children fairly bristle when their bottle is late and demand to be held throughout the day. Three o'clock in the morning is their favorite "playtime." Later, during toddlerhood, they resist all forms of authority and their greatest delights include "painting" the carpet with Mom's makeup or trying to flush the family cat down the toilet. Their frustrated parents wonder where they went wrong and why their child-rearing experience is so different from what they had expected. They desperately need a little coaching about what to do next.

That was the basic premise of my book back in 1978. But the years since then have passed very quickly, and the tough-as-nails kids about whom I was writing are now grown, having made the breathless journey from babyhood to adolescence and on into adulthood. Most of them now have strong-willed children of their own, which is rather humorous to contemplate. As kids, they gave their parents fits, but now the chickens have come home to roost. These new moms and dads are getting their just desserts, and they deserve everything their kids are doing to rattle their nerves. Their parents, to whom I addressed the original book, are likely to be grandparents now who have probably evolved into permissive pushovers just as my marvelous mom did when we made her a grandmother. And so the cycle of life continues, generation by generation, with each family member playing a prearranged part that feels entirely new, but which is actually rooted in antiquity.

It is with relish, therefore, that I return to this subject, which has been a lifelong fascination. Nearly 3 million copies of *The Strong-Willed Child* have sold in dozens of languages, but it became clear to me recently that the time had come to revise the manuscript. A wealth of new information has come to light since I first put my thoughts on paper (yes, on paper—I wrote the original manuscript with pencils on yellow pads, resulting in sheets that were taped together to produce a scroll that sometimes exceeded fifty feet. Inexplicably, I didn't get into the computer thing until the twentieth century was almost over).

But why did this book need to be retooled more than twenty-five years downstream? It is certainly not because the nature of children has changed since the seventies. Kids are kids and always will be. It is rather because the scientific understanding of inborn temperaments in little people is far greater now than it was two or three decades ago. Some of the more recent insights have come from careful research in the field of child development, and I will share those conclusions with you presently. For example, research on attention deficit/hyperactivity disorder (ADHD), or "hyperactivity," as it was previously called, was in its infancy when I first sat down to write. Little was known about the disorder in those days, much less how to deal with it. Given this and other newer developments, it is time to reconsider the strong-willed child and how best to raise him or her. Far from contradicting my basic thesis, however, the intervening years have only served to validate the principles I described as a young psychologist and professor.

The other reason I set about revising *The Strong-Willed Child* is because I've now had many more years to work with families and to compare the approaches that succeed with those that clearly do not. Those experiences have been interwoven into the fabric of this edition, in hopes that they will be of help and encouragement to today's parents and for generations to come. Who knows? Maybe the testy boys and girls who are challenging their parents today will grow up to read these words in the distant future, searching desperately for advice about handling their own bratty little kids. I hope so.

Let's begin by acknowledging that rearing boys and girls can be a difficult assignment, especially today when the culture is battling mightily with parents for the hearts and minds of their kids. To bring them up properly requires the wisdom of Solomon and the determination of an Olympic champion. Admittedly, the job looks much easier than it is in reality. Overconfident parents, particularly those who are new to the responsibility, remind me of a man watching the game of golf for the first time. He thinks, *This is going to be simple. All you have to do is hit that little white ball out there in the direction of the flag.* He then steps up to the tee, draws back his club, and dribbles the "little white ball" about nine feet to the left. *Maybe,* he says to himself, *I ought to swing harder. That's what Tiger Woods does.* But the more he hacks at the ball, the farther into the rough he goes. So it is with child rearing. There are sand traps and obstacles everywhere for parents who are blessed with strong-willed kids. What those moms and dads need is a well-designed "game plan" for the inevitable challenges they will face at home. Without such a plan, they will find themselves muddling through by trial and error.

Consider the experience of a friend of mine, who was a recreational pilot when he was younger. On one occasion, he flew his single-engine plane toward his home base at a small country airport. Unfortunately, he waited too long to start back and arrived in the vicinity of the field as the sun dropped behind a mountain. By the time he maneuvered his plane into position to land, he could not see the hazy runway below. There were no lights to guide him and no one on duty at the airport. He circled the field for another attempt to land, but by then the darkness had become even more impenetrable. For two desperate hours, he flew his plane around and around in the blackness of the night, knowing that probable death awaited him when he ran out of fuel. Then as greater panic gripped him, a miracle occurred. Someone on the ground heard the continuing drone of his engine and realized his predicament. That merciful man drove his car back and forth on the runway to show my friend the location of the airstrip. Then he let his lights cast their beam from the far end while the plane landed.

I think of that story now when I am descending at night in a commercial airliner. As I look ahead, I can see the green lights bordering the runway that tell the captain where to direct the plane. If he stays between those lighted boundaries, all will be well. But disaster lies to the left and to the right.

So it is with this challenging task of child rearing. What parents need are some runway lights—some reliable markers—that will illuminate the safe region between extremes. Two of those guiding principles are, quite simply, *love* and *control*. If they are understood and implemented properly by moms and dads, the relationship with their children is likely to be healthy—despite inevitable mistakes and shortcomings. But beware! It is often very difficult to balance love and control when dealing with a strong-willed child. The temptation is to tilt beyond one of the two boundaries—toward white-hot anger and oppressiveness, or toward permissiveness and disengagement. Why? Because the constant battles that these tougher kids precipitate can cause a parent to become a screamer and a tyrant or one who lets the child rule pathetically. There is danger for a youngster on either side of the "runway." If the parental plane comes down wide or short, it will bump through the cornfield with unpredictable consequences. We'll talk more about that presently.

The purpose of this book, then—both the original version and this revision—is to provide these and other understandings that will contribute to competent parenthood. We will deal specifically with the subject of discipline as it relates to the independent youngsters who are more challenging to raise.

Suffice it to say at this point that the rewards for doing a good job of parenting are worth all the blood, sweat, and tears that are invested in it. Although my children are now grown, the way they have turned out is the most satisfying accomplishment of my life. You can be sure I'll say more about that in pages to come.

Well, let's get started. It is my hope that this discourse will help illuminate the runway for those parents trying to pilot their children through the darkness.

James Dobson

James C. Dobson, Ph.D.

ONE

THE WILD & WOOLLY WILL

A T ONE TIME, the Dobson household consisted of a mother and a father, a boy and a girl, one hamster, one parakeet, one lonely goldfish, and two hopelessly neurotic cats. We all lived together in relative harmony with a minimum of conflict and strife. But there was another member of our family who was less congenial and cooperative. He was a stubborn, twelve-pound dachshund named Sigmund Freud (Siggie), who honestly believed that he owned the place. All dachshunds tend to be independent, I'm told, but Siggie was a confirmed revolutionary. He was not vicious or mean; he just wanted to run things—and the two of us engaged in a power struggle throughout his lifetime.

Siggie was not only stubborn, but he wouldn't pull his own weight in the family. He wouldn't bring in the newspaper on cold mornings; he refused to chase a ball for the children; he didn't keep the gophers out of the garden; and he didn't do any of the usual tricks that most cultured dogs perform. Alas, Siggie refused to engage in any of the self-improvement programs that I initiated on his behalf. He was content just to trot through life, watering and sniffing and barking at everything that moved.

Sigmund was not even a good watchdog. This fact was confirmed the night we were visited by a prowler who entered our backyard at three o'clock in the morning. I suddenly awoke from a deep sleep, got out of bed, and felt my way through the house without turning on the lights. I knew someone was on the patio and Siggie knew it too, because the coward was crouched behind me! After listening to the thumping of my heart for a few minutes, I reached out to take hold of the rear doorknob. At that moment, the backyard gate quietly opened and closed. Someone had been standing three feet from me and that someone was now tinkering in my garage. Siggie and I held a little conversation in the darkness and decided that he should be the one to investigate the disturbance. I opened the back door and ordered my dog to "Attack!" But Siggie had just had one! He stood there throbbing and shaking so badly that I couldn't even push him out the back door. In the noise and confusion that ensued, the intruder escaped (which pleased both dog and man).

Please don't misunderstand me: Siggie was a member of our family and we loved him dearly. And despite his anarchistic nature, I did finally teach him to obey a few simple commands. However, we had some classic battles before he reluctantly yielded to my authority. The greatest confrontation occurred when I had been in Miami for a three-day conference. I returned to observe that Siggie had become boss of the house while I was gone. But I didn't realize until later that evening just how strongly he felt about his new position as captain.

At eleven o'clock that night, I told Siggie to go get into his bed, which was a permanent enclosure in the family room. For six years, I had given him that order at the end of each day, and for six years Siggie had obeyed. On that occasion, however, he refused to budge. He was in the bathroom, seated comfort-

ably on the furry lid of the toilet seat. That was his favorite spot in the house, because it allowed him to bask in the warmth of a nearby electric heater. Incidentally, Siggie had to learn the hard way that it was extremely important that the *lid be down* before he left the ground. I'll never forget the night he learned that lesson. He came thundering in from the cold and sailed through the air—and nearly drowned before I could get him out.

On the night of our great battle, I told Sigmund to leave his warm seat and go to bed. Instead, he flattened his ears and slowly turned his head toward me. He braced himself by placing one paw on the edge of the furry lid, then hunched his shoulders, raised his lips to reveal the molars on both sides, and uttered his most threatening growl. That was Siggie's way of saying, "Get lost!"

I had seen this defiant mood before and knew that I had to deal with it. The only way to make Siggie obey was to threaten him with destruction. Nothing else worked. I turned and went to my closet and got a small belt to help me "reason" with 'ol Sig. My wife, who was watching this drama unfold, told me that as soon as I left the room, Siggie jumped from his perch and looked down the hall to see where I had gone. Then he got behind her and growled.

When I returned, I held up the belt and again told the angry dog to get into his bed. He stood his ground so I gave him a firm swat across the rear end, and he tried to bite the belt. I popped him again and he tried to bite me. What developed next is impossible to describe. That tiny dog and I had the most vicious fight ever staged between man and beast. I fought him up one wall and down the other, with both of us scratching and clawing and growling. I am still embarrassed by the memory of the entire scene. Inch by inch I moved him toward the family room and his bed. As a final desperate maneuver, Siggie jumped on the couch and backed into the corner for one last snarling stand. I eventually got him into his bed, but only because I outweighed him two hundred to twelve!

The following night I expected another siege of combat at Siggie's bedtime. To my surprise, however, he accepted my command without debate or complaint and simply trotted toward the family room in perfect submission. In fact, Siggie and I never had another "go for broke" stand.

It is clear to me now that Siggie was saying on the first night, in his canine way, "I don't think you're tough enough to make me obey." Perhaps I seem to be humanizing the behavior of a dog, but I think not. Veterinarians will confirm that some breeds of dogs, notably dachshunds and shepherds, will not accept the leadership of their masters until human authority has stood the test of fire and proved itself worthy. I got that message across to Siggie in one decisive encounter, and we were good friends for the rest of his life.

This is not a book about the discipline of dogs. But there is an important aspect of my story that is highly relevant to the world of children. Just as surely as a dog will occasionally challenge the authority of his leaders, a child is inclined to do the same thing, only more so. This is no minor observation, for it represents a characteristic of human nature that has escaped the awareness of many experts who write books on the subject of discipline. When I wrote twenty-five years ago, there was hardly a text for parents or teachers that adequately acknowledged the struggle—the confrontation of wills—that strong-willed children seem to love. For them, adult leadership is rarely accepted unchallenged; it must be tested and found worthy before it is respected. It is one of the frustrating aspects of child rearing that most parents have to discover for themselves.

THE HIERARCHY OF STRENGTH AND COURAGE

But why do some children, particularly those who are strong-willed, have such a pugnacious temperament? One of the simplistic answers (there is a more complete explanation in chapter 3) is that it reflects the admiration boys and girls have for strength and courage. They will occasionally disobey parental instructions for the precise purpose of testing the determination of those in charge. Why? Because they care deeply about the issue of "who's toughest." This helps explain the popularity of superheroes—Robin Hood and Tarzan and Spider-Man and Superman—in the folklore of children. It also explains why they often brag, "My dad can beat up your dad!" (One child said in response, "That's nothing, my mom can beat up my dad too!")

Whenever a youngster moves into a new neighborhood or a new school district, he usually has to fight (either verbally or physically) to establish himself in the hierarchy of strength. This respect for power and courage also makes children want to know how tough their leaders are. Thus, whether you are a parent, a grandparent, a Scout leader, a bus driver, or a schoolteacher, I can guarantee that sooner or later, one of the children under your authority will clench his little fist and take you on. Like Siggie at bedtime, he will say with his manner: "I don't think you are tough enough to make me obey." You had better be prepared to prove him wrong in that moment, or the challenge will happen again and again.

This defiant game, which I call Challenge the Chief, can be played with surprising skill by very young children. A father told me of taking his three-year-old daughter to a basketball game. The child was, of course, interested in everything in the gym except the athletic contest. Dad permitted her to roam free and climb on the bleachers, but he set definite limits regarding how far she could stray. He took her by the hand and walked with her to a stripe painted on the gym floor. "You can play all around the building, Janie, but don't go past this line," he instructed her. He had no sooner returned to his seat than the toddler scurried in the direction of the forbidden territory. She stopped at the border for a moment, then flashed a grin over her shoulder to her father, and deliberately placed one foot over the line as if to say, "Whatcha gonna do about it?" Virtually every parent the world over has been asked the same question at one time or another.

The entire human race is afflicted with the same tendency toward willful defiance that this three-year-old exhibited. Her behavior in the gym is not so different from the folly of Adam and Eve in the Garden of Eden. God had told them they could eat anything in the Garden except the forbidden fruit ("do not go past this line"). Yet they challenged the authority of the Almighty by deliberately disobeying His commandment. Perhaps this tendency toward self-will is the essence of original sin that has infiltrated the human family. It certainly explains why I place such stress on the proper response to willful defiance during childhood, for that rebellion can plant the seeds of personal disaster. The weed that grows from it may become a tangled briar patch during the troubled days of adolescence.

When a parent refuses to accept his child's defiant challenge, something changes in their relationship. The youngster begins to look at his mother and father with disrespect; they are unworthy of her allegiance. More important, she wonders why they would let her do such harmful things if they really loved her. The ultimate paradox of childhood is that boys and girls want to be led by their parents but insist that their mothers and fathers earn the right to lead them.

On behalf of those readers who have never experienced such a confrontation, let me describe how a determined kid is typically constructed. At birth he looks deceptively like his more compliant sibling. He weighs seven pounds and is totally dependent on those who care for him. Indeed, he would not survive for more than a day or two without their attention. Ineffectual little arms and legs dangle aimlessly in four directions, appearing to be God's afterthoughts. What a picture of vulnerability and innocence he is!

Isn't it amazing, given this beginning, what happens in twenty short months? Junior then weighs twenty-five pounds and he's itching for action. This kid who couldn't even hold his own bottle less than two years earlier now has the gall to look his two-hundred-pound father straight in the kisser and tell him where to get off? What audacity! Obviously, there is something deep within his soul that longs for control. He will work at achieving it for the rest of his life.

When our children were young, we lived near one of these little spitfires. He was thirty-six months old at the time and had already bewildered and overwhelmed his mother. The contest of wills was over. He had won it. His sassy talk, to his mother and anyone else who got in his way, was legendary in the neighborhood. Then one day my wife watched him ride his tricycle down the driveway and into the street, which panicked his mother. We lived on a curve and the cars came around that bend at high speed. The woman rushed out of the house and caught up with her son as he pedaled down the street. She took hold of his handlebars to redirect him, and he came unglued.

"Get your dirty hands off my tricycle!" he screamed. His eyes were squinted in fury. As Shirley watched in disbelief, this woman did as she was told. The life of her child was in danger, yet this mother did not have the courage to make him obey her. He continued to ride down the street while she trailed along behind, hoping for the best.

How could it be that a tiny little boy at three years of age was able to buffalo his thirty-year-old mother in this way? Clearly, she had no idea how to manage him. He was simply tougher than she—and they both knew it. This mild-mannered woman had produced an iron-willed youngster who was willing to fight with anyone who tried to run him in, and you can be sure that his mom's physical and emotional resources were continually drained by his antics. We lost track of this family, but I'm sure this kid's adolescent years were something to behold.

A LESSON IN A SUPERMARKET

In thinking about the characteristics of compliant and defiant children, I sought an illustration to explain the vastly differing thrusts of human temperaments. I found an appropriate analogy in a supermarket. Imagine yourself in a grocery store, pushing a cart up the aisle. You give the basket a small shove, and it glides at least nine feet out in front and then comes to a gradual stop. You walk along happily tossing in the soup and ketchup and loaves of bread. Grocery shopping is such an easy task, for even when the cart is burdened with goods, it can be directed with one finger.

But buying groceries is not always so blissful. On other occasions, you select a cart that ominously awaits your arrival at the front of the market. When you push the stupid thing forward, it tears off to the left and knocks over a stack of bottles. Refusing to be outmuscled by an empty cart, you throw all your weight behind the handle, fighting desperately to keep the ship on course. It seems to have a mind of its own as it darts toward the eggs and careens back in the direction of a terrified grandmother in green tennis shoes. You are trying to do the same shopping assignment that you accomplished with ease the week before, but the job feels more like combat duty today. You are exhausted by the time you herd the contumacious cart toward the checkout counter.

What is the difference between the two shopping baskets? Obviously, one has straight, well-oiled wheels that go where they are guided. The other has crooked, bent wheels that refuse to yield.

Do you get the point? We might as well face it; some kids have crooked wheels! They do not want to go where they are led, because their own inclinations take them in other directions. Furthermore, the parent who is pushing the cart must expend seven times the energy to make it move, compared with the parent of a child with straight wheels. (Only mothers and fathers of strong-willed children will fully comprehend the meaning of this illustration.)

But how is the strength of the will distributed among children? My original assumption was that this aspect of human temperament is represented by a typical bell-shaped curve. In other words, I presumed that a relatively small number of very compliant kids appeared at one end of the continuum and an equally small number of defiant youngsters were represented at the other. The rest, comprising the majority, were likely to fall somewhere near the middle of the distribution, like this:

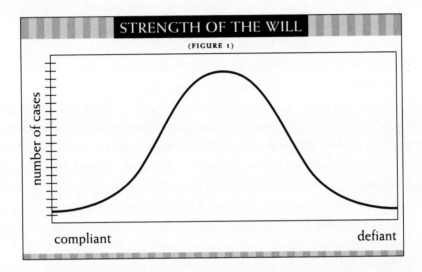

However, having talked to at least 100,000 harried parents, I'm convinced that my supposition was wrong. The true distribution probably looks more like this:

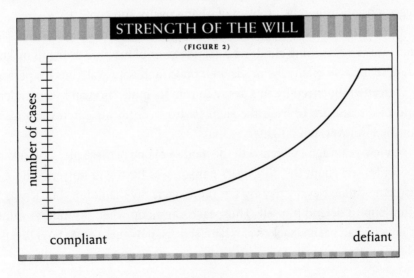

Don't take this observation too literally. Maybe it only *seems* that the majority of toddlers are confirmed anarchists. Furthermore, there is a related phenomenon regarding sibling relationships that I have never been able to explain. When there are two children in the family, one is likely to be compliant and the other defiant. Who knows why it works out that way. There they are, born to the same parents, but as different as though they came from different planets. One cuddles to your embrace and the other kicks you in the navel. One is a natural sweetheart and the other goes through life like hot lava. One follows orders and the other gives them. Quite obviously, they are marching to a different set of drums.

Former U.S. president Franklin Roosevelt was clearly a strong-willed child and grew up to be a very strong-willed man. When he was a boy, he once strung a string across the top of the stairs where it could not be seen. Predictably, his nurse came along carrying a supper tray and tripped, making what must have been a spectacular plunge downward. The record does not reveal what punishment he received for this wicked trick. We are told, however, that Franklin was very bossy with his peers and that he liked to win at everything. When he was once scolded for the way he treated other children, he said, "Mummie, if I didn't give the orders, nothing would happen."[1] *That* is a strong-willed child.

Temperamental differences often create serious relational problems within the family. The strong-willed child faces constant discipline and is subjected to many threats and finger-wagging lectures, while his angelic brother, little Goody Two-shoes, polishes his halo and soaks up the warmth of parental approval. They are pitted against each other by the nature of their divergent personalities and may spend a lifetime scratching and clawing one another. (Chapter 9 offers specific suggestions regarding the problem of sibling rivalry and conflict.)

I have described the approach to life taken by the tougher kids. Let's look quickly at the easygoing child, who spends most of his time trying to make his parents happy. In reality, he needs their praise and approval; thus his personality is greatly influenced by this desire to gain their affection and recognition. A word of displeasure or even the slightest frown from his parents can disturb him. He is a lover, not a fighter.

A few years ago I talked with the mother of one of these pleasant kids. She was concerned about the difficulties her son was having in nursery school. He was being bullied every day by the more aggressive children, but it was not within him to defend himself. Thus, each afternoon when his mother came to get him, he had been whacked and harassed again by these other boys. Even the girls were joining in the fun.

"You must defend yourself!" his mother said again and again. "Those other children will keep hitting you until you make them stop!"

Each day she urged her little lover to be more assertive, but it contradicted his nature to do so. Finally, his frustration became so great that he began reaching for the courage to follow his mother's advice. As they rode to school one morning he said, "Mom! If those kids pick on me again today, I'm—I'm—I'm going to beat them up! Slightly."

How does one beat up someone else "slightly"? I don't know, but it made perfect sense to this compliant child. He didn't want to use any more force than was absolutely necessary to survive. Why? Because he had a peace-loving nature. His parents didn't teach it to him. It was rooted deep within his psyche.

I must make it clear that the compliant child is not necessarily wimpy or spineless. That fact is very important to our understanding of his nature and how he differs from his strong-willed sibling. The distinction between them is not a matter of confidence, willingness to take risks, sparkling personalities, or other desirable characteristics. Rather, the issue under consideration here is focused on the strength of the will—on the inclination of some children to resist authority and determine their own course, as compared with those who are willing to be led. It is my supposition that these temperaments are prepackaged before birth and do not have to be cultivated or encouraged. They will make themselves known soon enough.

By the way, there is another category of temperaments in children that some parents will recognize instantly. These kids are not really strong-willed—at least, their assertiveness is not expressed in the same way. The distinction here is not one of independence and aggressiveness. It is a matter of tactics. They rarely challenge the authority of their parents or teachers in a stiff-necked manner, but they are willful nonetheless. I call them "sneaky." Adults think these youngsters are going along with the program, but inside, there's subversion afoot. When no one is looking, they break the rules and push the limits. When caught, as inevitably they are, they may lie or rationalize or seek to hide the evidence. The appropriate approach to these sneaky kids is not appreciably different from handling the strong-willed child. Sooner or later, his or her self-will can be expected to break into the open, usually during early adolescence. Then it's "Katie, bar the door."

I'll close this introductory chapter by offering two more observations for parents who are raising strong-willed children. First, it is very common for these moms and dads to feel great guilt and self-condemnation. They are trying so hard to be good parents, but the struggle for control that goes on at home day after day leaves them frustrated and fatigued. No one told them that parenthood would be this difficult, and they blame themselves for the tension that arises. They had planned to be such loving and effective parents, reading fairy tales by the fireplace to their pajama-clad angels, who would then toddle happily off to bed. The difference between life as it is and life as it ought to be is distressing. We'll talk more about that presently.

Second, I have found that the parents of compliant children don't understand their friends with defiant youngsters. They intensify guilt and embarrassment by implying, "If you would raise your kids the way I do mine, you wouldn't be having those awful problems." May I say to both groups that willful children can be difficult to manage even when parents handle their responsibilities with great skill and dedication. It may take several years to bring such a youngster to a point of relative obedience and cooperation within the family unit, and indeed a strong-willed child will be a strong-willed individual all her life. While she can and must be taught to respect authority and live harmoniously with her neighbors, she will always have an assertive temperament. That is not a bad thing. It simply "is." During the childhood years, it is important for parents not to panic. Don't try to "fix" your tougher boy or girl overnight. Treat that child with sincere love and dignity, but require him or her to follow your leadership. Choose carefully the matters that are worthy of confrontation, then accept her challenge on those issues and win decisively. Reward every positive, cooperative gesture she makes by offering your attention, affection, and verbal praise. Then take two aspirin and call me in the morning.

Well, that is the subject of our discussion. In the chapters to come, we will explore ways of leading the toughie, approaches to discipline at each age level, reasons why he is the way he is, and many other aspects of child rearing. There's so much to share.

Before pressing on, however, let me give you an update on our little dachshund, Siggie, whom people still ask me about. This delightful dog lived for seventeen years and gave our family so much pleasure, despite his revolutionary tendencies. Shortly before he died, some teenagers drove through our neighborhood at three o'clock in the morning and tossed a hapless pup out of their car. She showed up at our front door the next morning, scared, hungry, and lost. We didn't want another dog at the time, even though Siggie had seen his better days. We were especially disinterested in owning a cur whose daddy had been a traveling man. Nevertheless, we couldn't bring ourselves to take her to the pound. While we were trying to find her another home, we fell head over heels in love with this gentle, vulnerable animal that our daughter named Mindy.

Mindy grew to become the most beautiful, noble dog I've ever owned. She simply had no will of her own, except to do the bidding of her masters. Probably because of the unknown horrors of her puppyhood, she could not stand any expression of displeasure on my part. If scolded, she would jump in my lap and hide her eyes in the crook of my arm. Her only wish was to be with her human companions. Many times as I sat reading or studying at my desk, Mindy would quietly slip in beside me and rest her head on my knee. I'll tell you, I'm a sucker for any living thing with that kind of need. When forced to stay outside, Mindy would sit and stare at us through the family-room window. My wife would get uncomfortable with the dog's pleading brown eyes focused on her every move, so she actually pulled down the shades. Then Shirley would mutter in exasperation, "Mindy, get a life!"

An incident occurred several years later that illustrated Mindy's sweet nature. Our family had gone on a two-week vacation and left her alone in the backyard. A neighbor boy came by once each day to feed her and give her fresh water. Thus, her physical needs were met, but we underestimated the loneliness she must have experienced throughout those fourteen days. Why else would

this forty-pound dog have gone into our garage and dug through the boxes of toys that our children, Danae and Ryan, had outgrown? She found the stuffed animals that had long since been discarded and brought them one at a time to her bed near the house. When we arrived home, Mindy was lying on her blanket with eight of these furry friends arranged in front of her.

I know! I know! No dog deserves the affection our family bestowed on this ol' hound, and some of my readers will think it foolish. For my part, however, I believe God designed this species specifically for companionship and devotion to man. (Who knows why the Lord made cats?) Surprisingly, it is believed that the death rate for people who have lost a spouse is 500 percent lower the first year for those who own a dog. Take my advice: If you need something to love, go to the nearest pound and look for a furry little pup who'll think you're the neatest boss in the world! That's what Mindy thought about the Dobsons.

But, alas, this beautiful animal is also gone. My wife, Shirley, called her one day and she failed to come. That had never happened before. We found her lying by the side of the house where she had fallen. Mindy died of lymphoma that had spread throughout her body. And so ended a twelve-year love affair between a devoted dog and her affectionate masters. Good-bye, gentle friend.

I have shared these two dog stories, describing Siggie and Mindy, to illustrate the difference in temperaments between the two animals we have loved. One of them was determined to run the world and the other was deliriously happy just to be part of the family. They represented opposite ends of the canine universe.

Well, I hope the analogy is clear. In this book, we're focusing not on dogs but on the varied and infinitely complex personalities of children. We'll talk in subsequent chapters about what those temperaments mean for parents and how that understanding helps us raise our children properly.

(By the way, I was only kidding when I asked why God created cats. It was a joke. Honest. I didn't mean it. Please don't write and say hateful things to me. Like Mindy, I can't stand to be criticized.)

TWO

MOTHERS SHARE THEIR STORIES

There was a little girl,
Who had a little curl,
Right in the middle of her forehead.
When she was good,
She was very good indeed,
But when she was bad, she was horrid.[1]

TO BETTER UNDERSTAND the nature of strong-willed children (and I am referring now to those who are *very* strong-willed), I invited several parents into the Focus on the Family radio studio a few years ago to discuss their experiences in child rearing. What resulted was an enlightening, and sometimes tearful, discussion of these tough-as-nails kids and what it was like dealing with them on a daily basis. If you are not yet convinced that such youngsters exist or that leading them successfully can be one of life's great challenges, then read on. I think the recollections of the moms you're about to meet will be insightful and helpful. What follows is a transcript of the interchange that occurred in our studio during a two-hour dialogue.

JCD: First, we are pleased to welcome Debra Merritt, mother of four children. She brought her seventeen-year-old strong-willed daughter, Lizz, with her today, and I'm anxious to get her perspective. Also with us is Kristen

NOTE: *This transcript was edited somewhat to transform the imprecise "spoken language" into the more readable "written language," while being faithful to the context.*

Walker, who has four children. And, finally, Joy Solomon is here, who is a homemaker with two grown kids. These three moms have raised ten children between them, and they learned some valuable lessons along the way.

Let me begin by providing the background for this program. Shirley and I went to Alabama for a visit several years ago, and while there, we were invited to have lunch with about twenty people. We happened to be seated across from Joy and her husband, Davey, whom we had never met. Immediately, the four of us found common ground. Joy, what do you remember about that lunch?

Joy: Well, our conversation started when you said, "Hi, I'm Jim," as if we wouldn't recognize that voice immediately. I said, "Well, I'm Joy, but I'm surprised you don't remember me because you lived with us for a while." You said, "I did?" I said, "Yes, for about three years when we were really struggling with our strong-willed child." Then you said, "Oh, you have one of those." I said, "Yes," and you asked how old he was. I said, "Well, it's a she and she is now nineteen and doing very well, but we had some dark days along the way—no, we had some very, very dark days back then.

JCD: That is the reason I asked you to be here today, Joy, because you are the quintessential mother of a strong-willed child. You experienced many of the frustrations that I have written about through the years, including guilt, self-condemnation, and self-doubt.

Joy: All of them.

JCD: How soon after your daughter was born did you know that she was going to be hard to handle?

Joy: I think she slept through the night at maybe fifteen months old. At eighteen months old, you could tell her no and she would fall on the floor, throw a fit, and roll around. We would sit and watch her for a while because we weren't going to give in. We were going to be strong. She would stand up, and she would have that beautiful angelic face, and she would say, "I'm sorry." She would come over and lay her head in my lap, and then she would bite me. That was the first clue because it was a manipulation. She made sure that you weren't worried about what she was going to do, and then she would bite. She was very, very tough.

JCD: Does she know that you're here today?

Joy: Yes, she does. She has given her permission for me to tell this story. We've been on a difficult journey. When you combine a keen intelligence with our daughter's strong will, and especially when her spirit turned more defiant at sixteen, we were in a world of hurt.

JCD: Now, Joy, I really want you to help folks who have never dealt with a very strong-willed child begin to understand. There are some families with four or six kids, and none of them have a defiant temperament like we are describing. Their children are generally happy, cooperative, and obedient. Such moms and dads are inclined to assume that parents who struggle to maintain control at home are just weak or ineffective. Sometimes that is an accurate assessment, but in other cases, the difficulties result from the nature of a particular child. You need to help people grasp how difficult it can be to raise a defiant youngster. Your daughter didn't simply disobey occasionally. Every child does that. You were in a war of wills with Dana almost from the very earliest moments of life.

Joy: Yes. I remember a key time for us was when she was five years old and she was a physically strong child. There was an episode where she had been out throwing rocks at cars. I called her in and I said, "Dana, why were you throwing rocks at cars?" She said, "Well, I did warn them. I told them they didn't belong on my street. As they went down the road I told them if they came back by, that I'd have to throw a rock at their car. So I threw rocks at them."

I said, "We live on a cul-de-sac. Where were they going?" She had that look that she would give you when you just really weren't understanding what she was saying, and she said, "That's not my fault." What she did was entirely understandable to her. It wasn't her fault that someone had built the street that way. I took her in to spank her and she said, "You're not going to spank me. I'm going to wait until my daddy gets home." Well, you've met Davey. He is a large man.

She knew the longer she could put off a spanking, the longer she had to work up her defense. I said, "No, I'm going to spank you now." She said, "No, you're not. You will not spank me." I said, "Yes, I will." That day, I think, was a terrifying day because I physically could not control her. She threw every ounce of strength and determination into fighting me. It was a battle that probably lasted an hour and a half—and this child was five years old.

JCD: How did it end?

Joy: It ended with me putting her out in the garage. She was walking around screaming. Then she rang the doorbell, and she said, "I'll take my spanking now." I did spank her, because I knew if I ever let her win one of those battles, I would never have control of her again. But it was a constant struggle.

I went to see a good friend of ours, a pastor in Columbus, and said to him, "I'm at my wit's end. I don't know how to control this child." He said, "Every night when you put her to bed, I want you and Davey to go in and lay your hands on her while she's asleep. What you're going to pray is for the Holy Spirit to conquer the strong will while not destroying her spirit, because that's what makes Dana who she is."

We did that every night. We would go in and pray over her and lay hands on her. It was about six months later she got up one morning and she said, "You know, I'm bad sometimes." I said, "I know." She said, "I don't mean the things I say. I'm not going to do that anymore." For about the next ten years, she was able to control it. Then she hit adolescence.

JCD: When we were having lunch together in Alabama, you told me a story that I want you to share. It involved your son, who decided to run away from home.

Joy: We called it lovingly "the Dr. Dobson spiel," where I would say, "Oh, Mother loves you so much, and you have to be my big boy." I would go through that every time he would say, "I'm going to run away from home." Well, one night it just struck me, "Okay, this is it." So he was in his little pajamas and he said, "If you make me go to bed, I'm going to run away from home." So I said, "Well, we'll see you later, buddy. Have a nice trip." So he walked out the door but quickly rang the doorbell, and he said, "I didn't mean tonight." I said, "Well, I do. I am really tired of this. It's time for you to go, but let me pack you a bag. You'll need pajamas and things."

He said, "Well, I might need to think about this." I said, "Well, you've got about three minutes while I go pack your bag. It's important to me that you stay here and be our son, but this is your decision. Either you run away, or I never want to hear you threaten to leave again. If you decide to live here, I don't want you to threaten to leave again." So I went and packed the suitcase. I don't think I put anything in it. I went back, and I opened the door, and he said, "Well, I've been thinking about it and I guess I'm gonna stay." I said, "But never say that to me again, do you understand?" He said, "Yes, ma'am." From then on, he would say, "If you make me do that, I . . . I . . . I'm not going to be your best friend." I'd say, "Well, that's sad."

What works for one has to work for the other, right? I was a stay-at-home mom and Dana was going through her own "I'm going to run away from home" routine. So one night I had had it, and I said, "Well, I'll see you later." It's funny the pictures that stay in your mind. She had on a Strawberry Shortcake robe and Strawberry Shortcake slippers, and her little blonde hair. Then she walked out the door. I went and sat down and Davey looked at me and he said, "Well, she's been out there about five minutes. Do you think—you know—maybe she should have rung the doorbell by now?" I said, "No, she's got that defiant spirit. We're going to give her about ten minutes." Then I went to the front door. There was nobody there. She was gone. By the grace of God, we lived on a cul-de-sac, because there was a street lamp and she was underneath it with her thumb out. She was hitching a ride! *(laughter and surprise from the panel)*

JCD: How old was she then?

Joy: She was six at the time and she had no fear whatsoever. There she was in her robe and slippers and nothing else. She was going to leave with no other clothes. I had to drag her into the house kicking and screaming because she was running away. "You told me I could run away." I thought, *This isn't what I'm supposed to be dealing with!*

JCD *(to the listening audience)*: Can you see why I wanted Joy here? I wanted people to understand that children who have Dana's brand of fortitude and determination are tough to handle, even if the parents use great wisdom and tact in raising them. A compliant child would never pull a stunt like that, but for the strong-willed youngster, it was just another challenge— just another opportunity to do battle—because they just love to go toe-to-toe-with their parents. They get their kicks by playing power games. That is what was happening in this instance.

I want to hear about Dana's adolescent years, Joy, but first, let me ask Kristen to tell us her story.

Kristen: Well, in hindsight, I think we knew shortly after birth that our daughter, Lizz, was strong-willed. At ten days old she was taken to the hospital with a case of spinal meningitis. As they were trying to get a spinal tap from her, she would arch her back instead of compliantly lying in a fetal position. They had to hold her down at ten days of age. The technicians ended up trying ten or twelve times before they could get untainted spinal fluid to culture so they could verify that she really had spinal meningitis. In fact, it was so bad they ended up going through a vein in her skull to get a sample. Then at eighteen months of age, we were visiting some friends for dinner. My two older kids were there, and our hostess had cut-glass candy dishes at each end of her couch. They didn't have any children yet so they could risk having something that fragile sitting out.

I told my two oldest children, "These are glass. They'll break. Don't touch them. Don't play rough around here." I didn't even mention them to Lizz. I thought, *I'll deal with that when the time comes.* When she finally saw the candy dishes after dinner, we told her emphatically, "No, you're not going to touch that." And again I said with conviction, "No, we're not going to touch it." After the battle was over, my friend said, "Do you realize, you slapped her hand nine times before she yielded?"

JCD: Did she eventually obey you?

Kristen: Yes, for that moment.

JCD: But she was saying emphatically, "I think I can outlast you."

Kristen: Oh yes. But the biggest fight we fought happened when she was five. I had been homeschooling the kids. Lizz decided she wasn't getting enough attention one day. So I pulled her up on my lap. While she was sitting on my lap and I was still trying to teach, she started kicking me with one of her legs. Well, I put her leg between my legs so she couldn't kick me anymore. Then she started kicking me with the other leg. I put both legs between mine, and she started pinching and scratching.

We ended up on the floor. She was actually spread-eagle on the floor. I was holding her down so that she could not hurt me or try to do damage to me. She was screaming, "Let go of me, let go of me," and I was saying, "We're here until you calm down." She'd quit crying and I'd start to pray, and she'd immediately start to scream again, "Don't you pray for me." So we'd start again. It turned out to be a forty-five-minute battle.

JCD: Lizz, do you remember that?

Lizz: I remember several times when I would just argue and end up on the floor with Mother on top of me. I was thinking, *Who's going to win?!* So it went on and on—I mean, it seemed like hours, sometimes.

JCD: Do you remember how you felt during those battles?

Lizz: I was just determined to win. My pride got in there too, you know? I believed I was stronger than Mom, and it was all about being rebellious and getting my own way.

JCD (*to the radio audience*): We're hearing some classic examples today of the battle of wills between parents and children. I have been witnessing conflicts of this sort within families for the past thirty years. What Lizz said about her determination to win over her mother goes right to the heart of what these little revolutionaries are after. Standing up to a big, powerful adult who is supposed to be in charge is fun for them. The winner of the "game," as every strong-willed child knows intuitively, is the one who either comes out on top or who reduces the other to tears. Quiet conversations and gentle explanations simply don't work.

Some authors contend that a child only acts naughty when she is frustrated over her circumstances. That certainly happens. But what we are dealing with in the illustrations we're hearing about today were not incidents motivated by frustration; they were driven by willful defiance.

[We'll talk more about that behavior and the proper parental response to it in subsequent chapters.]

Debra, let's hear your stories. Tell us about your strong-willed child.

Debra: Well, I had two of them, but one was really tough: I knew she was a strong-willed child before she was born. She was part of a twin set. I wanted her twin brother to be the football player and my daughter to be the nice, sweet, little cheerleader. As it turned out, she is the one being recruited by the football team, and my son is a wonderful child who writes tender poetry. He'll be the best pediatrician in the whole world. So my kids kind of flip-flopped.

The night before they were born, I was scheduled for a C-section because I don't dilate. I was playing table games with some friends next door, and I had this eruption, like a volcano or an earthquake, in my stomach. I know that it's probably not possible, but I swear my daughter switched places with my son. He was the lower child so he was expected to come out first, and she just went "shoo." I had this horrible experience the next morning. I woke up in a pool of blood. My baby girl was going to come out of that cervix whether it dilated or not. I was raced to the hospital and taken into emergency surgery. My daughter was going to come out no matter what the obstacles. So talk about being born smoking a cigar, yelling orders at the nursing staff, complaining about the temperature—that was my baby girl.

JCD: What was her babyhood like?

Debra: She was a challenge from the very first day! I had a five-year-old and a three-year-old, and then the twins were born. No grandparents lived close by. They would come and visit and help us, but I was a very busy young mother.

Christina would scream and scream and scream. I thought, *Well, she's sick. She must have medical problems, such as colic or whatever.* But then her dad would walk in the room and she would start baby flirting and cooing. You know, that sweet little thing. All she wanted was her dad. So I thought, *You can raise this child. I'll raise the other three.* Because she's stronger willed than I am by a long shot.

JCD: How difficult was that for you emotionally?

Debra: It was very difficult because I was a mother at heart. I'd always wanted to be a mom. I had good relationships with my other children. My second is precious. She does what she can to help me and to serve. She's just a wonderful child. Then I get this child who's like . . . well, my in-laws and others call her "the kid and a half."

JCD: There are very few experiences in life, I believe, that are more stressful than bringing a child into the world with one major goal—and that's to be a good mom or dad. You pour every effort and every resource into that assignment, only to have your beloved child reject your leadership almost from birth and engage in a never-ending battle of wills. That is terribly painful. It produces great guilt and self-condemnation, especially for the parents who care the most.

Debra: You're right. I believe firmly that strong-willed children love conflict. They just love the battle, and I don't love the battle. It was a very difficult experience for me because I'm not strong willed.

JCD: I conducted an extensive survey on this subject some years ago that involved thirty-five thousand parents. One of the things we observed was the enormous agitation that occurs when a compliant, loving mother, who would never have dreamed of disobeying her parents, gives birth to a kid who gets his greatest thrill out of fighting with his mother. Debra, you have tears in your eyes, don't you?

Debra: I do have tears in my eyes. But let me tell you a funny story. My husband and I used to count to three, and if the kids had not minded by then, they would have to face the wooden spoon. But, unfortunately, my kids are all very strong willed. One morning I put Elizabeth in her high chair so I could feed her. I was giving her Cheerios and fun things to eat. I was working around the house and I just wanted to keep her busy. Well, at some point during that time she became impatient, so she said, "Mother, I want to eat now. One, two, three . . . "

JCD: She was counting you down.

Debra: Right. And by the time she hit two, I had her dinner ready and my husband walked in the door. And I said, "John, it works. I had done everything that she wanted me to do before she got to three." *(laughter)*

Debra: And he said, "Yeah, that's all we need—a compliant mother and a strong-willed child." *(laughter)*

JCD: Joy, you saw the tears in Debra's eyes a minute ago.

Joy: Yes.

JCD: Did you ever cry when your daughter took you on?

Joy: I cried a lot when she was young. I cried even more during the teenage years. I was so shy as a child. And to please my parents was my greatest accomplishment in life—to make them proud of me and to please them. But Dana didn't feel that way about me. She could turn her back on me in a heartbeat. She was so tough. One day at preschool, there was a young handicapped boy whom the teachers were mainstreaming. Dana immediately befriended this child. More than anyone else in the class, she was drawn to that child. Another boy was making fun of this child, and Dana said, "I'm only going to warn you once. Don't make fun of him again, or I'm going to have to beat you up." Well, he came back and made fun of him again, and Dana said, "This was your last warning; I only give two warnings. Don't make fun of him again." Well, he came back, and before she was through with him, she had dragged him up one side of the playground and down the other. She had torn his shirt. She had torn his shorts, and he was screaming for Dana to let him go. And the teachers finally got ahold of her and said, "Dana, did you not hear him asking you to let him go?" And she said something I had said to her repeatedly, "I refuse to negotiate with a four-year-old." It came right back to me.

JCD: It is interesting that the same strong will that parents have to deal with is often expressed with peers. That temperament can be advantageous as the years unfold, because these youngsters are tough enough to withstand peer pressure and chart their own course.

This gets really personal, but tell me, Lizz, have you ever seen your mom cry in a moment of conflict?

Lizz: Hardly ever.

JCD: Kristen, you're obviously not a crier. But can you understand why the other two ladies here were so emotional?

Kristen: Oh yes, oh yes.

JCD: You just didn't express it the same way.

Kristen: I didn't express it in tears. I think I became more strong willed . . . "

JCD: In order to cope with it?

Kristen: Yes—in order to cope with it. I've always wanted to please people. I still do, but I was bound and determined that my children were not going to defeat me in anything. Yet there were days and weeks when all I did was defend my right to lead. My entire days were consumed with disciplining Lizz and trying to get her to follow the rules the way we had laid them out.

JCD: And the other children were not behaving quite that way.

Kristen: Oh no, no, not at all. You'd tell my oldest and my youngest not to do something, and they'd look up at you with their big blue eyes, and they'd say, "Oh, Mommy, I'm sorry." And they'd never do it again. Lizz would say, "Let's go for it."

JCD: There are millions of kids like you, Lizz, which raises an interesting question. Many parents have asked me whether their children's rebellious behavior is the result of parental mistakes and poor judgment, or whether there is something else responsible for it. Well, clearly, some moms and dads are more effective at handling kids than others are, and some of them regularly make a mess of things. Their children sometimes respond with increasingly testy behavior. Parenting is just like any other skill. It's given in greater portions to some than to others. Men, for example, just by their masculine presence, are typically better at handling tough kids than women are. If I may be candid, the three of you here today have described moments when you lost control of your children and were literally fighting physically to deal with your very difficult kids. It would appear that you were making some tactical errors at that point.

Nevertheless, a strong-willed child is a strong-willed child. The kids we are talking about here are born that way, and some of them are so tough that Hulk Hogan couldn't handle them without a struggle. As I indicated, these particularly contentious kids just love to reduce big powerful adults to tears and leave them shaken and discouraged. Their personalities are rooted in their genetic makeup.

I know I'm not giving Lizz much hope about the children she will bear. *(laughter)*

Kristen: Sorry, Lizz, you may have the mother's curse. You may produce a child just like you were.

JCD: Wait 'til you get your own.

Kristen: I've taken it further. I said to Lizz, "I hope all of yours are just like you."

Joy: I disagree. I have told Dana that I hope she never experiences what I went through because that would give me a strong-willed grandchild. *(laughter)*

JCD: It would, at that.

Joy: So, I'm looking for easier grandchildren.

JCD: Debra, do you have only one tough child?

Debra: Well, I have several who are strong-willed, plus I have one who trained another one to have a strong will. When you have twins and one of them is tough, you have double trouble. When they were little, we had difficulty keeping them in their cribs because Christina did not need to sleep. She was very strong physically. She could climb. She could walk. All my kids walked and ran at ten months old, and she would help her brother get out of the crib in the middle of the night. They were in the house running around unsupervised. And this is where our battles took place.

JCD: How did Christina spring her brother from the crib?

Debra: She would jump out of bed, and then she would collect whatever was in the room and put it in his crib, so he would step up on stuffed animals, or whatever she collected. And then, the two of them would be running loose while we slept.

Now, I was used to my other kids getting out of their crib, and it was no big deal; they would come and cuddle with us. But the twins had each other. They did not want me. We would, literally, find them in the kitchen, in the sink, playing with knives, opening the refrigerator, and throwing things around. It got to the point where keeping them alive was all I could do. I slept outside their door with a pillow and a blanket for a time because they would have to cross over me before they would leave the room. It was the only way I could protect them, and I just prayed for them. Like you, Joy, we laid hands on the kids and said, "Oh, Lord." I just prayed that they wouldn't kill themselves when they were little. And that sounds extreme, but it's true.

JCD: Debra, have you found yourself in moments like that with your face in your hands, saying, "I am a total failure as a mom"?

Debra: I did. I had four children, and a set of twins, and I was tired.

JCD: You just couldn't fight all the time.

Debra: I couldn't fight it. I just trusted in the power of prayer. The Lord is good. When my kids became saved and they were baptized by their own choice, they all changed. They all became new people in Christ.

JCD: Isn't that wonderful?

Debra: And their personalities changed, and that happened at about fourteen or fifteen for each one of them. And, truly, the Lord has done an incredible work, but I can't take any responsibility for it. I wish I'd been stricter. I wish I'd been firmer, but I did what I could in the midst of very difficult circumstances.

JCD: See, Debra, every one of us is inadequate as a parent. We all have to depend on the Lord. That reality hit me when my daughter was three. I saw that she would eventually make her own choices in life. My Ph.D. in child development was helpful to me, but it would not guarantee the eventual outcome. There are no certainties in raising a child. It is true for all parents. We come to the point where, even in our greatest strength, we have to say, "Lord, I need your help here." That's what being a parent is all about.

Did you depend on the Lord that way, Joy?

Joy: Oh, boy, did I ever.

JCD: So, it was a constant battle . . .

Joy: All day long, from the time she woke up until the time she went to bed. And there were times that she would be such an angel. She would be so caring and loving, and I would think, "Okay, okay, we're making progress. We're making progress." And then, thirty seconds later, one thing would trigger that defiant will, and she would be off and running. There were times, especially for me as a stay-at-home mom, when I felt like such a failure. I felt like, *This is a career I chose?* It's like starting a small business and watching it go under. Here I was looking at this child whom God had entrusted to me, and I couldn't even control her.

JCD: You said that after a period of time you and your husband, Davey, began praying for Dana—laying hands on her at night when she was asleep, and asking the Lord to help you bring that rebellious spirit under subjection. You said God answered those prayers and that Dana was able to control her behavior for four or five years. But you said she later went into adolescence and the rebelliousness resurfaced.

Joy: That is what we refer to as the dark period. She became very unhappy with herself. She didn't like her personal appearance because she was a heavy child. She had very curly hair, which no one else in our family has. Yet she was very intelligent. So, with the combination of her personality and intelligence, and being unhappy with her looks, she decided she was going to change everything. She began running around with kids who said, "Your parents are still trying to control you. Your parents don't really want you to be happy. Your parents want to live your life for you. They don't want you to leave home." She found a boyfriend who told her this and everything she wanted to hear. He said, "You're wonderful, but your parents don't understand you." And because she was so needy at that time, she became totally addicted to that relationship.

When I think back on our conversation in Alabama, I remember that you asked me if Dana had gotten into drugs and alcohol, and I said I didn't think so. And you said, "Well, we need to thank God for that." And I said, "We do, but when your child is addicted to a relationship, there is no help available." There was really nothing we could do about Dana's dependence on this guy, but it was as destructive as anything she could have been involved in.

JCD: How long did it go on?

Joy: Two and a half years.

JCD: And during that time, what were you doing?

Joy: I was crying every day. School didn't matter. *(crying)* I'm sorry.

JCD: That's all right.

Joy: She lost her relationship with her family and with God. School didn't matter. Soccer didn't matter, which had been a tremendous part of her life. The only thing that she could see in her future was that young man, and she totally built her life—her future life—around him. Her total existence depended on him.

JCD: Were you fasting and praying during that time?

Joy: We fasted. We prayed. We went for counseling. I was working at a Christian outlet store and people would come in—wonderful people—and they would say, "How are you doing today?" And I would say, "Fine, thanks, how are you?" One of the problems we had with Dana at that time was [that she was] lying constantly about everything. But I was lying too. I thought, *I lie every day. Every time I tell somebody that we're doing wonderful, thanks, I'm lying too.* Finally, I turned to someone who had asked that question and I said, "I'm sorry. I'm not trying to burden you with my problems, but I need to tell you I'm not okay. I'm losing a child." *(weeping)*

JCD: There are so many parents out there who have been through something like this, and others that are there right now. Some good, solid Christian families are crying with us today because they're experiencing the same thing. Most would give their lives for their children in a heartbeat. They've done everything they know to do, and they can't fix it. But the Lord still hears and answers prayer, and, Joy, He was hearing you all that time, wasn't He?

Joy: He heard all of my prayers, every one of them. The people who carried my child to the mercy seat, I can never thank them enough. There are no words to describe my gratitude, because the relationship we have with her now is so much better than I ever imagined when she was a child.

JCD: I want to hear more about that in a moment, but, Kristen, what was the low point for you and your husband?

Kristen: We finally had to go to the elders of our church at one point because our daughter would steal. She would take whatever she wanted, and we'd ask, "Lizz, why are you taking something that doesn't belong to you?" And she'd say, " 'Cause I want it." It was just amazing to me that a four- or a five-year-old could articulate the bottom line like that: "I wanted it. I took it." She'd steal money from the church or from the offering plate to buy a Coke from the Coke machine, and she stole some of the decorations out of the bathroom—just a little cinnamon stick, but she wanted it; therefore, she took it.

It got to the point where we took her back to the Scripture. My husband sat down with her and said, "This is what the Bible says. You've got to obey the leaders in your life, and if you don't, we've got to take you to a higher authority." And he went to the elders of our church and asked a couple of them who had children if they would be willing to sit down with Lizz. At that time, she was probably in kindergarten, maybe first grade. And these two godly men sat down with her and made her accountable—made her memorize Scripture. She had gotten to the point where she needed to know that there was a higher authority. That's why we went to the elders.

JCD: Lizz, that had a big impact on you, didn't it?

Lizz: Extremely, yes.

JCD: What do you remember about that time?

Lizz: I remember just being thoroughly embarrassed and having to be responsible for what I did to someone else and having to "'fess up" to that responsibility. Until probably second grade, I would take things from my teachers. I would get into their desks. If they had food in there, I would take their food. And I stole my kindergarten teacher's earrings. And eventually . . . you know, I was thinking, *Who cares? I'll be disciplined, but who cares?* And the discipline didn't bother me. It was when they said, "Okay, you have to go to your teacher. You have to go to the elders, and you have to apologize for doing that." And that's when I thought, *Oh no!* It was embarrassing and humbling, and I realized what I had done.

JCD: Punishment was not something that deterred you in any way.

Lizz: Didn't faze me, not a bit.

JCD: You just figured out a way to get around it.

Lizz: Uh-huh.

JCD: It was a challenge for you.

Lizz: Yeah. If I got grounded from the phone, I'd try to get on the phone. If I got grounded from the computer, I'd try to get on the computer. So, it was just something else to be defiant about.

JCD: To the parents who are raising such a child, it is important for you to figure out what the kid is thinking. You have to get behind the eyes of that child and see it the way that he or she sees it. Only then will you have a better idea of how to respond.

You know, Lizz, my mother was able to do that. She knew that I was messing around in school when I was in the ninth grade. I was a big disciplinary problem at that time, but my mother figured out how to get to me. She said one day, "You can behave any way you want to at school, and I'm not going to do anything about it. Nothing, that is, unless the school calls to tell me about it. If they do, I'm going to school with you the next day. I will sit beside you in class, and I will be in the hall when you are standing with your friends. I'm going to be right there all day, and you will not be able to get rid of me." Man, that shaped me up in a big hurry. That would have been social suicide to have my mom trailing along behind me; I absolutely could not run the risk of her standing around with my friends. It shaped me up in one day.

Joy: A parent has to get very creative in response to the challenges that come his or her way. When we were riding in the family car and Dana was in trouble and knew what was waiting for her at home, she would put both hands on the window and scream at people when we stopped at red lights. She would shout, "Save me! Save me!"

JCD: You are kidding, Joy.

Joy: No, no. I'm not kidding. I was thinking, *If the police pull me over, I'm going to have to show them that this really is my child.*

JCD: Well, we've heard some pretty scary things here today about several very tough kids. But our purpose is not to depress everyone. In fact, there is good news for us to share about each of the children we have discussed. That's why we're here, because there is reason for hope. And, Joy, the update on your story that you shared with me when we met in Alabama is very inspirational. As we sat at the table, you took a crumpled piece of paper out of your purse that day and read something to me.

Joy: I did.

JCD: I don't think you intended to share that note with me on that day.

Joy: No, I had no idea.

JCD: You just happened to have it with you.

Joy: Well, it didn't just happen. I take it everywhere I go. I keep this with me. It is such a reminder.

JCD: Tell everyone what the note says.

Joy: Well, Dana was in her first year in college, and she wrote me this note in midyear:

Dear Mom,

Hey there. This is going to be a weird letter. I've been doing a lot of lifelong thinking. Mom, sometimes I wonder where I would be and what life would be like if I hadn't come back from the dark side. You know, I never thought that I would consider my mother to be my best friend, but you are. I would never trade this closeness I've gained with you for anything in the world. You and Dad used to say that if I would just wait until it was time for me to move out, that you would be behind me 100 percent. Now I understand. I know that you and I were growing, even when I was at home, but I don't think that I ever truly appreciated you until now. At least, not as much as you deserve to be appreciated. I miss you every day. I mean, I thought that when I went to school that I would never want to go home or even call. But I don't like to go through the day without talking to you. You know, I hope that one day I will be as successful as Daddy. I want to be as keen and respected in my field as he is in his. But you, above all, had the hardest profession of all. You had to raise me. Mom, I hope that you understand what a gift God gave you. He gave you the will and the power to raise me. You showed me the kinds of things that no college or professional school could ever teach me. I can only pray that one day God will make me the kind of mother you have been and will always be to me. I just wanted to take a minute to say, "Thank you" and "I love you."

Your baby girl,
Dana

(Joy was crying as she read.)

JCD: Oh, Joy. That was worth a million dollars, wasn't it? Would you have ever believed that Dana would send you a loving letter like that when you were going through your struggles with her?

Joy: Never.

JCD: Lizz, do you sense a mother's heart here?

Lizz: Yes, very much.

JCD: That's what you've heard today.

Lizz: Um-hmm.

JCD: Do you want to be a mother someday?

Lizz: Absolutely.

JCD: And can you imagine bringing a child into the world as dedicated to your baby as you hope to be, and then having this kind of conflict take place?

Lizz: I'm sure it'll happen. I do want to say one thing about strong-willed children like me. God has this amazing, amazing way of saying, "I want you, and I want you to be strong-willed for Me." And instead of being rebellious and disobedient, He wants us to be strong-willed for Him.

JCD: Do you remember actually having those thoughts?

Lizz: Oh, absolutely. I went out with a bunch of my friends, and I was being stupid. And I had come home, and then I just sat down, and I just felt the presence of God. I looked at myself, and I was thinking, "My life has been pointless. I've spent all of my life being strong-willed and wanting to win every battle." And then, God just grabbed me. It was as though He said, "Leave it behind, Lizz," you know?

JCD: Kristen, you were praying for Lizz at that time, weren't you?

Kristen: Oh, I am a lot like Joy. We had all prayed as a family. Her grandparents have been faithful prayer partners. Rich and I pray continually for her. Everybody we know . . . we have not hidden from her the fact that she has been a strong-willed child, so, it is not necessarily an uncommon topic of conversation among people whom we have dealt with this. So, yes, we've had many people praying as well. I am really blessed by the fact that I have seen what God can do and still have time with my daughter to build a relationship that every parent wants. So, I do cry when I think about that.

JCD: Debra, you were praying during your difficulties too, weren't you?

Debra: Oh yes, and my oldest daughter, who's getting married in a month, has become the mentor for my second strong-willed child, and that has been an answer to prayer because their relationship was tainted. When you're an only child or a firstborn child and then your position is usurped by a younger sister, that's a big deal. And so, they were not friends when my oldest daughter was in high school. But now they have become close friends. Elizabeth has mentored Christina to where she is today. And she helped her understand herself and her place in the family.

We had a similar experience last summer. Christina had just gone crazy. I listened to her scream at me until about two in the morning for no reason. And, all of a sudden, it was like the Holy Spirit came over her, and she started repeating things that I would have said to her if I had been talking. And she said, "Mom, I will fight a battle all the way because I want to win." But, she said, "Don't ever be scared to put boundaries in my way because I need rules. I need boundaries. And I respect everything you've done—"

And then she said something else. She said, "I know who I am in God. And I know that I will make right choices." She said, "I've had a bad year. I'm going to change this next year," and she has. She's a different person this year. She said, "You have trained me well. You have given me the stability of a Christian school and a church and a Christian family." She said, "I will choose wisely, and I want to live my life because you've modeled it for me with Jesus."

JCD: Let me say it again: I'm telling our listeners and readers that there is hope here. That is the reason I wanted to address this topic on our program. On their behalf, I want to ask you, the three mothers here, a very important question. The Scripture says that children are a blessing from the Lord. Do you still feel that way, even though raising your kids was a struggle for you? Was it worth it?

Joy: Children are a treasure. That is what I told my children when they were young. . . . But, for a while, Dana forgot that, or she didn't seem to believe it. Now, I think she is to the point where she understands that she truly is a treasure to us. The strong will that she has will be an asset to her in life. She wants to be an attorney. That will be wonderful, because she'll argue with a rock. (*laughter*)

JCD: And the Lord's going to use that temperament.

Joy: I believe He will. I am so blessed.

JCD: How about the other two?

Kristen: Worth every minute, every battle, every ounce of energy that I put into it. I would never, never trade anything.

JCD: Debra?

Debra: One of my children's names means "house of God," another means "great woman of God," and the third means "precious gift of God." So, I did tell each of them that they were gifts. I didn't know if I could have children. They were all tremendous miracles and blessings. Absolutely, every minute was worth it, even the conflicts we had, because I know that God is sufficient, I know He's able, and I know He's going to use them mightily.

JCD: You know, anyone can raise the easy kids. I'm reminded of a very difficult time when I was asked to interview convicted serial murderer Ted Bundy at the Florida State Prison. We had more than nine hundred requests for media appearances in three days, and there was tremendous pressure on me. Added to that was the emotion of dealing with a man who had killed at least twenty-eight women and girls in cold blood. I remember the morning before I went to talk to Bundy that I didn't want to do it. At that point the Lord seemed to speak to me, and He said, *I sent you to do this job because I knew you could handle it. I selected you for this difficult assignment.*

This is my point. When parents bring one of these tough youngsters into the world, they need to recognize that while raising that child may be difficult for a time, it is worth their effort to do the job right. Their attitude should be, "The Lord gave me this challenging child for a purpose. He wants me to mold and shape this youngster and prepare him or her for a life of service to Him. And I'm up to the task. I'm going to make it with the Lord's help." That's the healthy way of looking at parenting when the pressure is on. There is a tendency, I think, for parents of strong-willed children to feel cheated and oppressed because other moms and dads seem to have smooth sailing with their children, whereas they are at war every day of the week. But if they can perceive their task as a God-given assignment and believe that He's going to help them to fulfill it, then the frustrations become more manageable.

Let me give you one other word of encouragement. Just as the three mothers have now experienced, most strong-willed children tend to come around when they get through adolescence. Don't be too quick as a parent to brand yourself as a failure. Kids do grow up, and you will find out later that the values and principles that you tried so hard to instill were actually going inside and sticking. It may be that your difficult children will become your best friends, as it is now for Joy and Dana, if . . . if you persevere. So, when your child's behavior is saying "I hate you" in every way possible, hang in there. Keep your courage. Don't panic. Better days are coming.

Joy: We were at home one day recently and Dana was home. She said, "Why did you never give up on me?" And I said, "Because you're a treasure. God gave you to us. I could never have given up on you." She said, "A lot of people would." And I said, "Not if they believed in the power of God and the power of prayer, because I wasn't sure how soon it was going to be, but I always believed that you would come back." I had tremendous hope and faith.

Another thing happened when Dana was at home. She said, "You know, I remember one night when it was really, really bad, and there was a big fight. You were crying. I got used to you crying because you did it all the time." But then Dana said what really got to her that night was that she made her daddy cry. Her father's tears touched her heart. *(There were tears around the table at that point.)*

JCD: Debra, what advice do you have for the mother out there today who is experiencing what you were feeling when your kids were small?

Debra: Well, I think what I'm going to do is quote your book. I think it's page 24 of *The Strong-Willed Child*. You said, in effect, "Pick your battles. Win decisively. Take two aspirin and call me in the morning." *(laughter)*

JCD: Well, do all that, but don't call me. *(laughter)*

Debra: I think I lived on your broadcasts when my children were little. I used to wash my floors and pick up the food that had been thrown on the floor while they were eating, and I would sob through the broadcasts. But it helped me because I knew that other people were also struggling. I knew that God was in control, and I knew there were people out there who understood.

Now I go to people like Kristen, because we share an office together, and we talk about our strong-willed daughters, and we pray for you very regularly, and we watch you, and we love you, and we nurture you together.

JCD: The folks here at Focus on the Family get the credit for that, but this is why we're here. A reporter came to my office yesterday for an interview about the ministry. As far as I know, she is not a Christian. After we talked for almost an hour, she asked, "Why do you do this? You've said that you care about all those people who reach out for help. Why have you invited hundreds of thousands of them every month to bring their troubles here? Why do you put yourself and your staff through this?" I tried to explain that this is the essence of my Christian faith. Jesus said, "Inasmuch as ye have done it unto one of the least of these my brethren, ye have done it unto me" (Matthew 25:40, KJV). It gives me a great deal of satisfaction to put an arm around a mom who's depressed or discouraged or hopeless and to offer support and encouragement to her. As I talked, I noticed that this tough reporter got big tears in her eyes. So I'm just thankful that we have this opportunity to express care and concern for those who are hurting. And, Debra, I'm pleased that you were one of them.

Let me say one last thing to you, Lizz. I think you're going to make a great mom. I can just see it. You're very bright, and you're very dedicated, and the fact that you've landed on your feet this early is a very good sign. I trust that you will have a good year in school next year, and then go on into college. Then I want you to write your mom an e-mail that will make her cry. She's not a crier, but I'll bet you could bring "happy tears" to her eyes.

Joy, you brought a Bible with you today. That's been your mainstay, hasn't it?

Joy: It has.

JCD: Well, come back and see us when you've got grandkids who are strong-willed children, will you? *(laughter)*

JCD: Thanks for being with us.

Panel: Thank you.

Final post-interview comments: I'm sure this interchange has been unsettling to some readers, particularly those who have young children and envision a future of all-out warfare with their irritable kids, much like that described by our panel. Let me hasten to say that the children whom we have read about in this chapter are at the far end of the continuum with regard to the strength of the will. Most boys and girls, even those who qualify for the title *strong-willed,* are less determined and more easily led. My purpose in providing what might be called a worst-case scenario, therefore, is to illustrate the varying ways children respond to authority, and to give hope and direction to those who are, in fact, raising one or more little revolutionaries. The good news, as we saw, is that the outcome even for those youngsters can be positive and deeply satisfying in the long run.

THREE

WHAT MAKES THEM THE WAY THEY ARE?

HAVING HEARD FROM THE MOTHERS on our panel, who no doubt represent millions of other moms who have struggled to control their children, one has to wonder why so many "experts" on parenting have failed to notice that some children are tougher to raise than others. One would never get that impression from reading the advice offered by this army of permissive psychologists, counselors, pediatricians, psychiatrists, and columnists for women's magazines, who are convinced that raising kids is as simple as falling off a log. All parents need to do, they have been saying for decades, is give them a lot of space, treat them like adults, and if absolutely necessary, explain every now and then why they might want to consider behaving better. How nice it would be if that were true. Unfortunately, this rosy view is cruel nonsense. It leaves Mom and Dad with the impression that every other parent in the world finds it easy to lead children, and those who are having trouble with it are miserable failures. In most cases, it is not fair and it is not true.

Misguided advice on child rearing has been prominent in the literature for at least seventy-five years. For example, best-selling author of books for parents John Caldwell Holt wrote a terrible text in 1974 entitled *Escape from Childhood*.[1] It was straight out of left field. Jim Stingley reviewed the book for the *Los Angeles Times*:

> In the latest one, [Holt] plainly advocates the overthrow of parental authority in just about every area. He sets forth that children, age whatever, should have the right to: experience sex, drink and use drugs, drive, vote, work, own property, travel, have a guaranteed income, choose their guardians, control their learning, and have legal and financial responsibility. In short, Holt is proposing that parents

discard the protectorate position they have held over their children in this and other countries over the past several hundred years, and thrust them, or rather let them thrust themselves—when they feel like they want to—into the real-life world.[2]

Doesn't that sound utterly foolish? Even the *Los Angeles Times* reviewer, a supposedly unbiased journalist, implies that Holt's ideas are ludicrous. Can you imagine a six-year-old girl driving her own car to an escrow office, where she and her preschool male friend will discuss the purchase of a new home over a martini or two? Can you visualize a teary-eyed mother and father standing in the doorway, saying good-bye to their five-year-old son who has decided to pack his teddy bear and go live with someone else? Have we gone completely mad? Discard the protectorate position, indeed! The surprising thing is that this man and his cockamamy theories were taken seriously by many people during the revolutionary days of the late sixties and seventies. In fact, Holt was quoted in the *Times* article as saying:

> "Oddly enough, the chapter on the matter of drinking and drugs, letting young people do whatever older people do, as well as manage their own sex lives, hasn't brought as much flak as I would have expected. . . . The understanding, sympathetic responses [from readers] have clearly outweighed the negative or hostile ones," he said.

About the time the Holt book came along, an article appeared in *Family Circle* that also revealed the permissiveness of the day. Its title, "A Marvelous New Way to Make Your Child Behave," should have been the first clue as to the nature of its content.[3] (If its recommendations were so fantastic, why hadn't they been observed in more than five thousand years of parenting?) The subtitle was even more revealing: "Rewards and Punishment Don't Work." Those two Pollyannaish headlines revealed the primrose path down which the authors were leading its readers. Never once did they admit that a child is capable of the kind of rebellion described by the three mothers we just met. Instead, the examples given in the article focused on relatively minor incidents of childish irresponsibility, such as a child not washing his hands before dinner or wearing improper clothing or not taking out the garbage. Responsible behavior is a noble objective for our children, but let's admit that the more difficult task is shaping the child's will in moments of rebellion.

A more current example of permissive approaches to child rearing is referred to as "positive discipline," or the "positive parenting" movement. It sounds good, but it is little more than repackaged permissive claptrap. Consider the following advice, featured on the Oklahoma State Department of Health's "Positive Discipline" Web page. It reads, "The goal of discipline is not to control children and make them obey but to give them skills for making decisions, gradually gaining self-control, and being responsible for their own behavior." Instead of telling a child, "Don't hit the kitty" or "Stop kicking the table," they suggest that parents say, "Touch the kitty gently" or "Keep your feet on the floor." The Web site goes on to assert that "Giving a child choices allows him some appropriate power over his life and encourages decision making." Parents are advised to "redirect" childish behavior. For example, if a child is throwing a truck around the house, instead of telling him to stop, they suggest you say to him, "I can't let you throw your truck, but you may throw the ball outside." Or if the child is kicking a door, you are to tell him, "You may not kick the door, but you may kick this ball or plastic milk jug." Their suggestion for dealing with willful defiance is to ignore it or to allow the child to engage in "something pleasant" until he cools off.[4]

What ridiculous advice that is. Notice how hard the parent is supposed to work to avoid being the leader at home. What's wrong with explaining to a child exactly what you want him or her to do and expecting obedience in return? Why is it unacceptable for a parent to insist that a child engaging in destructive or irritating behavior immediately cease and desist? Why not tell the child, "Kitties have feelings just like you do. You will not hit the kitty"? A youngster whose parent has never taken charge firmly is being deprived of a proper understanding of his mom's or dad's authority. It also keeps him from comprehending other forms of authority that will be encountered when he leaves the safety of his permissive cocoon. Sooner or later, that boy or girl is going to bump into a teacher, a police officer, a Marine Corps drill sergeant, or an employer who never heard of positive discipline and who will expect orders to be carried out as specified. The child who has only heard "suggestions" for alternative behavior through the years, which he may choose to accept or reject, is not prepared for the real world.

Here's yet another example of bad parental advice, also reflecting the positive discipline philosophy. Lini Kabada, writing for the Knight-Ridder newspaper chain, relayed this advice:

[Karen] Gatewood once spanked and called "time-out." Now she talks about her children's feelings. When the girls act up, she sweetly and calmly suggests alternative activities and offers support ("I know you're sad") in the midst of tantrums, a touchy-feely technique called "time-in."

    Ms. Gatewood . . . allows what positive-parenting attitudes call "natural and logical consequences" of behavior to flow. For example, [her daughter] Amanda recently wanted to take a favorite piece of string on an outing. Ms. Gatewood warned that she might lose it, but didn't argue with the child. She allowed the natural and logical consequence to unfold. Sure enough, Amanda lost the string and she cried.

    Ms. Gatewood didn't ignore Amanda's feelings, as pediatricians suggest in the face of a tantrum. "I said, 'That is sad. It's horrible,' because to her it was horrible. She said, 'I won't bring my toys next time.'"[5]

How utterly simplistic and unworkable! Ms. Gatewood doesn't know much about children apparently, and she is certainly confused about how to manage them. What if little Amanda had wanted to take Mom's wedding ring on the outing instead of a piece of worthless string? What if she refused to go to bed until she collapsed in exhaustion night after night? What if she began regularly pouring her Cream of Wheat and orange juice into the television set? What if she refused to take necessary medication? Somewhere along the way, parental leadership has to make a showing. Boys and girls must be taught what is and is not acceptable behavior; the responsibility to establish those boundaries is an assignment given to moms and dads by the creator of families. Parents can't always just wait around for logical consequences to do a job they should be doing themselves.

Of course, logical consequences have a place in child rearing. But one very logical consequence of misbehavior might be sitting his wiggly bottom on a chair with instructions to think about why he must never spit in Mommy's face or run down a busy street or drive nails in the furniture or try to flush baby sister down the toilet. The "positive-parenting" books don't admit that these misbehaviors and a thousand others do happen—regularly in some families. They won't acknowledge that some mothers and fathers go to bed at night with pounding, throbbing headaches, wondering how raising kids became such an exhausting and nerve-racking experience. Instead, the Karen Gatewoods of the world offer squishy advice and touchy-feely explanations, such as "time-in," that leave parents confused, misinformed, and guilt ridden. My colleague, John

Rosemond, with whom I am usually in strong agreement, gave the best assessment of the positive-parenting concept: "That's horse manure," he said, "and that's my most polite term. It's wimp parenting."

Let's examine now a more thorough answer to the fundamental question about willful defiance: Why is it that most children seem to have a need to take on those in authority over them? Why can't they just be satisfied with quiet discussions and patient explanations and gentle pats on the head? Why won't they follow reasonable instructions and leave it at that? Good questions.

I hope I have made the case by now that willfulness is built into the nature of some kids. It is simply part of their emotional and intellectual package brought with them into the world. This aspect of inborn temperament is not something boys and girls *learn*. It is something they *are*. Mothers know this instinctively. Virtually every mom with two or more children will affirm that she noticed differences in their personality—a different "feel"—the first time she held them. They'll tell you that some of them were tough and some were easy. But each was unique.

The early authorities in the field of child development denied what their eyes told them. They thought they had a better idea, concluding that babies come into the world devoid of individuality. Children, they said, are blank slates upon which the environment and experience will be written. John Locke and Jean-Jacques Rousseau, among others, promoted this notion and thereby confused the scientific understanding of children for decades. Most of the best-known psychologists in the world ascribed to this theory at one time or another, and many are still influenced by it. The more accurate view, however, based on careful research, recognizes that while experience is very important in shaping the human personality, the "blank slate" hypothesis is a myth. Children don't start life at the same place. They bring with them an individuality that is uniquely their own, different from that of every other individual who has ever lived. Let me say again that one of their innate characteristics is what I have termed "the strength of the will," which varies from child to child. If you have regular contact with children, you will be able to see this aspect of temperament, more or less, in living color.

A classic study of inborn temperaments was conducted more than twenty-five years ago by psychiatrists Stella Chess and Alexander Thomas and outlined in their excellent book, *Know Your Child*.[6] The authors reported that not only do babies differ significantly from one another at the moment of birth, but those differences tend to be rather persistent throughout childhood. Even more interestingly, they observed three broad categories or patterns of temperaments into which the majority of children can be classified. First, they referred to the "difficult child," who is characterized by negative reactions to people, intense mood swings, irregular sleep patterns and feeding schedules, frequent periods of crying, and violent tantrums when frustrated.[7] This is the youngster I have designated the "strong-willed child." Chess and Thomas described the second category as the "easy child," who exhibits a positive approach to people, quiet adaptability to new situations, regular sleep patterns and feeding schedules, and a willingness to accept the rules of the game.[8] The authors concluded, "Such a youngster is usually a joy to his or her parents, pediatrician, or teachers."[9] Amen. My term for the easy child is "compliant."

Chess and Thomas called the third personality pattern "slow to warm up" or "shy."[10] Youngsters in this category respond negatively to new situations and adapt slowly. However, they are less intense than difficult children, and they tend to have regular sleeping and feeding schedules. When they are upset or frustrated, they typically withdraw from the situation and react mildly rather than explode with anger and rebellion.

Not every child fits into one of these categories, of course, but according to Drs. Chess and Thomas, approximately 65 percent do.[11] The researchers also emphasized that babies are fully human at birth, being able immediately to relate to their parents and learn from their environment.[12] Blank slates at birth? Hardly!

We know now that heredity plays a much larger role in the development of human temperament than was previously understood. This is the conclusion of meticulous research conducted over many years at institutions like the University of Minnesota. The researchers there identified more than one hundred sets of identical twins that had been separated near the time of birth. They were raised in varying cultures, religions, and locations. They did not know each other, however, until they were grown. Because each set of twins shared the same DNA, or genetic material, and the same architectural design, it became possible for the researchers to examine the impact of inheritance by comparing their similarities and their differences on many variables. From these and other studies, it became clear that much of the personality, perhaps 70 percent or more, is inherited.[13] Our genes influence such qualities as creativity, wisdom, loving-kindness, vigor, longevity, intelligence, and even the joy of living.

Consider the brothers known in the Minnesota study as the "Jim twins," who were separated until they were thirty-nine years old. Their similarities were astonishing. Both married a woman named Linda. Both had a dog named Toy.

Both suffered from migraine headaches. Both chain-smoked. Both liked the same brand of beer. Both drove Chevys, and both served as sheriff's deputies. Their personalities and attitudes were virtual carbon copies.[14] Though this degree of symmetry is exceptional, it illustrates the finding that most identical twins reveal surprising similarities in personality that are linked to heredity.

A person's genetic structure is thought to even influence the stability of his or her marriage. If an identical twin gets a divorce, the risk of the other also divorcing is 45 percent.[15] However, if a fraternal twin, who shares only half as many genes, divorces, the risk to the other twin is only 30 percent.[16]

What do these findings mean? Are we mere puppets on a string, playing out a predetermined course without free will or personal choices? Of course not. Unlike birds and mammals that act according to instinct, humans are capable of rational thought and independent action. We don't act on every sexual urge, for example, despite our genetic underpinnings. What is clear is that heredity provides a nudge in a particular direction—a definite impulse or inclination—but one that can be brought under the control of our rational processes. In fact, we must learn early in life to do just that.

What do we know specifically about children with particularly strong wills? That question has intrigued me for years. There has been very little written about these youngsters and almost no research on which to base an understanding. That dearth of information left parents of difficult children to muddle through on their own. In response, I conducted a survey of thirty-five thousand parents, mentioned earlier, to learn what their experiences have been. It was not a "scientific" investigation, since there was no randomized design or availability of a control group.[17] Nevertheless, what I learned was fascinating to me and, I hope, will be useful to you. Here is a summary of a huge volume of information that was provided by the people who have the most knowledge of kids who are as hardheaded as mules—the parents who live with them every day.

- We found that there are nearly three times as many strong-willed kids as those who are compliant. Nearly every family with multiple children has at least one who wants to run things. Male strong-willed children outnumber females by about 5 percent, and female compliant children outnumber males by about 6 percent. Thus, there is a slight tendency for males to have tougher temperaments and for females to be more compliant, but it can be, and often is, reversed.
- Birth order has nothing to do with being strong-willed or compliant.

These elements of temperament are basically inherited and can occur in the eldest child or in the baby of the family.

- Most parents know they have a strong-willed child very early. One-third can tell at birth. Two-thirds know by the youngster's first birthday, and 92 percent are certain by the third birthday. Parents of compliant children know it even earlier.

- The temperaments of children tend to reflect those of their parents. Although there are many exceptions, two strong-willed parents are more likely to produce tough-minded kids and vice versa.

- Parents of strong-willed children can expect a battle during the teen years, even if they have raised them properly. Fully 74 percent of strong-willed children rebel significantly during adolescence. The weaker the authority of the parents when the kids are young, the greater the conflict is in later years.

- Incredibly, only 3 percent of compliant children experience severe rebellion in adolescence, and just 14 percent go into even mild rebellion. They start out life with a smile on their face and keep it there into young adulthood.

- The best news for parents of strong-willed children is the rapid decrease in their rebellion in young adulthood. It drops almost immediately in the early twenties and then trails off even more from there. Some are still angry into their twenties and early thirties, but by then the fire is gone for the majority. They peacefully rejoin the human community.

- The compliant child is much more likely to be a good student than the strong-willed child. Nearly three times as many strong-willed children made Ds and Fs during the last two years of high school as did compliant children. Approximately 80 percent of compliant children were A and B students.

- The compliant child is considerably better adjusted socially than the strong-willed child. It would appear that youngsters who are inclined to challenge the authority of their parents are also more likely to behave offensively with their peers.

- The compliant child typically enjoys higher self-esteem than the strong-willed child. It is difficult to overestimate the importance of this finding. Only 19 percent of compliant teenagers either disliked themselves (17 percent) or felt extreme self-hatred (2 percent). Of the very strong-willed teenagers, 35 percent disliked themselves and 8 percent experienced extreme self-hatred. The strong-willed child seems compelled from within to fuss, fight, test, question, resist, and challenge.

Obviously, the findings I have shared in this chapter are of enormous significance to our understanding of children. They and related concepts are described in greater detail in my book *Parenting Isn't for Cowards*.[18]

QUESTIONS AND ANSWERS

Q: Tell me why some kids with every advantage and opportunity seem to turn out bad, while others raised in terrible homes become pillars in the community. I know one young man who grew up in squalid circumstances, yet he is such a fine person today. How did his parents manage to raise such a responsible son when they didn't even seem to care?

A: That illustrates just the point I have been trying to make. Neither heredity nor environment will account for all human behavior. There is something else there—something from within—that also operates to make us who we are. Some behavior is caused, and some plainly isn't.

Several years ago, for example, I had dinner with two parents who had unofficially "adopted" a thirteen-year-old boy. This youngster followed their son home one afternoon and asked if he could spend the night. As it turned out, he stayed with them for almost a week without receiving so much as a phone call from his mother. It was later learned that she worked sixteen hours a day and had no interest in her son. Her alcoholic husband had divorced her several years earlier and left town without a trace. The boy had been abused, unloved, and ignored through much of his life.

Given this background, what kind of kid do you think he is today—a druggie? a foul-mouthed delinquent? a lazy, insolent bum? No. He is polite to adults; he is a hard worker; he makes good grades in school; and he enjoys helping around the house. This boy is like a lost puppy who desperately wants a good home. He begged the family to adopt him officially so he could have a real father and a loving mother. His own mom couldn't care less.

How could this teenager be so well-disciplined and polished despite his lack of training? I don't know. It is simply within him. He reminds me of my wonderful friend David Hernandez. David and his parents came to the United

States illegally from Mexico more than fifty years ago and nearly starved to death before they found work. They eventually survived by helping to harvest the potato crop throughout the state of California. During this era, David lived under trees or in the open fields. His father made a stove out of an oil drum half-filled with dirt. The open campfire was the centerpiece of their home.

David never had a roof over his head until his family finally moved into an abandoned chicken coop. His mother covered the boarded walls with cheap wallpaper, and David thought they were living in luxury. Then the city of San Jose condemned the area, and David's "house" was torn down. He couldn't understand why the community would destroy so fine a place.

Given this beginning, how can we explain the man that David Hernandez became? He graduated near the top of his class in high school and was granted a scholarship to college. Again, he earned high marks and four years later entered Loma Linda University School of Medicine. Once more, he scored in the top 10 percent of his class and continued in a residency in obstetrics and gynecology. Eventually, he served as a professor of obstetrics and gynecology at both Loma Linda University and the University of Southern California medical schools. Then, at the peak of his career, his life began to unravel.

I'll never forget the day Dr. Hernandez called me after he'd been released from the hospital following a battery of laboratory tests. The diagnosis? Sclerosing cholangitis, a liver disorder that was invariably fatal at that time. The world lost a fine husband, father, and friend six years later when he was only forty-three. I loved him like a brother, and I still miss him today.

Again, I ask how such discipline and genius could come from these infertile circumstances. Who would have thought that this deprived boy sitting in the dirt would someday become one of the most loved and respected surgeons of his era? Where did the motivation originate? From what bubbling spring did his ambition and thirst for knowledge flow? He had no books, took no educational trips, knew no scholars. Yet he reached for the sky. Why did it turn out this way for David Hernandez and not the youngster with every advantage and opportunity?

Why have so many children of prominent and loving parents grown up in ideal circumstances only to reject it all for the streets of Atlanta, San Francisco, or New York? Good answers are simply not available. It apparently comes down to this: God chooses to use individuals in unique ways. Beyond that mysterious relationship, we must simply conclude that some kids seem born to make it and others are determined to fail. Someone reminded me recently that the same boiling water that softens the carrot also hardens the egg. Likewise, some individuals react positively to certain circumstances and others negatively. We don't know why.

Two things are clear to me from this understanding. First, parents have been far too quick to take the credit or blame for the way their children turn out. Those with bright young superstars stick out their chests and say, "Look what we accomplished." Those with twisted and irresponsible kids wonder, *Where did we go wrong?* Well, neither is entirely accurate. No one would deny that parents play an important role in the development and training of their children. But they are only part of the formula from which a young adult is assembled.

Second, behavioral scientists have been far too simplistic in their explanation of human behavior. We are more than the aggregate of our experiences. We are more than the quality of our nutrition. We are more than our genetic heritage. We are more than our biochemistry. And we are more than our parents' influence. God has created us as unique individuals, capable of independent and rational thought that is not attributable to any other source. That is what makes the task of parenting so challenging and rewarding. Just when you think you have your kids figured out, you had better brace yourself! Something new is coming your way.

Q: Does Scripture confirm that babies have temperaments or personalities before birth?
A: Yes, in several references we learn that God knows and relates to unborn children as individuals. He said to the prophet Jeremiah, "Before I formed you in the womb I knew you, and before you were born I consecrated you; I appointed you a prophet to the nations" (Jeremiah 1:5, RSV). The apostle Paul said we were also chosen before birth (see Ephesians 1:4). And in a remarkable account, we are told of the prenatal development of the twins Jacob and Esau. As predicted before their birth, one turned out to be rebellious and tough while the other was something of a mama's boy. They were fighting before they were born and continued in conflict through much of their lives (see Genesis 25:22-27). Then later, in one of the most mysterious and disturbing statements in the Bible, the Lord said, "Jacob have I loved, but Esau have I hated" (Romans 9:13, KJV). Apparently, God discerned a rebellious nature in Esau before he was born and knew that he would not be receptive to the divine Spirit.

These examples tell us that unborn children are unique individuals with whom God is already acquainted. They also confirm, for me at least, the wickedness of abortion, which destroys those embryonic little personalities.

Q: How can you say that precious little newborns come into the world inherently evil? I agree with the experts who say that babies are born good and they only learn to do wrong later.

A: Please understand that the issue here is not with the purity or innocence of babies. No one would question their preciousness as creations of God. The point of disagreement concerns the tendencies and inclinations they have inherited. People who believe in innate goodness would have us believe that human beings are naturally unselfish, honest, respectful, kind to others, self-controlled, obedient to authority, etc. Children, as you indicated, then subsequently learn to do wrong when they are exposed to a corrupt and misguided society. Bad *experiences* are responsible for bad behavior. To raise healthy kids, then, it is the task of parents to provide a loving environment and then stay out of the way. Natural goodness will flow from within.

This is the humanistic perspective on childish nature. Millions of people believe it to be true. Most psychologists have also accepted and taught this notion throughout the twentieth century. There is only one thing wrong with the concept. It is entirely inaccurate.

Q: How can you be so sure about the nature of children? What evidence do you have to support the belief that their tendency is to do wrong?

A: We'll start with what the "owner's manual" has to say about human nature. Only the Creator of children can tell us how He made them, and He has done that in Scripture. It teaches that we are born in sin, having inherited a disobedient nature from Adam. King David said, "In sin did my mother *conceive* me" (Psalm 51:5, KJV, italics added), meaning that this tendency to do wrong was transmitted genetically. Paul said this sinful nature has infected every person who ever lived. "For *all* have sinned, and come short of the glory of God" (Romans 3:23, KJV, italics added). Therefore, with or without bad associations, children are naturally inclined toward rebellion, selfishness, dishonesty, aggression, exploitation, and greed. They don't have to be taught these behaviors. They are natural expressions of their humanness.

Although this perspective is viewed with disdain by the secular world today, the evidence to support it is overwhelming. How else do we explain the pugnacious and perverse nature of every society on earth? Bloody warfare has been the centerpiece of world history for more than five thousand years. People of every race and creed around the globe have tried to rape, plunder, burn, blast, and kill each other century after century. Peace has been but a momentary pause when they have stopped to reload! Plato said more than 2,350 years ago: "Only dead men have seen an end to war."[19] He was right, and it will continue that way until the Prince of Peace comes.

Not only have nations warred against each other since the beginning of time, we also find a depressing incidence of murder, drug abuse, child molestation, prostitution, adultery, homosexuality, and dishonesty among individuals. How would we account for this pervasive evil in a world of people who are naturally inclined toward good? Have they really drifted into these antisocial and immoral behaviors despite their inborn tendencies? If so, surely *one* society in all the world would have been able to preserve the goodness with which children are born. Where is it? Does such a place exist? No, although admittedly some societies are more moral than others. Still, none reflect the harmony that might be expected from the natural goodness theorists. Why not? Because their basic premise is wrong.

Q: What, then, does this biblical understanding mean for parents? Are they to consider their babies guilty before they have done anything wrong?
A: Of course not. Children are not responsible for their sins until they reach an age of accountability—and that time frame is known only to God. On the other hand, parents should not be surprised when rebellious or mischievous behavior occurs. It *will* happen, probably by the eighteenth month or before. Anyone who has watched a toddler throw a temper tantrum when she doesn't get her way must be hard-pressed to explain how the phrase "innate goodness" became so popular! Did her mother or father model the tantrum for her, falling on the floor, slobbering, kicking, crying, and screaming? I would hope not. Either way, the kid needs no demonstration. Rebellion comes naturally to her entire generation—although in some individuals it is more pronounced than in others.

For this reason, parents can and must train, mold, correct, guide, punish, reward, instruct, warn, teach, and love their kids during the formative years. Their purpose is to shape that inner nature and keep it from tyrannizing the entire family. Ultimately, however, only Jesus Christ can cleanse it and make it wholly acceptable to the Master. This is what the Bible teaches about people, and this is what I firmly believe.

Q: If it is natural for a toddler to break all the rules, should he be disciplined for his defiance?
A: You are on to something important here. Many of the spankings and slaps given to toddlers can and should be avoided. Toddlers get in trouble most fre-

quently because of their natural desire to touch, bite, taste, smell, and break everything within their grasp. However, this exploratory behavior is not aggressive. It is a valuable means for learning and should not be discouraged. I have seen parents slap their two-year-olds throughout the day for simply investigating their world. This squelching of normal curiosity is not fair to the youngster. It seems foolish to leave an expensive trinket where it will tempt him and then scold him for taking the bait. If little fat fingers insist on handling the trinkets on the lower shelf, it is much wiser to distract the child with something else than to discipline him for his persistence. Toddlers cannot resist the offer of a new plaything. They are amazingly easy to interest in less fragile toys, and parents should keep a few alternatives available for use when needed.

When, then, should the toddler be subjected to mild discipline? When he openly defies his parents' spoken commands! If he runs the other way when called, purposely slams his milk glass onto the floor, dashes into the street while being told to stop, screams and throws a tantrum at bedtime, hits his friends—these are the forms of unacceptable behavior that should be discouraged. Even in these situations, however, all-out spankings are not often required to eliminate the behavior. A parent's firm rap to the fingers or command to sit in a chair for a few minutes will convey the same message just as convincingly. Spankings should be reserved for a child's moments of greatest antagonism, usually occurring after the third birthday.

The toddler years are critical to a child's future attitude toward authority. He should be taught to patiently obey without being expected to behave like a more mature child.

Without watering down anything I have said earlier, I should also point out that I am a firm believer in the judicious use of grace (and humor) in parent-child relationships. In a world in which children are often pushed to grow up too fast and too soon, their spirits can dry out like prunes beneath the constant gaze of critical eyes. It is refreshing to see parents temper their inclination for harshness with a measure of unmerited favor. There is always room for more loving forgiveness within our home. Likewise, there's nothing that rejuvenates the parched, delicate spirit of a child faster than when a lighthearted spirit pervades the home and regular laughter fills its halls. Heard any good jokes lately?

FOUR

SHAPING THE WILL

THE YOUNG MOTHER of a defiant three-year-old girl once approached me in Kansas City to thank me for my books and tapes. She told me that a few months earlier her little daughter had become increasingly defiant and had managed to buffalo her frustrated mom and dad. They knew she was manipulating them but couldn't seem to regain control. Then one day they were in a bookstore and happened upon a copy of my first book, *Dare to Discipline* (now revised and called *The New Dare to Discipline*).[1] They bought a copy and learned that it is appropriate, from my perspective, to spank a child under certain well-defined circumstances. My recommendations made sense to these harassed parents, who promptly used that technique the next time their daughter gave them reason to do so. But the little girl was just bright enough to figure out where they had picked up the new idea. When the mother awoke the next morning, she found her copy of *Dare to Discipline* floating in the toilet! That darling little girl had done her best to send my book off to the sewer where it belonged. I suppose that is the strongest editorial comment I've received on any of my writings!

This incident with the toddler was not an isolated case. Another child selected my book from an entire shelf of possibilities and threw it into the fireplace. I could easily become paranoid about these hostilities. Dr. Benjamin Spock, the late pediatrician who wrote the widely acclaimed *Dr. Spock's Baby and Child Care,* was loved by millions of children who grew up under his influence.[2] But I have apparently been resented by two generations of kids who wanted to catch me in a blind alley on some cloudy night.

I continue to receive the most delightful mail from children and their parents about the subject of discipline. A college student approached me with a smile and handed me a poem written just for me. It read: "Roses are red, Violets are blue. When I was a kid, I got spanked 'cause of you." Sorry about that, sir!

A mother wrote to tell me that she took her daughter to the doctor for her routine childhood inoculations. The youngster came home that evening and told her father, "I just got my shots for mumps, measles, and rebellion." Don't you wish there was an injection for that type of behavior? I would have had my adolescents given a big dose at least once a week.

A little eight-year-old girl mailed me this note:

Dear Dobinson
You are a mean and curle thing. You and your dumb sayings won't take you to Heaven.

Kristy P.

P.S. Kids don't like wippens.

It is obvious that children are aware of the contest of wills between generations, which can become something of a game. Lisa Whelchel, former child actress on the television sitcom *The Facts of Life,* described a funny encounter with her four-year-old boy, Tucker. She related the story in her excellent book, *Creative Correction.* Lisa and her husband were going out to dinner and left the children with a babysitter. As they were standing at the door, she said to her son, "I really want you to do your best to obey the babysitter tonight."

Tucker immediately replied, "Well, Mom, I just don't know if I can do that."

"Why not?" she asked.

With a straight face, he answered, "There's so much foolishness built up in my heart, I don't think there is any room for goodness and wisdom."

"Well," Lisa said, "maybe we need to step into the bathroom and drive that foolishness out."

With that, Tucker replied, "W-wait a minute. I feel the foolishness going away all by itself—the goodness is coming in right now!"[3]

Lisa's encounter with her son did not represent a serious challenge to her authority and should have been (and, in fact, was) responded to with a smile. But when a real donnybrook occurs between generations, it is extremely important for the parents to "win." Why? A child who behaves in ways that are disrespectful or harmful to himself or others often has a hidden motive. Whether he recognizes it or not, he is usually seeking to verify the existence and stability of the boundaries. This testing has much the same function as a police officer in years past who turned doorknobs at places of business after dark. Though he tried to open the doors, he hoped they were locked and secure. Likewise, a child who defies the leadership of his parents is reassured when they remain confident and firm under fire. It creates a sense of security for a kid who lives in a structured environment in which the rights of other people (and his own) are protected by well-defined limits.

With that said, let's hurry along now to the how-tos of shaping a child's will. I've boiled this complex topic down to six straightforward guidelines that I hope will be helpful, the first of which is most important and will be dealt with in greater detail.

FIRST: BEGIN TEACHING RESPECT FOR AUTHORITY WHILE CHILDREN ARE VERY YOUNG

The most urgent advice I can give to the parents of an assertive, independent child is to establish their positions as strong but loving leaders when Junior and Missy are in the preschool years. This is the first step toward helping them learn to control their powerful impulses. Alas, there is no time to lose. As we have seen, a naturally defiant youngster is in a high-risk category for antisocial behavior later in life. She is more likely to challenge her teachers in school and question the values she has been taught. Her temperament leads her to oppose anyone who tries to tell her what to do. Fortunately, this outcome is not inevitable, because the complexities of the human personality make it impossible to predict behavior with complete accuracy. But the probabilities lie in that direction. Thus, I will repeat my most urgent advice to parents: that they begin shaping the will of the particularly aggressive child very early in life. (Notice that I did not say to crush his will or to destroy it or to snuff it out, but to rein it in for his own good.) But how is that accomplished?

Well, first let me tell you how *not* to approach that objective. Harshness, gruffness, and sternness are not effective in shaping a child's will. Likewise, constant whacking and threatening and criticizing are destructive and counterproductive. A parent who is mean and angry most of the time is creating resentment that will be stored and come roaring into the relationship during adolescence or beyond. Therefore, every opportunity should be taken to keep the tenor of the home pleasant, fun, and accepting. At the same time, however, parents should display confident firmness in their demeanor. You, Mom and Dad, are the boss. You are in charge. If you believe it, the tougher child will accept it also. Unfortunately, many mothers today are tentative and insecure in approaching their young children. If you watch them with their little boys and girls in supermarkets or airports, you will see these frustrated and angry moms who are totally confused about how to handle a given misbehavior. Temper tantrums throw them for a loop, as though they never expected them. Actually, they have been coming on for some time.

A pediatrician friend told me about a telephone call he received from the anxious mother of a six-month-old baby.

"I think he has a fever," she said nervously.

"Well," the doctor replied, "did you take his temperature?"

"No," she said. "He won't let me insert the thermometer."

There is trouble ahead for this shaky mother. There is even more danger for her son in the days ahead. He will quickly sense her insecurity and step into the power vacuum she has created. From there, it will be a wild ride all the way through adolescence.

Here are some nuts-and-bolts suggestions for avoiding the trouble I have described. Once a child understands who is in charge, he can be held accountable for behaving in a respectful manner. That sounds easy, but it can be very difficult. In a moment of rebellion, a little child will consider his parents' wishes and defiantly choose to disobey. Like a military general before a battle, he will calculate the potential risk, marshal his forces, and attack the enemy with guns blazing. When that nose-to-nose confrontation occurs between generations, it is extremely important for the adult to display confidence and decisiveness. The child has made it clear that he's looking for a fight, and his parents would be wise not to disappoint him! Nothing is more destructive to parental leadership than for a mother or father to equivocate during that struggle. When parents consistently lose those battles, resorting to tears and screaming and other signs of frustration, some dramatic changes take place in the way they are seen by their children. Instead of being secure and confident leaders, they become spineless jellyfish who are unworthy of respect or allegiance.

Susanna Wesley, mother of eighteenth-century evangelists John and Charles Wesley, reportedly bore nineteen children. Toward the end of her life, John asked her to describe in writing her philosophy of mothering for him. Copies of her reply are still in existence today. As you will see from the excerpts that follow, her beliefs reflect a traditional understanding of child rearing. She wrote:

> In order to form the minds of children, the first thing to be done is to
> conquer the will, and bring them into an obedient temper. To inform

the understanding is a work of time, and must with children proceed by slow degrees as they are able to bear it; but the subjecting of the will is a thing which must be done at once, and the sooner the better!

For by neglecting timely correction, they will contract a stubbornness and obstinacy which is hardly ever after conquered, and never without using such severity as would be painful to me as to the children. In the esteem of the world, those who withhold timely correction would pass for kind and indulgent parents, whom I call cruel parents, who permit their children to get habits which they know must afterward be broken. Nay, some are so stupidly fond as in sport to teach their children to do things which in the after while, they must severely beat them for doing.

Whenever a child is corrected, it must be conquered; and this will be no hard matter to do, if it be not grown headstrong by too much indulgence. And, if the will of a child is totally subdued, and if it be brought to revere and stand in awe of the parents, then a great many childish follies and inadvertencies may be passed by. Some should be overlooked and taken no notice of, and others mildly reproved. But no willful transgressions ought ever to be forgiven children without chastisement, more or less as the nature and circumstances of the offense shall require.

I cannot dismiss this subject. As self-will is the root of all sin and misery, so whatever cherishes this in children insures their after wretchedness and faithlessness. Whatever checks and mortifies, promotes their future happiness and piety. This is still more evident if we further consider that Christianity is nothing less than doing the will of God, and not our own; that the one grand impediment to our temporal and eternal happiness being this self-will. No indulgence of it can be trivial, no denial unprofitable.[4]

Does that sound harsh by our modern standards? Perhaps. While I would have balanced the approach with greater compassion and gentleness, I believe that Mrs. Wesley's basic understanding was correct. If the strong-willed child is allowed by indulgence to develop "habits" of defiance and disrespect during his or her early childhood, those characteristics will not only cause problems for the parents, but will ultimately handicap the child whose rampaging will was never brought under self-control.

Does this mean that Mom or Dad should be snapping orders all day long, disregarding the feelings and wishes of the child? Certainly not! I would not want to be treated that way, and you wouldn't either. Most of the time, you can talk things through and come to a mutual understanding. Furthermore, there is nothing wrong with negotiating and compromising when disagreements occur between generations. Six-year-old Lance may voluntarily rest or nap in the afternoon so that he can watch a late evening children's program on television. Mom may offer to drive her ten-year-old daughter to soccer practice, provided she agrees to straighten and clean her room. There are countless situations such as these during childhood when a "no-win, no-lose" agreement can be reached without imposing constant demands and threats on a youngster. These mutually agreed-upon conclusions will not undermine parental leadership and won't reinforce a spirit of rebellion, even in a tough-minded child.

On the other hand, there is a time to speak in that tone of voice that says, kindly but firmly, "Please do it now, because I said so." One can't always negotiate with a child or give repetitive explanations and requests for cooperation. Every command doesn't have to end with a question mark, as in, "Would you like to go take your bath now?" Sometimes you simply have to step in and be the boss. As we saw in the last chapter, it is this expression of authority that many modern parental advisers resist tooth and nail. They never want moms and dads to sound as though they are in charge. Some even refer to that style of management as "power games." One writer of books for parents expressed his permissive philosophy this way:

> The stubborn persistence of the idea that parents must and should use authority in dealing with children has, in my opinion, prevented for centuries any significant change or improvement in the way children are raised by parents and treated by adults. Children resent those who have power over them. In short, children want to limit their behavior themselves, if it becomes apparent to them that their behavior must be limited or modified. Children, like adults, prefer to be their own authority over their behavior.[5]

I couldn't disagree more. God has installed parents as leaders for a finite period of time. When they are afraid or unwilling to fulfill that responsibility, the strong-willed child is positively driven to step to the front and begin running things. As we have seen, it is his passion to take charge anyway. If you as a mom or dad won't be the boss, I guarantee that your tough-as-nails kid will grab that role. That is the beginning of sorrows for both generations.

The New Testament, which the Scripture tells us is "God-breathed" (2 Timothy 3:16), speaks eloquently to this point. We read in 1 Timothy 3:4-5, "He [speaking of the father] must have proper authority in his own household, and be able to control and command the respect of his children" (Phillips). Colossians 3:20 expresses this divine principle to the younger generation: "Children, obey your parents in all things: for this is well pleasing unto the Lord" (KJV). I find no place in the Bible where our little ones are designated as codiscussants at a conference table, deciding what they will and will not accept from the older generation. Power games, indeed.

Why is parental authority so vigorously supported throughout the Bible? Is it simply catering to the whims of oppressive, power-hungry adults, as some would have us believe? No, the leadership of parents plays a significant role in the development of a child! By yielding to the loving authority (leadership) of his parents, a child learns to submit to other forms of authority that will confront him later in his life. Without respect for leadership, there is anarchy, chaos, and confusion for everyone concerned.

There is an even more important reason for the preservation of authority in the home. Children who are acquainted with it learn to yield to the benevolent leadership of God Himself. It is a fact that a child identifies his parents with God in the early days, whether the adults want that role or not. Specifically, most children see God the way they perceive their earthly fathers (and, to a lesser degree, their mothers). This fact was illustrated in our home when our son, Ryan, was just two years old. Since his babyhood, he had seen his sister, mother, and father say grace before eating our meals, because we always thank God for our food in that way. But because of his age, the little toddler had never been asked to lead the prayer. On one occasion when I was out of town, Shirley put the lunch on the table and spontaneously turned to Ryan, saying, "Would you like to pray for our food today?" Her request apparently startled him and he glanced around nervously, then clasped his little hands together and said, "I love you, Daddy. Amen."

When I returned home and heard about Ryan's prayer, it was immediately apparent that my son had actually confused me with God. And I'll confess, I wished he hadn't! I appreciated the thought, but I was uncomfortable with its implications. It was too big a job for an ordinary dad to handle. There were times when I'm sure I disappointed our children—times when I was too tired to be what they needed from me—times when my human frailties were all too apparent. The older they became, the greater was the gap between who I was and who they had thought I was—especially during the storms of adolescence. No, I didn't want to represent God to my son and daughter. But whether I liked it or not, they thought of me in those terms, and your younger children probably see you that way too!

In short, the Creator has given parents the awesome responsibility of representing Him to their children. As such, they should reflect two aspects of divine nature to the next generation. First, our heavenly Father is a God of unlimited love, and our children must become acquainted with His mercy and tenderness through our own love toward them. But make no mistake about it: our Lord is also the possessor of majestic authority! The universe is ordered by a sovereign God who requires obedience from His children and has warned that "the wages of sin is death" (Romans 6:23). To show our little ones love without authority is as serious a distortion of God's nature as to reveal an iron-fisted authority without love.

From this perspective, then, a child who has only "negotiated" with his parents and teachers during times of intense conflict has probably not learned to submit to the authority of the Almighty. If this youngster is allowed to behave disrespectfully to Mom and Dad, sassing them and disobeying their specific orders, then it is most unlikely that he will turn his face up to God about twenty years later and say humbly, "Here am I, Lord; send me!" To repeat, a child learns to yield to the authority of God by first learning to submit to (rather than bargain with) the leadership of his parents.

But what did the apostle Paul mean in his first letter to Timothy where he referred to parents having the "proper authority"? Was he giving them the right to browbeat their children, disregarding their feelings and instilling fear and anxiety in them? No. There is a wonderful balance taught by Paul in this letter and in Ephesians 6:4. It reads, "Fathers, do not exasperate your children; instead, bring them up in the training and instruction of the Lord."

We'll move more quickly now through the five other general guidelines for shaping the will of a child.

SECOND: DEFINE THE BOUNDARIES BEFORE THEY ARE ENFORCED
Preceding any disciplinary event is the necessity of establishing reasonable expectations and boundaries for the child. She should know what is and is not acceptable behavior before she is held responsible for it. This precondition will

eliminate the sense of injustice that a youngster feels when she is punished or scolded for violating a vague or unidentified rule.

THIRD: DISTINGUISH BETWEEN WILLFUL DEFIANCE AND CHILDISH IRRESPONSIBILITY

Let's return briefly to the letter written by Susanna Wesley, who recommended that a mother or father overlook "childish follies and inadvertencies" but never ignore "willful transgressions." What did she mean? She was referring to the distinction between what I would call childish irresponsibility and "willful defiance." There is a world of difference between the two. Understanding the distinction will be useful in knowing how to interpret the meaning of a behavior and how to respond to it appropriately. Let me explain.

Suppose little David is acting silly in the living room and falls into a table, breaking several expensive china cups and other trinkets. Or suppose Ashley loses her bicycle or leaves her mother's coffeepot out in the rain. Perhaps four-year-old Brooke reaches for something on her brother's plate and catches his glass of milk with her elbow, baptizing the baby and making a frightful mess on the floor. As frustrating as these occurrences are, they represent acts of childish irresponsibility that have little meaning in the long-term scheme of things. As we all know, children will regularly spill things, lose things, break things, forget things, and mess up things. That's the way kids are made. These behaviors represent the mechanism by which children are protected from adult-level cares and burdens. When accidents happen, patience and tolerance are the order of the day. If the foolishness was particularly pronounced for the age and maturity of the individual, Mom or Dad might want to have the youngster help with the cleanup or even work to pay for the loss. Otherwise, I think the event should be ignored. It goes with the territory, as they say.

There is another category of behavior, however, that is strikingly different. It occurs when a child defies the authority of the parent in a blatant manner. She may shout "I will not!" or "You shut up!" or "You can't make me." It may happen when Junior grabs a handful of candy bars at the checkout and refuses to give them back, or when he throws a violent temper tantrum in order to get his way. These behaviors represent a willful, haughty spirit and a determination to disobey. Something very different is going on in those moments. You have drawn a line in the dirt, and the child has deliberately flopped his bony little toe across it. You're both asking, *Who is going to win? Who has the most courage? Who is in charge here?* If you do not conclusively answer these questions for your strong-willed children, your child will precipitate other battles designed to ask them again and again. That's why you must be prepared to respond immediately to this kind of stiff-necked rebellion. It is what Susanna Wesley meant when she wrote, "Some [misbehavior] should be overlooked and taken no notice of [referring to childish irresponsibility], and others mildly reproved. But no willful transgressions ought ever to be forgiven children without chastisement, more or less as the nature and circumstances of the offense shall require." Susanna arrived at this understanding 250 years before I came along. She learned it from the nineteen kids who called her Mama.

Brace yourself now, because I'm about to recommend something to you that will be controversial in some circles. You may not even agree with it, but hear me out. On those occasions when you find yourself and your strong-willed child in one of those classic battles of the will, it is not the time to discuss the virtues of obedience. You shouldn't send Jack or Jane to his or her room to pout. Time-out doesn't work very well and time-in is a total failure. Bribery is out of the question. Crying and begging for mercy are disastrous. Waiting until tired ol' Dad comes home to handle matters at the end of the day will be equally unproductive. None of these touchy-feely responses and delaying maneuvers are going to succeed. It all comes down to this: When you have been challenged, it is time for you to take charge—to defend your right to lead. When mothers and fathers fail to be the boss in a moment like that, they create for themselves and their families a potential lifetime of heartache. Or as Susanna Wesley said, "No indulgence of [willful defiance] can be trivial, no denial unprofitable." Therefore, I believe a mild and appropriate spanking is the discipline of choice for a hot-tempered child between twenty months and ten years of age. I will talk at greater length in chapter 8 about corporal punishment, its advantages, its limitations, and the dangers of its misuse.

FOURTH: REASSURE AND TEACH
AFTER THE CONFRONTATION IS OVER

After a time of conflict during which the parent has demonstrated his right to lead (particularly if it resulted in tears for the child), the youngster between two and seven (or older) will probably want to be loved and reassured. By all means, open your arms and let him come! Hold him close and tell him of your love. Rock him gently and let him know again why he was punished and how he can avoid the trouble next time. This is a teachable moment, when the objective of your discipline can be explained. Such a conversation is difficult or impossible to achieve when a rebellious, stiff-necked little child is clenching her fist and taking you on. But after a confrontation has occurred—especially if it involved tears—the child usually wants to hug you and get reassurance that you really care for her. By all means, open your arms and let her snuggle to your breast. And for the Christian family, it is extremely important to pray with the child at that time, admitting to God that we have all sinned and no one is perfect. Divine forgiveness is a marvelous experience, even for a very young child.

FIFTH: AVOID IMPOSSIBLE DEMANDS

Be absolutely sure that your child is capable of delivering what you require. Never punish him for wetting the bed involuntarily or for not becoming potty trained by one year of age or for doing poorly in school when he is incapable of academic success. These impossible demands put the child in an irresolvable conflict: there is no way out. That condition brings unnecessary risks to the human emotional apparatus. Besides that, it is simply unjust.

SIXTH: LET LOVE BE YOUR GUIDE!

A relationship that is characterized by genuine love and affection is likely to be a healthy one, even though some parental mistakes and errors are inevitable.

These six steps should, in my view, form the foundation for healthy parent-child relationships. There is one more ingredient that will round out the picture. We will read about it in the next chapter.

QUESTIONS AND ANSWERS

Q: You said we need to interpret the intent of children so that we can know how to discipline properly. What if I'm not sure? What if my child behaves in ways that may or may not be willfully defiant? How can I tell the difference?
A: That question has been asked of me dozens of times. A mother will say, "I think Garrett was being disrespectful when I told him to take his bath, but I'm not sure what he was thinking."

There is a very straightforward solution to this parental dilemma: Use the next occasion for the purpose of clarifying. Say to your son, "Garrett, your answer to me just now sounded disrespectful. I'm not sure how you intended it. But just so we understand each other, don't talk to me like that again." If it occurs again, you'll know it was deliberate. Most confusion over how to discipline results from parents' failure to define the limits properly. If you're hazy on what is acceptable and unacceptable, then your child will be doubly confused.

Most children will accept the boundaries if they understand them and are sure you mean business when you set them up.

Q: If you had to choose between a very authoritarian style of parenting and one that is permissive and lax, which would you prefer? Which is healthier for kids?

A: Both extremes leave their characteristic scars on children, and I would be hard-pressed to say which is more damaging. At the oppressive end of the continuum, a child suffers the humiliation of total domination. The atmosphere is icy and rigid, and he lives in constant fear. He is unable to make his own decisions, and his personality is squelched beneath the hobnailed boot of parental authority. Lasting characteristics of dependency, deep-seated anger, and serious adolescent rebellion often result from this domination.

But the opposite extreme is also damaging to kids. In the absence of adult leadership, the child is her own master from earliest babyhood. She thinks the world revolves around her heady empire, and she often has utter contempt and disrespect for those closest to her. Anarchy and chaos reign in her home. Her mother is often the most frazzled and frustrated woman on the block. It would be worth the hardship and embarrassment she endures if her passivity produced healthy, secure children. It typically does not.

The healthiest approach to child rearing is found in the safety of the middle ground between disciplinary extremes. I attempted to illustrate that reasonable parenting style on the cover of my first book, *Dare to Discipline,* which included this little diagram:

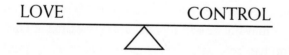

LOVE   CONTROL

Children tend to thrive best in an environment where these two ingredients, love and control, are present in balanced proportions. When the scale tips in either direction, problems usually begin to develop at home.

Unfortunately, parenting styles in a culture tend to sweep back and forth like a pendulum from one extreme to the other.

Q: I could use some advice about a minor problem we're having. Tim, my six-year-old, loves to use silly names whenever he speaks to my husband and me. For example, this past week it's been "you big hot dog." Nearly every time he sees me now he says, "Hi, hot dog." Before that it was "dummy," then "moose" (after he studied M for moose in school). I know it's silly and it's not a huge problem, but it gets so annoying after such a long time. He's been doing this for a year now. How can we get him to talk to us with more respect, calling us Mom or Dad, instead of hot dog and moose? Thank you for any advice you can offer.

A: What we have here is a rather classic power game, much like those we have discussed before. And contrary to what you said, it is not so insignificant. Under other circumstances, it would be a minor matter for a child to call his parents a playful name. That is not the point here. Rather, strong-willed Tim is continuing to do something that he knows is irritating to you and your husband, yet you are unable to stop him. That is the issue. He has been using humor as a tactic of defiance for a full year. It is time for you to sit down and have a quiet little talk with young Timothy. Tell him that he is being disrespectful and that the next time he calls either you or his father a name of any kind, he will be punished. You must then be prepared to deliver on the promise, because he will continue to challenge you until it ceases to be fun. That's the way he is made. If that response never comes, his insults will probably become more pronounced, ending in adolescent nightmares. Appeasement for a strong-willed child is an invitation to warfare.

Never forget this fact: The classic strong-willed child craves power from the time he's a toddler and even earlier. Since Mom is the nearest adult who is holding the reins, he will hack away at her until she lets him drive his own buggy. I remember a mother telling me of a confrontation with her tough-minded four-year-old daughter. The child was demanding her own way and the mother was struggling to hold her own.

"Jenny," said the mother, "you are just going to have to do what I tell you to do. I am your boss. The Lord has given me the responsibility for leading you, and that's what I intend to do!"

Jenny thought that over for a minute and then asked, "How long does it have to be that way?"

Doesn't that illustrate the point beautifully? Already at four years of age, this child was anticipating a day of freedom when no one could tell her what to do. There was something deep within her spirit that longed for control. Watch for the same phenomenon in your child. If he's a toughie, it will show up soon.

Q: Isn't a mother manipulating the child by using rewards and punishment to get him to do what she wants?

A: No more than a factory supervisor manipulates his employees by docking their pay if they arrive late. No more than a police officer manipulates a speeding driver by giving him a traffic ticket. No more than an insurance company manipulates that same driver by increasing his premium. No more than the IRS manipulates a taxpayer who files his return one day late by charging a penalty for his tardiness. The word *manipulation* implies a sinister or selfish motive of the one in charge. I don't agree.

Q: You have described the nature of willfully defiant behavior and how parents should handle it. But does all unpleasant behavior result from rebellion and disobedience?

A: No. Defiance can be very different in origin from the "challenge" response I've been describing. A child's negativism may be caused by frustration, disappointment, fatigue, illness, or rejection and therefore must be interpreted as a warning signal to be heeded. Perhaps the toughest task in parenthood is to recognize the difference between these behavioral messages. A child's resistant behavior always contains a message to his parents, which they must decode before responding.

For example, a disobedient youngster may be saying, *I feel unloved now that I'm stuck with that screaming baby brother. Mom used to care for me; now nobody wants me. I hate everybody.* When this kind of message underlies the defiance, the parents should move quickly to pacify its cause. The art of good parenthood, then, revolves around the interpretation of behavior.

Q: I'm never completely certain how to react to the behavior of my children. Can you give some specific examples of misbehaviors that should be punished, as well as others that can be ignored or handled differently?

A: Let me list a few examples at various age levels, asking that you decide how you would handle each matter before reading my suggestions. (Most of these items represent actual situations posed to me by parents.)

Example: I get very upset because my two-year-old boy will not sit still and be quiet in church. He knows he's not supposed to be noisy, but he hits his toys on the pew and sometimes talks out loud. Should I spank him for being disruptive?

My reply: The mother who wrote this question revealed a rather poor understanding of toddlers. Most two-year-olds can no more fold their hands and sit quietly in church than they can swim the Atlantic Ocean. They squirm and churn and burn every second of their waking hours. No, this child should not be punished. He should be left in the nursery where he can shake the foundations without disturbing the worshippers.

Example: My four-year-old son came into the house and told me he had seen a lion in the backyard. He was not trying to be funny. He really tried to convince me that this lie was true and became quite upset when I didn't believe him. I want him to be an honest and truthful person. Should I have spanked him?

My reply: Definitely not. There is a very thin line between fantasy and reality in the mind of preschool children, and they often confuse the two. I remember, for example, the time I took my son to Disneyland when he was three years of age. He was absolutely terrified by the wolf who stalked around with the three pigs. Ryan took one look at those sharp, jagged teeth and screamed in terror. I have a priceless video of him scrambling for the safety of his mother's arms. After we returned home, I told Ryan there was a "very nice man" inside the wolf suit who wouldn't hurt anyone. My son was so relieved by that news that he needed to hear it repeatedly.

He would say, "Dad?"

"What, Ryan?"

"Tell me 'bout that nice man!"

You see, Ryan was not able to distinguish between the fantasy character and a genuine threat to his health and safety. I would guess that the lion story related in the question above was a product of the same kind of confusion. The child may well have believed that a lion was in the backyard. This mother would have been wise to play along with the game while making it perfectly clear that she didn't believe the story. She could have said, "Oh, my goodness! A lion in the backyard. I sure hope he is a friendly old cat. Now, Jonathan, please wash your hands and come eat lunch."

Example: John is in the second grade and is playing around in school. Last month his teacher sent home a note telling us of his misbehavior, and he threw it away. We discovered at open house the following week that he had lied to us and destroyed the note. What would you have done?

My reply: That was a deliberate act of disobedience. After investigating the facts, I probably would have given John a spanking for his misbehavior in school and for being untruthful to his parents. I would then talk to his teacher about why he was cavorting in school and consider why he was afraid to bring home the note.

FIVE

PROTECTING THE SPIRIT

I MUST OFFER a very important clarification and precaution at this point related to the task of shaping the will of strong-willed children. The reader might conclude from what I have written that I think of "little people" as the villains and their parents as the inevitable good guys. Of course that is not true. Children, including those who regularly challenge authority, are delightful little creatures who need buckets of love and understanding every day of their life. Furthermore, it is vitally important to establish a *balanced* environment for them, wherein discipline and occasional punishment are matched by patience and respect and affection. The "slap 'em across the mouth" approach to child management, even for a kid who is determined to break all the rules, is a disaster. It wounds not only the body but inflicts permanent damage on the spirit as well.

Our objective, then, is not simply to shape the will, but to do so without breaking the spirit. To understand this dual objective of parenting, we need to clarify the distinction between the will and the spirit. The will, as we have seen, represents one's deeply ingrained desire to have his or her way. The intensity of this passion for independence varies from person to person, but it exists to one degree or another in almost all human beings. It may not show up in very compliant individuals until the twenties, thirties, or even beyond, but the telltale signs are there, nonetheless, waiting to be expressed when the circumstances are right. The eating disorder anorexia, for example, is believed to be related to this muted self-will that eventually asserts itself over the issue of food. At least in this arena, the "good little girl," and relatively fewer "nice little boys," can gain a measure of control over his or her circumstances in adolescence or young adulthood, despite agonizing pleas and warnings of parents, doctors, and friends.

The self-will of a very independent child, by contrast, may be fully operational at birth. It is remarkable how early it can make its presence known. Studies of the neonatal period indicate that at two or three days of age, an infant is capable of manipulating parents to get what he wants and needs. In 1999, psychologist Amanda Woodward, a professor at the University of Chicago, released a study concluding that long before the child can talk, he or she is able to size up adults and learn how to interact with them to his or her advantage.[1] This finding would not be surprising to the parents of strong-willed infants who have walked the floor in the wee small hours, listening to their tiny baby making his wishes abundantly clear.

A year or two later, some toddlers can become so angry that they are capable of holding their breath until they lose consciousness. Anyone who has ever witnessed this full measure of rage has been shocked by its power. It can also be quite audacious. The mother of one headstrong three-year-old told me her daughter refused to obey a direct command because, as she put it, "You're just a mommy, you know!" Another toddler screamed every time her mother grabbed her hand to guide her through a parking lot. She would yell at the top of her lungs: "Let go! You're hurting me!" The embarrassed mother, who was just trying to ensure her child's safety, would then have to deal with the hostile looks of other shoppers who thought she was abusing her child.

Truly, willfulness is a fascinating component of the human personality. It is not fragile or wobbly. It can and must be molded, shaped, and brought under the authority of parental leadership. Haven't you read news stories describing suicidal adults who stood on ledges or bridges, threatening to jump? Some of them have defied the combined forces of the Army, the Navy, and the Marine Corps, which sought desperately to save their lives. Even though these people had been emotionally sandbagged by life, their determination to control their own destiny remained intact and functional. My point is that parents will not harm a child by taking steps to gain control of a child's rebellious nature, even though it sometimes involves confrontation, sternness, warnings, and, when appropriate, reasonable punishment. Only by accepting the inevitable challenges to parental authority and then by "winning" at those critical moments can parents teach a headstrong boy or girl civilized behavior. And only then will that child be given the ability to control his or her own impulses in the years to come.

Now that we've discussed the necessity of shaping the will during early childhood, let's consider the other parental obligation that must be given emphasis. Whereas the will is made of titanium and steel, the human spirit is a million times more delicate. It reflects the self-concept or the sense of worthiness that a child feels. It is the most fragile characteristic in human nature and is especially vulnerable to rejection, ridicule, and failure. It must be handled with great care.

How, then, are we to shape the will while preserving the spirit? It is accomplished by establishing reasonable boundaries in advance and then enforcing them with love, while avoiding any implications that a child is unwanted, unnecessary, foolish, ugly, dumb, burdensome, embarrassing, or a terrible mistake. Any accusation or reckless comment that assaults the worth of a child, such as "You are so stupid!" can do lifelong damage. Other damaging remarks include "Why can't you make decent grades in school like your sister?" "You have been a pain in the neck ever since the day you were born!" "I told your mother it was stupid to have another child," "There are times when I would like to put you up for adoption," and "How could anyone love a fat slob like you?" Would parents actually say such hurtful things to a child? Unfortunately, they can, and they do. We are all capable of hurling harsh words at a child or teenager when we are intensely angry or frustrated. Once such mean, cutting words have left our lips, even though we may be repentant a few hours later, they have a way of burning their way into a child's soul where they may remain alive and virulent for the next fifty years.

This topic is so vitally important that I made it a centerpiece of my book *Bringing Up Boys.* Let me quote from a portion of that discussion, which should be especially relevant for parents who are dealing with a sometimes irritating strong-willed child.

> [Words] are so easy to utter, often tumbling out without much reason or forethought. Those who hurl criticism or hostility at others may not even mean or believe what they have said. Their comments may reflect momentary jealousy, resentment, depression, fatigue, or revenge. Regardless of the intent, harsh words sting like killer bees. Almost all of us, including you and me, have lived through moments when a parent, a teacher, a friend, a colleague, a husband, or a wife said something that cut to the quick. That hurt is now sealed forever in the memory bank. That is an amazing property of the spoken word. Even though a person forgets most of his or her day-by-day experiences, a particularly painful comment may be remembered for decades. By contrast, the individual who did the damage may have no memory of the encounter a few days later.

[Senator] Hillary Rodham Clinton told a story about her father, who never affirmed her as a child. When she was in high school, she brought home a straight-A report card. She showed it to her dad, hoping for a word of commendation. Instead, he said, "Well, you must be attending an easy school." Thirty-five years later the remark still burns in Mrs. Clinton's mind. His thoughtless response may have represented nothing more than a casual quip, but it created a point of pain that has endured to this day.[2]

If you doubt the power of words, remember what John the disciple wrote under divine inspiration. He said, "In the beginning was the Word, and the Word was with God, and the Word was God" (John 1:1). John was describing Jesus, the Son of God, who was identified personally with words. That makes the case about words as well as it will ever be demonstrated. Matthew, Mark, and Luke each record a related prophetic statement made by Jesus that confirms the eternal nature of His teachings. He said, "Heaven and earth will pass away, but my words will never pass away" (Matthew 24:35). We remember what He said to this hour, more than two thousand years later. Clearly, words matter.

There is additional wisdom about the impact of words written in the book of James. The passage reads:

> *When we put bits into the mouths of horses to make them obey us, we can turn the whole animal. Or take ships as an example. Although they are so large and are driven by strong winds, they are steered by a very small rudder wherever the pilot wants to go. Likewise the tongue is a small part of the body, but it makes great boasts. Consider what a great forest is set on fire by a small spark. The tongue also is a fire, a world of evil among the parts of the body. It corrupts the whole person, sets the whole course of his life on fire, and is itself set on fire by hell. (James 3:3-6)*

Have you ever set yourself on fire with sparks spraying from your tongue? More important, have you ever set a child's spirit on fire with anger? All of us have made that costly mistake. We knew we had blundered the moment the comment flew out of our mouth, but it was too late. If we tried for a hundred years, we couldn't take back a single remark. The first year Shirley and I were married, she became very angry with me about something that neither of us can recall. In the frustration of the moment she said, "If this is marriage, I don't want any part of it." She didn't mean it and regretted her words almost immediately. An hour later we had reconciled and forgiven each other, but Shirley's statement could not be taken back. We've laughed about it through the years and the issue is inconsequential today. Still, there is nothing either of us can do to erase the utterance of the moment.

Words are not only remembered for a lifetime, but if not forgiven, they endure beyond the chilly waters of death. We read in Matthew 12:36: "I tell you that men will have to give account on the day of judgment for every careless word they have spoken." Thank God, those of us who have a personal relationship with Jesus Christ are promised that our sins—and our harsh words—will be remembered against us no more and will be removed "as far as the east is from the west" (Psalm 103:12). Apart from that atonement, however, our words will follow us forever.

I didn't intend to preach a sermon here, because I am not a minister or a theologian. But I find great inspiration for all family relationships within the great wisdom of the Scriptures. And so it is with the impact of what we say. The scary thing for us parents is that we never know when the mental videotape is running during our interactions with children and teens. A comment that means little to us at the time may stick and be repeated long after we are dead and gone. By contrast, the warm and affirming things we say about our sons and daughters may be a source of satisfaction for decades. Again, it is all in the power of words.

Here's something else to remember. The circumstances that precipitate a hurtful comment for a child or teen are irrelevant to their impact. Let me explain. Even though a child pushes you to the limit, frustrating and angering you to the point of exasperation, you will nevertheless pay a price for overreacting. Let's suppose you lose your poise and shout, "I can't stand you! I wish you belonged to someone else." Or "I can't believe you failed another test. How could a son of mine be so stupid!" Even if every normal parent would also have been agitated in the same situation, your child will not focus on his misbehavior or failure in the future. He is likely to forget what he did to cause your outburst. But he will recall the day you said you didn't want him or that he was stupid. It isn't fair, but neither is life.

I know I'm stirring a measure of guilt into the mix with these comments. (My words are powerful too, aren't they?) My purpose, however, is not to hurt you but to make you mindful that everything you say has lasting meaning for a child. He may forgive you later for "setting the fire," but how much better it would have been to have stayed cool. You can learn to do that with prayer and practice.

It will also help to understand that we are most likely to say something hurtful when we are viscerally angry—when we are so perturbed that we aren't thinking rationally. The reason is because of the powerful biochemical reaction going on inside. The human body is equipped with an automatic defense system called the fight-or-flight mechanism, which prepares the entire organism for action. When we're upset or frightened, adrenaline is pumped into the bloodstream, setting off a series of physiological responses within the body. In a matter of seconds, the individual is transformed from a quiet condition to an "alarm reaction" state. The result is a red-faced father or mother who shouts things he or she had no intention of saying.

These biochemical changes are involuntary, operating quite apart from conscious choice. What is voluntary, however, is our reaction to them. We can learn to take a step back in a moment of excitation. We can choose to hold our tongue and remove ourselves from a provoking situation. As you have heard, it is wise to count to ten (or five hundred) before responding. It is extremely important to do this when we're dealing with children who anger us. We can control the impulse to lash out verbally or physically and avoid doing what we will certainly regret when the passion has cooled.

What should we do when we have lost control and said something that has deeply wounded a child? We should begin to repair the damage as quickly as possible. I have many fanatic golfing friends who have tried in vain to teach me their crazy game. They never give up even though it is a lost cause. One of them told me that I should immediately replace the divot after digging yet another hole with my club. He said that the quicker I could get that tuft of grass back in place, the faster its roots would reconnect. My friend was talking about golf, but I was thinking about people. When you have hurt someone, whether a child, a spouse, or a colleague, you must dress the wound before infection sets in. Apologize, if appropriate. Talk it out. Seek to reconcile. The longer the "divot" bakes in the sun, the smaller its chances for recovery will be. Isn't that a wonderful thought? Of course, the apostle Paul beat us to it. He wrote almost two thousand years ago, "Do not let the sun go down while you are still angry" (Ephesians 4:26). That Scripture has often been applied to husbands and wives, but I think it is just as valid with children.[3]

One more time: The goal in dealing with a difficult child is to shape the will without breaking the spirit. Hitting both targets is sometimes easier said than done. Perhaps it will help to share a letter from a mother who was having a terrible time with her son Jake. Her description of this child and her responses to him illustrate precisely how not to deal with a difficult boy or girl. (Note: The details of this letter have been changed slightly to conceal the identity of the writer.)

Dear Dr. Dobson:

More than anything else in this world, I want to have a happy family. We have two girls, ages three and five, and a boy who is ten. They don't get along at all. The boy and his father don't get along either. And I find myself screaming at the kids and sitting on my son to keep him from hitting and kicking his sisters.

His teacher of the past year thought he needed to learn better ways of getting along with his classmates. He had some problems on the playground and had a horrible time on the school bus. And he didn't seem to be able to walk from the bus stop to our house without getting in a fight or throwing rocks at somebody. So I usually pick him up and bring him home myself.

He is very bright but writes poorly and hates to do it. He is impulsive and quick-tempered (we all are now). He is tall and strong. Our pediatrician says he has "everything going for him." But Jake seldom finds anything constructive to do. He likes to watch television, play in the water, and dig in the dirt.

We are very upset about his diet but haven't been able to do anything about it. He drinks milk and eats Jell-O and crackers and toast. In the past he ate lots of hot dogs and bologna, but not much lately. He also craves chocolate and bubble gum. We have a grandma nearby who sees that he gets lots of it. She also feeds him baby food. We haven't been able to do anything about that, either.

Jake's teachers, the neighbor children, and his sisters complain about his swearing and name-calling. This is really an unfortunate situation because we're always thinking of him in a bad light. But hardly a day goes by when something isn't upset or broken. He's been breaking windows since he was a toddler. One day in June he came home early from school and found the house locked, so he threw a rock through his bedroom window, broke it, and crawled in. Another day recently he tried the glass cutter on our bedroom mirror. He spends a great deal of time at the grandma's who caters to him. We feel she is a bad influence, but so are we when we're constantly upset and screaming.

Anyhow, we have what seems to be a hopeless situation. He is growing bigger and stronger but not any wiser. So what do we do or where do we go?

My husband says he refuses to take Jake anywhere ever again until he matures and "acts like a civilized human being." He has threatened to put him in a foster home. I couldn't send him to a foster home. He needs people who know what to do with him. Please help us if you can.

Mrs. T.

P.S. Our children are adopted and there isn't much of anything left in our marriage.

This was a very sad plea for help, because the writer was undoubtedly sincere when she wrote, "more than anything else in this world, I want to have a happy family." From the tone of her letter, however, it was unlikely that she *ever* realized that greatest longing. In fact, that specific need for peaceful coexistence and harmony apparently led to many of her problems with Jake. She lacked the courage to do battle with him. It's possible that he suffered from ADHD (attention deficit/hyperactivity disorder), which I will discuss in an upcoming chapter. However, for the sake of our discussion here, let's look at the two very serious mistakes this mom made with her son.

First, Mr. and Mrs. T. failed to shape Jake's will, although he was begging for their intervention. It is an unsettling thing to be your own boss at ten years of age—unable to find even one adult who is strong enough to earn your respect. Why else would Jake have broken every rule and attacked every symbol of authority? He waged war on his teacher at school, but she was also baffled by his challenge. All she knew to do was call his trembling mother and report, "Jake needs to learn better ways of getting along with his classmates." (That was a kind way of putting it. I'm sure there were more caustic things the teacher could have said about this boy's classroom behavior!)

Jake was a brat on the school bus, he fought with his classmates on the way home, he broke windows and cut mirrors, he used the foulest language, and he tormented his sisters. He ate junk food and refused to complete his academic assignments or accept any form of responsibility. Can there be any doubt that Jake was screaming, "Look! I'm doing it all wrong! Doesn't anyone love me enough to care? Can't anyone help me? I hate the world and the world hates me!"

Mrs. T. and her husband were totally perplexed and frustrated. She responded by "screaming at the kids" and "sitting on [her] son" when he misbehaved. No one knew what to do with him. Even Grandma was a bad influence. Mom resorted to anger and high-pitched weeping and wailing. There is *no* more ineffective approach to child management than volcanic displays of anger, as we will see in the following chapter.

In short, Mrs. T. and her husband had totally abdicated their responsibility to provide leadership for their family. Note how many times she said, in essence, *we are powerless to act.* These parents were distressed over Jake's poor diet but wrote that they "haven't been able to do anything about it." Jake's grandmother fed him junk food and bubble gum, but they weren't able to do anything about that either. Likewise, they couldn't stop him from swearing or tormenting his sisters or breaking windows or throwing rocks at his peers. One has to ask "Why not?" Why was the family ship so difficult to steer? Why did it end up dashed to pieces on the rocks? The problem was that the ship and the crew had no captain! They drifted aimlessly in the absence of a leader—a decision maker who could guide them to safe waters.

The T. family not only failed to shape Jake's rampaging will, they also assaulted his wounded spirit with every conflict. Not only did they scream and cry and wring their hands in despair, but they demeaned his sense of personal worth and dignity. Can't you hear his angry father shouting, "Why don't you grow up and act like a civilized human being? Well, I'll tell you something! I'm through with you, boy! I'll never take you anywhere again or even let anyone know that you are my son. As a matter of fact, I'm not sure you are going to *be* my son for very long. If you keep acting like a lawless thug we're going to throw you out of the family—we're going to put you into a foster home. Then we'll see how you like it!" And with each accusation, Jake's self-esteem moved down another notch. But did these personal assaults make him sweeter and more cooperative? Of course not! He just became meaner and more bitter and more convinced of his own worthlessness. You see, Jake's spirit had been crushed, but his will still raged at hurricane velocity. And sadly, he then turned his self-hatred on his peers and family.

If circumstances had permitted (in other words, if I had been married to someone else), it would have been my pleasure to have had Jake in our home for a period of time. I don't believe it was too late to save him, and I would have felt challenged by the opportunity to try. How would I have approached this defiant youngster? By giving him the following message as soon as his suitcase was unpacked: "Jake, there are several things I want to talk over with you, now that you're a member of the family. First, you'll soon learn how much we love you in this house. I'm glad you're here, and I hope these will be the happiest days of your life. And you should know that I care about your feelings and problems and concerns. We invited you here because we wanted you to come, and you will receive the same love and respect that is given to our own children. If you have something on your mind, you can come right out and say it. I won't get angry or make you regret expressing yourself. Neither my wife nor I will ever intentionally do anything to hurt you or treat you unkindly. You'll see that these are not just empty promises that you're hearing. This is the way people act when they care about each other, and we already care about you.

"But, Jake, there are some other things you need to understand. There are going to be some definite rules and acceptable ways of behaving in this home, and you are going to have to live within them, just as our other children do. I will have them written for you by tomorrow morning. You will carry your share of responsibilities and jobs, and your schoolwork will be given high priority each evening. And you need to understand, Jake, that my most important job as your guardian is to see that you behave in ways that are healthy to yourself and others. It may take you a week or two to adjust to this new situation, but you're going to make it and I'm going to be here to see that you do. And when you refuse to obey, I will punish you immediately. In fact, I'm going to be right on your neck until you figure out that you can't beat the system. I have many ways to make you miserable, and I'm prepared to use them when necessary. This will help you change some of the destructive ways you've been acting in recent years. But even when I must discipline you, know that I will love you as much as I do right now. Nothing will change that."

The first time Jake disobeyed what he knew to be my definite instructions, I would have reacted decisively. There would have been no screaming or derogatory accusations, although he would quickly discover that I meant what I said. The following morning we would have discussed the issue rationally, reassuring him of our continuing love, and then started over.

Even the most delinquent children typically respond well to this pairing of love and consistent discipline! And it is a prescription for use in your own home too. I strongly suggest that you give it a go.

QUESTIONS AND ANSWERS

Q: My husband and I are divorced, so I have to handle all the discipline of the children myself. How does this change the recommendations you've made about discipline in the home?
A: Not at all. The principles of good discipline remain the same, regardless of the family setting. The procedures do become somewhat harder for one parent to implement since he or she has no additional support when the children become testy. Single mothers and fathers have to play both roles, which is not easily done. Nevertheless, children do not make allowances for difficult circumstances. As in any family, parents must earn their respect or they will not receive it.

Q: What do you think of the phrase "Children should be seen and not heard"?
A: That statement reveals a profound ignorance of children and their needs. I can't imagine how any loving adult could raise a vulnerable little boy or girl by that philosophy.

Q: Would you go so far as to apologize to a child if you felt you had been in the wrong?
A: I certainly would—and indeed, I have. A number of years ago I was burdened with pressing responsibilities that fatigued me and made me irritable. One particular evening I was especially grouchy and short-tempered with my ten-year-old daughter. I knew I was not being fair but was simply too tired to correct my manner. Through the course of the evening, I blamed Danae for things that were

not her fault and upset her needlessly several times. After going to bed, I felt bad about the way I had behaved, and I decided to apologize the next morning. After a good night of sleep and a tasty breakfast, I felt much more optimistic about life. I approached my daughter before she left for school and said, "Danae, I'm sure you know that daddies are not perfect human beings. We get tired and irritable just like other people, and there are times when we are not proud of the way we behave. I know I wasn't fair with you last night. I was terribly grouchy, and I want you to forgive me."

Danae put her arms around me and shocked me down to my toes. She said, "I knew you were going to have to apologize, Daddy, and it's okay; I forgive you."

Can there be any doubt that children are often more aware of the struggles between generations than their busy, harassed parents are?

SIX

THE MOST COMMON MISTAKE

IN OUR DISCUSSION of Jake and his family, I said that trying to control children by displays of anger and verbal outbursts is *the* most ineffective approach to management. It not only doesn't work, but it actually makes things worse. Researchers at the University of Washington, Dr. Susan Spieker and colleagues, found that parents who attempt to control their children by yelling and insulting them are likely to cause even more disruptive and defiant behavior.[1] It makes sense, doesn't it? If you yell at your kids, they will yell back at you—and more! Furthermore, there is an interactive effect. As the child becomes more rebellious, the parent becomes even angrier.

Unfortunately, when frustrated *most* adults fall into precisely that pattern of parenting. Educators often make the same mistake. I once heard a teacher say on national television, "I like being a professional educator, but I hate the daily task of teaching. My children are so unruly that I have to stay mad at them all the time just to control the classroom." How utterly demoralizing to be required to be mean and bad-tempered day in and day out to keep kids from going wild. Yet many teachers (and parents) know of no other way to make them obey. Believe me, it is exhausting and counterproductive! Let's look at why anger doesn't work.

Consider your *own* motivational system. Suppose you are driving home from work one afternoon, exceeding the speed limit by forty miles per hour. A police officer is standing on the corner, but there isn't much he can do in response. He has no car, no motorcycle, no badge, no gun, and no authority to write tickets. All he can do is scream insults at you and shake his fist as you pass. Would that cause you to slow down? Of course not! You might smile and wave as you hurry by. The officer's anger only emphasizes his impotence.

On the other hand, imagine yourself tearing through a school zone one morning on the way to the office. You suddenly look in the rearview mirror and see a black-and-white squad car bearing down on you from behind. Eight red lights are flashing and the siren is screaming. The officer uses his loudspeaker to tell you to pull over to the curb. When you have stopped, he opens his door and approaches your window. He is six foot nine, has a voice like the Lone Ranger's, and wears a big gun on his hip. His badge is gleaming in the light. He is carrying a little leather-bound book of citations that you have seen before—last month. The officer speaks politely but firmly, "Sir, I have you on radar traveling sixty-five miles per hour in a twenty-mile-per-hour zone. May I see your driver's license, please?" The officer doesn't scream, cry, or criticize you. He doesn't have to. You become putty behind the wheel. You fumble nervously to locate the small plastic card in your wallet (the one with the picture you hate). Your hands get sweaty and your mouth is dry as a bone. Your heart pounds like crazy in your throat. Why are you so breathless? It is because the course of *action* that the police officer is about to take is notoriously unpleasant. It will dramatically affect your future driving habits or, if you do not change, even cause you to do a lot of walking in the days ahead.

Six weeks later you go before a judge to learn your fate. He is wearing a black robe and sits high above the courtroom. Again, you are a nervous wreck. Not because the judge yells at you or calls you names—but because he has the power to make your day a little more unpleasant.

Neither the police officer nor the judge need to rely on anger to influence your behavior. They have far more effective methods of getting your attention. Their serenity and confidence are part of the aura of authority that creates respect. But what if they fail to understand that and begin to cry and complain? What if one of them says, "I don't know why you won't drive right. We've told you over and over that you can't break the law like this. You just continue to disobey no matter what we do." Then getting red-faced, he adds, "Well, I'll tell you this, young man, we're not going to take this anymore. Do you hear? Believe me, you're going to regret this . . . "

I'm sure you get the point. Anger does not influence behavior unless it implies that something irritating is about to happen. By contrast, *disciplinary action* does cause behavior to change. Not only does anger not work, I am convinced that it produces a destructive kind of disrespect in the minds of our children. They perceive that our frustration is caused by our inability to control the situation. We represent justice to them, yet we're on the verge of tears as we flail the air with our hands and shout empty threats and warnings.

I am not recommending that parents and teachers conceal their legitimate emotions from their children. I am not suggesting that we be like bland and unresponsive robots that hold everything inside. There are times when our boys and girls become insulting or disobedient to us, and revealing our displeasure is entirely appropriate. In fact, it *should* be expressed at a time like that, or else we will appear phony and wimpy. But it should never become a *tool* to get children to behave when we have run out of options and ideas. It is ineffective and can be damaging to the relationship between generations.

Let me give you another illustration that may be helpful. It will represent any one of 20 million homes on a typical evening. Henry is in the second grade and a constant whirlwind of activity. He has been wiggling and giggling since he got up that morning, but incredibly, he still has excess energy that needs to be burned. His mom is not in the same condition. She has been on her feet since staggering out of bed at 5:30 A.M. She fixed breakfast for the family, cleaned up the mess, got Dad off to work, sent Henry to school, and if she is employed, dropped off the younger kids at a day care center and rushed off to work. Or if she is a stay-at-home mom, she settled into a long day of trying to keep the preschoolers from killing each other. By late afternoon, she has put in nine hours of work without a rest. (Toddlers don't take breaks, unless they are nappers, so why should their mothers?)

Despite Mom's fatigue, she can hardly call it a day. Dad comes home from work and tries to help, but he is tired too. Mom still has at least six hours of work left to do, including grocery shopping, cooking dinner, giving baths to the little ones, changing their diapers, tucking them into bed, and helping Henry with his homework. I get depressed just thinking about such weary moms still working as the day draws to a close.

Henry is not so sympathetic, however, and arrives home from school in a decidedly mischievous mood. He can't find anything interesting to do, so he begins to irritate his uptight mother. He teases his little sister to the point of tears, pulls the cat's tail, and spills the dog's water. Mom is nagging by this time, but Henry acts like he doesn't notice. Then he goes to the toy closet and begins tossing out games and boxes of plastic toys and dumping out enough building blocks to construct a small city. Mom knows that someone is going to have to clean up all that mess, and she has a vague notion about who will get that assignment. The intensity of her voice is rising again. She orders him to the bathroom to wash his hands in preparation for dinner. Henry is gone for fifteen minutes. When he returns, his hands are still dirty. Mom's pulse is pounding through her arteries by this time and there is a definite migraine sensation above her left eye. Does this sound familiar?

Finally, Henry's bedtime arrives. But he does not *want* to go to bed, and he knows it will take his harassed mother at least thirty minutes to get him there. Henry does not do *anything* against his wishes unless his mother becomes very angry and blows up at him. Henry is sitting on the floor, playing with his games. Mom looks at her watch and says, "Henry, it's nearly eight o'clock [a thirty-minute exaggeration], so gather up your toys and go take your bath." Now Henry and Mom both know that she didn't mean for him to immediately take a bath. She merely wanted him to start thinking about taking his bath. She would have fainted dead away if he had responded to her empty command.

Approximately ten minutes later, Mom speaks again. "Now, Henry, it's getting later and you have school tomorrow; I want those toys picked up and then I want you in that tub!" She still does not expect Henry to obey, and he knows it. Her real message is, "We're getting closer, Hank." Henry shuffles around and stacks a box or two to demonstrate that he heard her. Then he settles down for a few more minutes of play. Six minutes pass and Mom issues another command, this time with more passion and threat in her voice, "Now listen, young man, I told you to get a move on, and I meant it!" To Henry, this means he must get his toys picked up and m-e-a-n-d-e-r toward the bathroom door. If his mother rapidly pursues him, then he must carry out the assignment posthaste. However, if Mom's mind wanders before she performs the last step of this ritual, or if the phone miraculously rings, Henry is free to enjoy a few minutes' reprieve.

You see, Henry and his mother are involved in a familiar one-act play. They both know the rules and the role being enacted by the opposite actor. The entire scene is preprogrammed, scripted, and computerized. It's a virtual replay of a scenario that occurs night after night. Whenever Mom wants Henry to do something he dislikes, she progresses through graduated steps of phony anger, beginning with calmness and ending with a red flush and threats. Henry does not have to move until she reaches her flash point, which signals that she is ready to do something about it. How foolish this game is. Since Mom controls Henry with empty threats, she must stay half-irritated all the time. Her relationship with her children is contaminated, and she ends each day with a pulsing headache. She can never count on instant obedience, because it takes her at least twenty or thirty minutes to work up a believable degree of anger.

How much better it is to use action to achieve the desired behavior and avoid the emotional outburst. Hundreds of approaches will bring a desired response: some involve minor pain; others offer a reward to a less naughty child.

When a parent's calm request for obedience is ignored by a child, Mom or

Dad should have some means of making their youngster want to cooperate. For those who can think of no such device, I will suggest one: There is a muscle lying snugly against the base of the neck. Anatomy books list it as the trapezius muscle, and when firmly squeezed, it sends little messengers to the brain saying, "This hurts: Avoid recurrence at all costs." The pain is only temporary; it can cause no damage the way I am suggesting its use. But it is an amazingly effective and practical recourse for parents when their youngster ignores a direct command to move.

Let's return to the bedtime scene with Henry and suggest how it could have been replayed more effectively. To begin, his mother should have forewarned him that he had fifteen more minutes to play. No one, child or adult, likes a sudden interruption of his activity. It then would have been wise to set the alarm clock or the stove buzzer. When the fifteen minutes passed and the buzzer sounded, Mom should have quietly told Henry to go take his bath. If he didn't move immediately, she could have taken Henry's face in her hands, looked him straight in the eye and said with conviction but not with frustration, "Do it NOW. Do you understand?" If the lad believes in his heart of hearts that she is prepared to punish him for delaying, no punishment will be necessary. If Henry learns that this procedure or some other unpleasantness is invariably visited upon him in such a moment, he will move before the consequences ensue. Authority, you see, is a subtle thing. It is conveyed mostly by confidence and determination, and sometimes a little bluster.

As for the use of punishment, I know that some readers could argue that the deliberate, premeditated application of minor pain to a small child is a harsh and unloving thing to do. To others, it will seem like pure barbarism. I obviously disagree. Given a choice between a harassed, screaming, threatening mother who blows up several times a day and a mom who has a reasonable, controlled response to disobedience, I would certainly recommend the latter. In the long run, the quieter home is better for Henry, too, because of the avoidance of strife between generations.

On the other hand, when a youngster discovers there is no threat behind the millions of words he hears, he stops listening to them. The only messages he responds to are those reaching a peak of emotion, which means much screaming and yelling. The child is pulling in the opposite direction, fraying Mom's nerves and straining the parent-child relationship. In the absence of action early in the conflict, the parent usually ends up punishing anyway. The consequences are also more likely to be severe, because by then the adult is irritated and out of control. And instead of the discipline being administered in a calm and judicious manner, the parent has become unnerved and frustrated, swinging wildly at the belligerent child. There is no reason for a fight to have occurred. The situation could have ended very differently if Mom had exhibited an attitude of confident authority.

Let's go back to Henry and his mother. Speaking softly, almost pleasantly, Mom says, "You know what happens when you don't mind me; now I don't see any reason why I should have to make you uncomfortable just to get your cooperation tonight, but if you insist, I'll play the game with you. When the buzzer sounds you let me know what the decision is."

The child then has the choice to make, and the advantages to him of obeying his mother's wishes are clear. She need not scream. She need not threaten to shorten his life. She need not become upset. She is in command. Of course, Mother will have to prove two or three times that she will apply the pain or other punishment if necessary. Occasionally throughout the coming months, Henry will check to see if she is still at the helm. That question is easily answered.

Understanding the interaction between Henry and his mother can be very helpful to parents who have become screamers and don't know why. Let's look at their relationship during that difficult evening as diagrammed in figure 3. Note that Henry's mother greets him at the front door after school, which represents a low point of irritation. From that time forward, however, her emotion builds and intensifies until it reaches a moment of explosion at the end of the day.

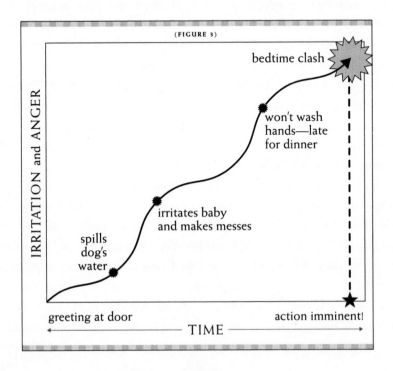

(FIGURE 3)

bedtime clash

won't wash hands—late for dinner

irritates baby and makes messes

spills dog's water

greeting at door

action imminent!

IRRITATION and ANGER

TIME

By her ultimate display of anger at bedtime, Mom makes it clear to Henry that she is through warning and is now ready to take definite action. You see, most parents (even those who are very permissive) have a point on the scale beyond which they will not be pushed; inevitable punishment looms immediately across that line. The amazing thing about children is that they know *precisely* where their parents typically draw the line. We adults reveal our particular points of action to them in at least six or eight subtle ways: Only at those moments do we use their middle names ("Jessica Emily Smith, get in that tub!"). Our speech becomes more staccato and abrupt ("Young! Lady! I! Told! You! . . . "). Our faces turn red (an important clue), we jump from our chair, and the child knows it is time to cooperate. It's all a game.

The other interesting thing about children is that, having identified the circumstances that immediately precede disciplinary action, they will take their parents directly to that barrier and bump it repeatedly but will *seldom* go beyond it deliberately. Once or twice Henry will ignore his mother's emotional fireworks, just to see if she has the courage to deliver on her promise. When that question has been answered, he will do what she demands in the nick of time to avoid punishment.

Now this brings us to the punch line of this important discussion. I must admit that what I am about to write is difficult to express and may not be fully understood by my readers. It may, however, be of value to parents who want to stop fighting with their children.

I have said that parental anger often signals to a child that the parents have reached their action line. Therefore, children obey, albeit reluctantly, only when Mom and Dad get mad, indicating that they will now resort to punishment. On the other hand, the parents observe that the child's surrender occurs simultaneously with their anger and inaccurately conclude that their emotional explosion is what forced the youngster to yield. Thus, their anger seems necessary for control in the future. They have grossly misunderstood the situation.

Returning one more time to the story of Henry, remember that his mother tells him repeatedly to take his bath. Only when she blows up does he get in the tub, leading her to believe that her anger produced his obedience. She is wrong! It was not her anger that sent Henry to the tub—it was the *action* he believed to be imminent. Her anger was nothing more than a tip-off that Mom was frustrated enough to spank his bottom. Henry *cares* about that!

I have written this entire chapter in order to convey this one message: You don't need *anger* to control children. You *do* need strategic action. Furthermore, you can apply the action anywhere on the time line that is convenient, and children will live contentedly within that boundary. In fact, the closer the action moves to the front of the conflict, the less punishment is required and the less often it is necessary. A squeeze of the trapezius muscle is not a sufficient deterrent at the end of a two-hour struggle, whereas it is more than adequate when the conflict is minimal. (Incidentally, I do not recommend that mothers weighing fewer than 120 pounds squeeze the shoulder muscles of their big teenagers. There are definite risks involved in that procedure. The general rule to follow is, if you can't reach it, don't squeeze it.)

The late Dr. Benjamin Spock, who wrote the perennial best seller, *Dr. Spock's Baby and Child Care,* was severely criticized for his laissez-faire approach to child rearing.[2] He was blamed for weakening parental authority and producing an entire generation of disrespectful and unruly children. To the man on the street, Dr. Spock became a symbol of permissiveness and overindulgence in parent-child relationships. It was a bum rap. I had lunch with him one day after we had been guests on a national television show and found our views to be surprisingly similar on most things not political.

Perhaps in response to the criticism that he experienced, Dr. Spock published a clarifying article entitled "How Not to Bring Up a Bratty Child." In it he wrote, "Parental submissiveness doesn't avoid unpleasantness; it makes it inevitable." A child's defiance, he said, "makes the parent increasingly more resentful, until it finally explodes in a display of anger."[3] He continued, "The way to get a child to do what must be done, or stop doing what should not be done, is to be clear and definite each time. . . . Parental firmness also makes for a happier child."[4] Finally, right before his death at ninety-three years of age, the old pediatrician was quoted as saying, "It's fine for parents to respect their children, but they often forget to ask for respect back."[5]

Dr. Spock was absolutely right. If you don't take a stand with your child early, she is *compelled* by her nature to push you further. Terrible battles are inevitable, especially during the adolescent years. The hesitant and guilt-ridden parent who is most anxious to avoid confrontation often finds himself or herself screaming and threatening throughout the day, and ultimately thrashing the child. Indeed, physical abuse may be the end result. However, if Mom and Dad have the courage and conviction to provide firm leadership from the earliest days of childhood, administering it in a context of genuine love, both generations will enjoy an atmosphere of harmony and respect. That is precisely what I have been trying to teach for over thirty years!

Contained in this simple explanation is an understanding of children that some adults comprehend intuitively, and which others never quite grasp. The concept involves the delicate balance between love and control, recognizing that implementing a reasonable and consistent action line does not assault self-worth; instead, it represents a source of security for an immature child.

I have had many mothers say to me over the years: "I don't understand my kids. They will do exactly what their father demands, but they won't mind me at all." There may be several reasons for this differential. First, fathers can be much more intimidating than mothers just by their "presence." The fact is that dads are often much bigger physically and have a deeper voice that has a way of encouraging a child to respond more quickly to their discipline. Second, children often look to their father for approval, and when he expresses his disappointment to them, they take it more to heart. Finally, and most pertinent here, because mothers usually spend more time with their children, they often get worn down and stop following through with discipline. When that's the case, children are bright enough to notice that Dad draws his action line earlier than Mom—and they'll behave accordingly.

There's another factor: Children often understand these forces better than their parents, who are bogged down with adult responsibilities and worries. That is why so many kids are able to win the contest of wills; they devote their *primary* effort to the game, while we grown-ups play only when we must. One father overheard his five-year-old daughter, Laura, say to her little sister, who was doing something wrong, "Mmmmm, I'm going to tell Mommy on you. No! I'll tell Daddy. He's worse!" Laura had evaluated the disciplinary measures of her two parents and concluded that one was more effective than the other.

This same child was observed by her father to have become especially disobedient and defiant. She was irritating other family members and looking for ways to avoid minding her parents. Her dad decided not to confront her directly about this change in behavior, but to punish her consistently for every offense until she settled down. For three or four days, he let Laura get away with nothing. She was spanked, stood in the corner, and sent to her bedroom. At the conclusion of the fourth day, she was sitting on the bed with her father and younger sister. Without provocation, Laura pulled the hair of the toddler, who was looking at a book. Her dad promptly took action and disciplined her. Laura did not cry, but sat in silence for a moment or two, and then said, "Hurrummph! All of my tricks are not working!"

If you think back to your own childhood years, you may remember similar events in which the disciplinary techniques of adults were consciously analyzed and their weaknesses probed. When I was a child, I once spent the night with a rambunctious friend who seemed to know every move his parents were going to make. Earl was like a military general who had deciphered the enemy code, permitting him to outmaneuver his opponents at every turn. After we were tucked into our own twin beds that night, he gave me an astounding description of his father's temper.

Earl said, "When my dad gets angry, he uses some really bad words that will amaze you." (He listed three or four startling examples.) I replied, "I don't believe it!" Mr. Walker was a very tall, reserved, Christian man who seemed to have it all together. I just couldn't conceive of him saying the words Earl had quoted.

"Want me to prove it to you?" said Earl mischievously. "All we have to do is keep on laughing and talking instead of going to sleep. My dad will come and tell us to be quiet over and over, and he'll get madder and madder every time he has to settle us down. Then you'll hear the cuss words. Just wait and see."

I was a bit dubious about the plan, but I did want to see the dignified Mr. Walker at his profane best. So Earl and I kept his poor father running back and forth like a yo-yo for over an hour. And as predicted, he became more intense and hostile each time he returned to our bedroom. I was getting very nervous and would have called off the demonstration, but Earl had been through it all before. He kept telling me, "It won't be long now."

Finally, about midnight, it happened. Mr. Walker's patience expired. He came thundering down the hall toward our room, shaking the entire house as his feet pounded the floor. He burst through the bedroom door and leaped on Earl's bed, flailing away at the boy, who was safely buried beneath three or four layers of blankets. Then from his lips came a stream of words that had seldom reached my tender ears. I was shocked, but Earl was delighted.

Even when his father was whacking the covers with his hand and screaming profanities, Earl raised up and shouted to me, "Did ya hear 'im? Huh? Didn't I tell ya? I told ya he would say it!" It's a wonder that Mr. Walker didn't kill his son at that moment!

I lay awake that night thinking about the episode and made up my mind *never* to let a child manipulate me like that when I grew up. Don't you see how important disciplinary techniques are to a child's respect for his parents? When a forty-five–pound bundle of trouble can deliberately reduce his powerful mother and father to a trembling, snarling mass of frustration, then something changes in the relationship. Something precious is lost. The child develops an attitude of contempt that is certain to erupt during the stormy adolescent years to come. I sincerely wish every adult understood that simple characteristic of human nature.

I've met a few wily grown-ups who had a great ability to lead kids. One of them lived near us in Arcadia, California. He owned and operated Bud Lyndon's Swim School and had a remarkable comprehension of the principles of discipline. I enjoyed sitting poolside just to watch the man work. However, there are few child developmentalists who could explain why he was so successful with the little swimmers in his pool. He was not soft and delicate in his manner; in fact, he tended to be somewhat gruff. When the kids got out of line, he splashed water in their faces and said sternly, "Who told you to move? Stay where I put you until I ask you to swim!" He called the boys "men of tomorrow" and other pet names. His class was regimented, and every minute was utilized purposefully. But would you believe it, the children loved Bud Lyndon. Why? Because they knew he loved them. Within his gruff manner was a message of affection that might escape the adult observer. Mr. Lyndon never embarrassed a child intentionally, and he covered for the youngster who swam poorly. He delicately balanced his authority with a subtle affection that attracted children like the pied piper. Mr. Bud Lyndon understood the meaning of discipline with love.

When I was in ninth grade I had an athletic coach who affected me in the same way. He was the master of the moment, and no one *dared* challenge his authority. I would have fought wild lions before tackling Mr. Ayers. Yes, I feared him. We all did. But he never abused his power. He treated me courteously and respectfully at a time when I needed all the dignity I could get. Combined with his acceptance of the individual was an obvious self-confidence and ability to lead a pack of adolescent wolves who had devoured less capable teachers. And that's why my ninth-grade gym coach had a greater influence on me than any other person during my fifteenth year. Mr. Craig Ayers understood discipline with love.

Not all parents can be like Mr. Lyndon or Mr. Ayers, and I would not suggest that they try. Nor would it be wise for a parent at home to display the same gruffness that is appropriate on the athletic field or at the pool. Parents must fit their disciplinary approach to their own personality patterns and the responses that feel natural. However, the overriding principle remains the same for men and women, mothers and fathers, coaches and teachers, pediatricians and psychologists: It involves discipline with love, a reasonable introduction to responsibility and self-control, parental leadership with a minimum of anger, respect for the dignity and worth of the child, realistic boundaries that are enforced with confident firmness, and a judicious use of rewards and punishments to those who challenge and resist. It is a system that bears the approval of the Creator Himself.

QUESTIONS AND ANSWERS

Q: It's easy for you to tell me not to get angry at my children, but there are times when they just make me furious. For example, I have a horrible time getting my ten-year-old daughter ready for school in the morning. She will get up when I insist, but she dawdles and plays as soon as I leave the room. I have to goad and push and warn her every few minutes or she will be late. So I get more and more angry and usually end up screaming insults at her. I know this is not the best way to handle her, but she makes me so mad! Tell me how I can get her moving without this emotion every day.

A: You are playing right into your daughter's hands by assuming the responsibility for getting her ready every morning. A ten-year-old should definitely be able to handle that task on her own, but your anger is not likely to bring about her independence. Let me offer a possible solution that has been helpful to others. It will focus on a child named Debbie.

Debbie's morning time problem related primarily to her compulsivity about her room. She would not leave for school unless her bed was made perfectly and every trinket was in its proper place. This was not something her mother taught her; Debbie was always very meticulous about her possessions. (I should add that her brother never had this problem.) Debbie could have easily finished those tasks on time if she was motivated to do so, but she was never in a particular hurry. So Mom began to fall into the same habit you described—warning, threatening, pushing, shoving, and ultimately becoming angry as the clock moved toward the deadline.

Debbie's mother and I discussed the problem and agreed that there had to be a better method of getting through the morning. I subsequently created a system that we called "checkpoints." It worked like this: Debbie was instructed to get out of bed before 6:30 each morning. It was her responsibility to set her alarm and get herself up. As soon as she got up, she immediately went to the kitchen, where a chart was taped to the refrigerator door. She then circled "yes" or "no" for the first checkpoint (getting up by 6:30) for that day. Even one minute late was considered a missed item. It couldn't have been more simple. She either did or did not get up by 6:30.

The second checkpoint occurred at 7:10. By that time, Debbie was required to have her room straightened to her own satisfaction, be dressed, have her teeth brushed and hair combed, and so forth, and be ready to practice the piano. Forty minutes was ample time for these tasks, which could actually be done in ten to fifteen minutes if she wanted to hurry. Thus, the only way she could miss the second checkpoint was to ignore it deliberately.

Now, what meaning did the checkpoints have? Did failure to meet them bring anger and wrath and gnashing of teeth? Of course not. The consequences were straightforward and fair. If Debbie missed one checkpoint, she was required to go to bed thirty minutes earlier than usual that evening. If she missed two, she hit her pillow an hour before her assigned hour. She was permitted to read during that time in bed, but she could not watch television or talk on the telephone. This procedure took all the morning pressure off of the mother and placed it on Debbie's shoulders, where it belonged. There were occasions when Mom would get up just in time to fix breakfast, only to find Debbie sitting soberly at the piano, clothed and ready for the day.

This system of discipline can serve as a model for parents whose children have similar behavioral problems. It was not oppressive; in fact, Debbie seemed to enjoy having a target to shoot for. The limits of acceptable performance were defined beyond question. The responsibility was clearly placed on the child. Consequences of noncompliance were fair and easily administered. And this system required no adult anger or foot stomping.

You can adapt this concept in order to resolve the thorny conflicts in *your* home too. The only limit lies in the creativity and imagination of the parent.

Q: Sometimes my husband and I disagree on our discipline and argue in front of our children about what is best. Do you think this is damaging?
A: Yes, I do. You and your husband should present a united front, especially when children are watching. If you disagree on an issue, it can be discussed later in private. Unless the two of you can come to a consensus, your children will begin to perceive that standards of right and wrong are arbitrary. They will also make end runs around the tougher parent to get the answer they want. There are even more serious consequences for boys and girls when parents are radically different in their approach.

Here's the point of danger: Some of the most hostile, aggressive teenagers I've seen come from family constellations where the parents have leaned in opposite directions in their discipline. Suppose the father is unloving and disinterested in the welfare of his kids. His approach is harsh and physical. He comes home tired and may knock them around if they get in his way. The mother is permissive by nature. She worries every day about the lack of love in the father-child relationships. Eventually she sets out to compensate for it. When Dad sends their son to bed without his dinner, Mom slips him milk and cookies. When he says no to a particular request, she finds a way to say yes. She lets the kids get away with murder because it is not in her spirit to confront them.

What happens under these circumstances is that the authority figures in the family contradict each other and cancel each other out. Consequently, the child is caught in the middle and often grows up hating both. It doesn't always work that way, but the probability for trouble is high. The middle ground between extremes of love and control must be sought if we are to produce healthy, responsible children.

Q: I see now that I've been doing many things wrong with my children. Can I undo the harm?
A: I doubt it is too late to do things right, although your ability to influence your children lessens with the passage of time. Fortunately we are permitted to make many mistakes with our kids. They are resilient, and they usually survive our errors in judgment. It's a good thing they do, because none of us can be a perfect parent. Besides, it's not the occasional mistakes that hurt a child—it is the consistent influence of destructive conditions throughout childhood that does the damage.

Q: My six-year-old has suddenly become mouthy and disrespectful at home. She told me to "buzz off" when I asked her to take out the trash, and she calls me names when she gets angry. I feel it is important to permit this emotional outlet, so I haven't tried to suppress it. Do you agree?
A: I'm afraid I don't. Your daughter is aware of her sudden defiance, and she's waiting to see how far you will let her go. If you don't discourage disrespectful behavior now, you can expect some wild experiences during the adolescent years to come.

With regard to your concern about emotional ventilation, you are right that your daughter needs to express her anger. She should be free to say almost anything to you provided it is said in a respectful manner. It is acceptable to say, "I think you love my brother more than me" or "You weren't fair with me, Mommy." There is a thin line between what is acceptable and unacceptable behavior at this point. The child's expression of strong frustration, even resentment and anger, should be encouraged if it exists. You certainly don't want her to bottle it inside. On the other hand, you should not permit your daughter to resort to name-calling and open rebellion. "Mom, you hurt my feelings in front of my friends" is an acceptable statement. "You stupid idiot, why didn't you shut up when my friends were here?!" is absolutely unacceptable.

If your daughter approaches you respectfully, as described in the first statement, it would be wise for you to sit down and try to understand the child's viewpoint. Be big enough to apologize if you have wronged her in some way. If you feel you are in the right, however, calmly explain why you acted as you did and tell your daughter how she can avoid a collision next time. It is possible to ventilate feelings without sacrificing parental respect, and the child should be taught how to do it. This communication tool will be very useful later in life, especially in marriage.

SEVEN

GEARING DISCIPLINE TO THE NEEDS OF CHILDREN

YVONNE, A MOTHER FROM SAN ANTONIO, wrote, "I was at the library with my twenty-month-old, Christy. I asked the librarian to help me locate *The Strong-Willed Child*, which was new at the time. As the librarian was filling out a form to request the book from a neighboring library, Christy threw herself on the floor in a tantrum because I wouldn't let her run between the shelves. The lady looked at me and asked, 'Shall we put *RUSH* on it?'"

While the broad principles I have provided to this point are widely applicable to children, each boy and girl is different, requiring his or her parents to interpret and apply them individually to the complex personality patterns evident in that particular youngster. Added to that challenge is the fact that the target is always moving. Developmental stages are in constant flux, so that Mom and Dad must be prepared to zig and zag year by year. An approach that is entirely appropriate and effective at age five may be obsolete by six or seven, creating a need for something entirely different. Then adolescence comes crashing onto the scene, and everything is thrown up for grabs. The best I can do to assist you in responding to this ever-changing pattern is to offer some guidelines for each age category and suggest that you use them to formulate your own techniques and understanding.

Let's begin at birth and weave our way through the childhood years. Please understand that this discussion is by no means exhaustive and merely suggests the general nature of disciplinary methods at specific periods.

BIRTH TO SEVEN MONTHS

No *direct* discipline is necessary for a child under seven months of age, regardless of the behavior or circumstance. Many parents do not agree and find themselves swatting a child of six months for wiggling while being diapered or for crying at midnight. This is a serious mistake. A baby is incapable of comprehending his offense or associating it with the resulting punishment. At this early age, infants need to be held, loved, touched, and soothed with the human voice. They should be fed when hungry and kept clean and dry and warm. It is probable that the foundation for emotional and physical health is laid during this first six-month period, which should be characterized by security, affection, and warmth.

On the other hand, it is possible to create a fussy, demanding baby by rushing to pick him up every time she utters a whimper or sigh. Infants are fully capable of learning to manipulate their parents through a process called reinforcement, whereby any behavior that produces a pleasant result will tend to recur. Thus, a healthy baby can keep her mother or father hopping around her nursery twelve hours a day (or night) by simply forcing air past her sandpaper larynx. To avoid this consequence, you need to strike a balance between giving your baby the attention she needs and establishing her as a tiny dictator. Don't be afraid to let her cry for a reasonable period of time (which is thought to be healthy for the lungs). It is necessary, though, to listen to the tone of her voice to determine if she's crying because of random discontent or genuine distress. Most parents learn to recognize this distinction very quickly.

In keeping with our theme, I need to say the obvious: Yes, Virginia, there *are* easy babies and difficult babies! Some seem determined to dismantle the homes into which they were born; they sleep cozily during the day and then howl in protest all night; they are often colicky and spit up the vilest stuff on their clothes (usually on the way to church); they control their internal plumbing until you hand them to friends, and then they let it blast. Instead of cuddling into the fold of the arms when being held, they stiffen rigidly in search of freedom. And parents who wonder shortly after birth, "Will this baby survive?" may find themselves leaning sock eyed over a vibrating crib at 3 A.M., asking, "Will *we* survive?"

Both generations usually recover before long, and this disruptive beginning becomes nothing but a dim memory for the parents. And from that demanding tyrant will grow a thinking, loving human being with an eternal soul and a special place in the heart of the Creator. To the exhausted and harassed parents, let me say, "Hang tough! You're doing *the* world's most important assignment."

EIGHT TO FOURTEEN MONTHS

Many children will begin to test the authority of their parents during the second seven-month period. The confrontations will be minor and infrequent before the first birthday, yet the beginnings of future struggles can be seen. Our daughter, Danae, for example, challenged Shirley for the first time when she was just nine months old. My wife was waxing the kitchen floor when Danae crawled to the edge of the linoleum. Shirley said, "No, Danae," gesturing to the child not to enter the kitchen. Since our daughter began talking very early, she clearly understood the meaning of the word *no*. Nevertheless, she crawled straight onto the sticky wax. Shirley picked her up and sat her down in the doorway, while saying *no* more firmly. Not to be discouraged, Danae scrambled back onto the newly mopped floor. My wife took her back, saying *no* even more firmly as she put her down. Seven times this process was repeated, until Danae finally yielded and crawled away in tears. As best as we can recall, that was the first direct collision of wills between my daughter and wife. Many more encounters were to follow.

How do parents discipline a one-year-old? Very carefully and gently! Children at this age are easy to distract and divert. Rather than jerking a china cup from their hands, show them a brightly colored alternative—and then be prepared to catch the cup when it falls. When unavoidable confrontations occur, as with Danae crawling onto the waxy floor, win them by firm persistence—not by punishment. Again, don't be afraid of the child's tears, which can become a potent weapon to avoid naptime or bedtime or a diaper change. Have the courage to lead the child without being harsh or mean or gruff.

Before leaving this dynamic time of life, I must share with you the findings of a ten-year study of children between the ages of eight and eighteen months. While this investigation, known as Harvard University's Preschool Project, was completed more than twenty-five years ago, its findings are still relevant for today. The researchers, led by Dr. Burton White, studied the young children intently during the ten-year period, hoping to discover how experiences in the early years of life contribute to the development of a healthy, intelligent human being. The conclusions from this exhaustive effort are summarized below, as reported originally in the *American Psychological Association Monitor:*[1]

- It is increasingly clear that the origins of human competence are to be found in a critical period of development between eight and eighteen months of age. The child's experiences during these brief months do more to influence future intellectual competence than any time before or after.
- The single most important environmental factor in the life of the child is the mother. According to Dr. White, "she is on the hook" and carries

more influence on her child's experiences than any other person or circumstance.

- The amount of *live* language directed to a child (not to be confused with television, radio, or overheard conversations) is vital to her development of fundamental linguistic, intellectual, and social skills. The researchers concluded, "Providing a rich social life for a twelve- to fifteen-month-old child is the best thing you can do to guarantee a good mind."

- Those children who are given free access to living areas of their homes progress much faster than those whose movements are restricted.

- The nuclear family is the most important educational delivery system. If we are going to produce capable, healthy children, it will be by strengthening family units and by improving the interactions that occur within them.

- The best parents in the study were those who excelled at three key functions:

  1. They were superb designers and organizers of their children's environments.

  2. They permitted their children to interrupt them for brief thirty-second episodes, during which personal consultation, comfort, information, and enthusiasm were exchanged.

  3. They were "firm disciplinarians while simultaneously showing great affection for their children." (I couldn't have said it better myself.)

These findings speak eloquently about the issues that matter most in early childhood. I hear within them an affirmation and validation of the concepts to which I have devoted my professional life.

FIFTEEN TO TWENTY-FOUR MONTHS

It has been said that all human beings can be classified into two broad categories: those who would vote yes to the various propositions of life and those who would be inclined to vote no. I can tell you with confidence that each toddler around the world would definitely cast a negative vote! If there is one word that characterizes the period between fifteen and twenty-four months of age, it is *no!* No, they don't want to eat their cereal. No, they don't want to play with their building blocks. No, they don't want to take a bath. And you can be sure that, no, they don't want to go to bed, ever. It is easy to see why this period of life has been called "the first adolescence," because of the negativism, conflict, and defiance of the age.

Dr. T. Berry Brazelton authored a helpful book called *Toddlers and Parents* that included an insightful description of the "terrible twos."[2] Quoted below is his classic description of a typical eighteen-month-old boy named Greg. Although I have never met this little fellow, I know him well . . . as you will when your child becomes a toddler.

When Greg began to be negative in the second year, his parents felt as if they had been hit by a sledge hammer. His good nature seemed submerged under a load of negatives. When his parents asked anything of him, his mouth took on a grim set, his eyes narrowed, and, facing them squarely with his penetrating look, he replied simply, "no!" When offered ice cream, which he loved, he preceded his acceptance with a "no." While he rushed out to get his snowsuit to go outside, he said "no" to going out.

His parents' habit of watching Greg for cues now began to turn sour. He seemed to be fighting with them all of the time. When he was asked to perform a familiar chore, his response was, "I can't." When his mother tried to stop him from emptying his clothes drawer, his response was, "I have to." He pushed hard on every familiar imposed limit, and never seemed satisfied until his parent collapsed in defeat. He would turn on the television set when his mother left the room. When she returned, she turned it off, scolded Greg mildly, and left again. He turned it on. She came rushing back to reason with him, to ask him why he'd disobeyed her. He replied, "I have to." The intensity of her insistence that he leave it alone increased. He looked steadily back at her. She returned to the kitchen. He turned it on. She was waiting behind the door, swirled in to slap his hands firmly. He sighed deeply and said, "I have to." She sat down beside him, begging him to listen to her to avoid real punishment. Again he presented a dour mask with knitted brows to her, listening but not listening. She rose wearily, he walked over to the machine to turn it on. As she came right back, tears in her eyes, to spank him, she said, "Greg, why do you want me to spank you? I hate it!" To which he replied, "I have to." As she crumpled in the chair, weeping softly with him across her lap, Greg reached up to touch her wet face.

After this clash, Mrs. Lang was exhausted. Greg sensed this and began to try to be helpful. He ran to the kitchen to fetch her mop and her dustpan, which he dragged in to her as she sat in her chair. This reversal made her smile and she gathered him up in a hug.

Greg caught her change in mood and danced off gaily to a corner, where he slid behind a chair, saying "hi and see." As he pushed the chair out, he tipped over a lamp which went crashing to the floor. His mother's reaction was, "No, Greg!" He curled up on the floor, his hands over his ears, eyes tightly closed, as if he were trying to shut out all the havoc he had wrought.

As soon as he was put into his high chair, he began to whine. She was so surprised that she stopped preparation of his food, and took him to change him. This did not settle the issue, and when she brought him to his chair again, he began to squirm and twist. She let him down to play until his lunch was ready. He lay on the floor, alternately whining and screeching. So unusual was this that she . . . felt his forehead for fever. . . . Finally, she returned to fixing his lunch. Without an audience, Greg subsided.

When she placed him in his chair again, his shrill whines began anew. She placed his plate in front of him with cubes of food to spear with his fork. He tossed the implement overboard, and began to push his plate away, refusing the food. Mrs. Lang was nonplussed, decided he didn't feel well, and offered him his favorite ice cream. Again, he sat helpless, refusing to feed himself. When she offered him some, he submissively allowed himself to be fed a few spoonfuls. Then he knocked the spoon out of her hand and pushed the ice cream away. Mrs. Lang was sure that he was ill.

Mrs. Lang extracted Greg from his embattled position, and placed him on the floor to play while she ate lunch. This, of course, wasn't what he wanted either. He continued to tease her, asking for food off her plate, which he devoured greedily. His eagerness disproved her theory of illness. When she ignored him and continued to eat, his efforts redoubled. He climbed under the sink to find the bleach bottle which he brought to her on command. He fell forward onto the floor and cried loudly as if he'd hurt himself. He began to grunt as if he were having a bowel movement and to pull on his pants. This was almost a sure way of drawing his mother away from her own activity, for she'd started trying to "catch" him and put him on the toilet. This was one of his signals for attention, and she rushed him to the toilet. He smiled smugly at her, but refused to perform. Mrs. Lang felt as if she were suddenly embattled on all fronts—none of which she could win.

When she turned to her own chores, Greg produced the bowel movement he'd been predicting.[3]

This, my friends, was not a description of a typical toddler. Greg was a classic strong-willed child. He was having fun at the expense of his mama, and he almost took the measure of her. I'll talk in a moment about how such a child should be handled.

The picture painted by Dr. Brazelton sounds pretty bleak, and admittedly, there are times when a two-year-old can dismantle the peace and tranquility of a home. (Our son, Ryan, loved to blow bubbles in the dog's water dish—a game that horrified us.) However, with all of its struggles, there is no more delightful time in life than this period of dynamic blossoming and unfolding. New words are being learned daily, and the cute verbal expressions of that age will be remembered for a half century. It is a time of excitement over fairy tales and make-believe and furry puppy dogs. And most important, it is a precious time of loving and warmth that will scurry by all too quickly. There are millions of older parents with grown children today who would give all they possess to relive those bubbly days with their toddlers.

Let me make a few recommendations about discipline that will, I hope, be helpful when a toddler is on the warpath. I must hasten to say, however, that the negativism of this turbulent period is both normal and healthy, and *nothing* will make an eighteen-month-old act like a five-year-old. Time is the only real "cure."

Now, let's talk about Greg. His kind of misbehavior is what Mrs. Susanna Wesley was referring to when she wrote, "In order to form the minds of children, the first thing to be done is to conquer the will, and bring them into an obedient temper. To inform the understanding is a work of time, and must with children proceed by slow degrees as they are able to bear it; but the subjecting of the will is a thing which must be done at once, and the sooner the better!" I'm not sure Mrs. Lang accomplished that purpose.

When times of confrontation occur with a strong-willed toddler such as

Greg, mild slaps on the bottom or the hand can begin between fifteen and eighteen months of age. They should be relatively infrequent and must be reserved for the kind of defiance he displayed over the television set. He understood what was expected of him but he refused to comply. This behavior is what I have been referring to as willful defiance. Greg was clearly taunting his mother and testing the limits of her endurance. Mrs. Lang mishandled the situation. I'm not being critical of her. I fully understand her frustration and am sure that most mothers would have responded similarly. Nevertheless, she needed to win that battle decisively in order to avoid endless recurrences down the road, but she failed to get that done.

Look again at the mistakes this mother made. When Greg turned the television set on after she had pointedly turned it off, Mrs. Lang "scolded Greg mildly." He did it again and she "came rushing back to reason with him." Then she asked him why he disobeyed her. He said "I have to" and turned the television on again. Finally, Mom "swirled in to slap his hands firmly." Slapping Greg's hands was the right thing to do, but it came far too late. She should have done that after he had been warned once and then disobeyed again. Mrs. Lang's other measures were not only ineffective, but they made things worse. It is a total waste of time to "reason" with a toddler in a moment of defiance, and certainly, one does not whine and ask him "why?" You will never get a satisfactory answer to that question. If Greg had had a few more years on him and told the truth, he would have said, "Because I'm trying to drive you nuts, that's why." Mrs. Lang wound up begging her strong-willed boy to listen and obey, and then cried when he forced her to punish him. Those were all the wrong things to have done.

I have concentrated on this story because it is applicable to millions of parents who have been led to believe that mild punishment is somehow harmful to children, and that even if it is applied, it should be a last resort after scolding, whining, begging, crying, explaining repeatedly, and trying to reason. These responses to blatant misbehavior undermine authority and put the parent on the same level with the child. What heady stuff it is for a two-year-old to take on a powerful adult and reduce her to tears.

Mrs. Lang should have come back into the room after the television set went on the second time and sat down with a word of advice for her little boy. She should have put her hands on either side of his head, looked him straight in the eyes, and said firmly, "Listen to me, Greg. Mommy does not want you to touch the television set again. Do you hear me? DON'T TOUCH IT AGAIN. Do you understand?" What she would have been doing in that moment was drawing the boundary lines vividly in Greg's mind. Then if he went back to the set for round three, she should have been standing nearby. The hand-slapping response should have occurred right then. It would not have been necessary to explain or reason. It would have been enough that his mother had given him an order. For most children, tears would have occurred and quenched the rebellious mood Greg was in. In most cases, that would have ended the matter. If he was especially tough, Greg might have tested his mother again. Without screaming or crying or begging, she would have needed simply to outlast him, no matter how long it took. Remember that Dr. Brazelton said Greg never seemed satisfied until his mother collapsed in defeat. That is why Mom should never have let that happen. This toddler should have come out of this encounter with the shocking belief that *Mom means business. I don't like what happened to me. I'd better do what she says.*

This response by the mother *must* be done without abusing the child physically or emotionally. I am convinced from my many years of working with parents that a frustrated woman like Mrs. Lang is less likely to do something unthinkable if she is empowered to handle the challenge early—before it becomes a donnybrook—rather than wait until she is too frazzled to control herself.

Let me caution parents not to punish toddlers for behavior that is natural and necessary to learning and development. Exploration of their environment, for example, is of great importance to intellectual stimulation. You and I will look at a crystal trinket and obtain whatever information we seek from that visual inspection. Toddlers, however, will expose it to all their senses. They will pick it up, taste it, smell it, wave it in the air, pound it on the wall, throw it across the room, and listen to the pretty sound it makes when shattering. By that process, they learn a bit about gravity, rough versus smooth surfaces, the brittle nature of glass, and some startling things about their parent's anger. (This is not what Greg was doing. He was not exploring. He was disobeying.)

Am I suggesting that kids, strong-willed or otherwise, be allowed to destroy a home and all of its contents? No, but neither is it right to expect curious toddlers to keep their fat little fingers to themselves. Parents should remove those items that are fragile or particularly dangerous and then strew their children's path with fascinating objects of all types. Permit them to explore everything that is not breakable. Do not ever punish them for touching something, regardless of its value, that they *did not know was off-limits*. With respect to dangerous items, such as electric plugs and stoves, as well as a few untouchable objects such as the TV controls, it is possible and necessary to teach and enforce the command "Don't touch!" After making it clear what is expected, a slap on the hand will usually discourage repeat episodes.

Entire books have been written about disciplining young children. I wrote a couple of them. I have only touched on the subject here to give a flavor of the proper approach to management of toddlers—even a confirmed revolutionary like Greg.

TWO TO THREE YEARS OF AGE

Perhaps the most frustrating aspect of raising children between two and three is their tendency to spill things, destroy things, eat horrible things, fall off things, flush things, kill things, and get into things. They also have a knack for doing embarrassing things, like sneezing on the man seated near them at McDonald's. During the toddler years, any unexplained silence of more than thirty seconds can throw an adult into a sudden state of panic. What mother has not had the thrill of opening the bedroom door, only to find Hurricane Hannah covered with lipstick from the top of her head to the carpet on which she stands? Beside her is a red handprint she has placed in the center of the carpet. Throughout the room is the aroma of Chanel No. 5, with which she has anointed a younger sibling. Wouldn't it be interesting to hold a national convention sometime, bringing together all the mothers who have experienced similar traumas?

When my daughter was two years of age, she was fascinated the first time she watched me shave in the morning. She stood captivated as I put the shaving cream on my face and began using the razor. That should have been my first clue that something was up. The following morning, Shirley came into the bathroom to find our dog, Siggie, sitting in his favorite spot on the furry lid of the toilet seat. Danae had covered his head with lather and was systematically shaving the hair from his shiny skull! Shirley screamed, "Danae!" which sent Siggie and his barber scurrying for safety. It was a hilarious sight to see the little wiener dog standing in the bedroom with nicks and bald spots on his head.

When Ryan was the same age, he had an incredible ability to make messes. He could turn something over and spill it faster than any kid I've ever seen, especially at mealtime. (Once while eating a peanut-butter sandwich, he thrust his hand through the bottom side. When his fingers emerged at the top they were covered with peanut butter, and Ryan didn't recognize them. The poor lad clamped down severely on his index finger.) Because of this destructive inclination, Ryan heard the word *mess* repeatedly from Shirley and me. It became one of the most important words in his vocabulary. One evening while taking a shower I left the door ajar and got some water on the floor. As you might expect, Ryan came thumping around the corner and stepped in it. He looked up at me and said in the gruffest voice he could manage, "Whuss all this mess in hyere?"

You *must* keep a sense of humor during the twos and threes in order to preserve your own sanity. But you must also proceed with the task of instilling obedience and respect for authority. Thus, most of the comments written in the preceding section also apply to the child between twenty-two and thirty-six months of age. Although the older toddler is much different physically and emotionally than he was at eighteen months, the tendency to test and challenge parental authority is still very much in evidence. In fact, when young toddlers consistently win the early confrontations and conflicts, they become even more difficult to handle in the second and third years. Then a lifelong disrespect for authority often begins to settle into their young minds. Therefore, I cannot overemphasize the importance of instilling two distinct messages within your child before she is forty-eight months of age:

- "I love you more than you can possibly understand. You are precious to me and I thank God every day He let me raise you!"
- "Because I love you, I must teach you to obey me. That is the only way I can take care of you and protect you from things that might hurt you. Let's read what the Bible tells us: 'Children, obey your parents in the Lord, for this is right'" (Ephesians 6:1).

The broad principle, which appears throughout this book, bears repeating. Healthy parenting can be boiled down to those two essential ingredients: love and control. They must operate in a system of checks and balances. Any concentration on love to the exclusion of control usually breeds disrespect and contempt. Conversely, an authoritarian and oppressive home atmosphere is deeply resented by the child who feels unloved or even hated. The objective for the toddler years is to strike a balance between mercy and justice, affection and authority, love and control.

Specifically, how does one discipline a naughty two- or three-year-old child? One possible approach is to require her to sit in a chair and think about what she has done. This is the concept often referred to as a time-out. Most children of this age are bursting with energy and absolutely hate to spend ten dull minutes with their wiggly posteriors glued to a chair. To some individuals, this form of punishment can be even more effective than a spanking and is remembered longer.

Parents to whom I have recommended using time-outs have often asked, "But what if they won't stay in the chair?" The same question is asked with reference to the child's tendency to pop out of bed after being tucked in at night. These are examples of the direct confrontation I have been describing. Parents who cannot require a toddler to stay on a chair for a few minutes or in bed at the end of the day are not yet in command of the child. There is no better time than now to change the relationship.

I would suggest that the youngster be placed in bed and given a little speech, such as, "Brandon, this time Mommy means business. Are you listening to me? Do *not* get out of this bed. Do you understand me?" Then when his feet touch the floor, give him one swat on the legs or backside with a small paddle or belt. (I'll explain later why a neutral object is better, in my opinion, than using the hand.) Put the paddle on the dresser where the child can see it, and promise him one more stroke if he gets up again. Walk confidently out of the room without further comment. If he rebounds again, fulfill your promise and offer the same warning if he doesn't stay in bed. Repeat the episode until the child acknowledges that you are boss. Then hug him, tell him how you love him, and remind him how important it is for him to get rest so that he won't be sick, etc.

Your purpose in this painful exercise (painful for both parties) is not only to keep the child in bed but to confirm your leadership in his mind. It is my opinion that too many parents lack the courage to win these confrontations and are kept off balance and on the defensive ever after. Remember: You are the benevolent boss. Act like it.

FOUR TO EIGHT YEARS

By the time a child reaches four years of age, the focus of discipline should not only be on his or her behavior, but also on the *attitudes* motivating it. The task of shaping this expression of the personality can be relatively simple or incredibly difficult, depending on the basic temperament of a particular child. Some youngsters are naturally warm and loving and trusting, while others sincerely believe the world is out to get them. Some enjoy giving and sharing, while their siblings may be selfish and demanding. Some smile throughout the day while others complain about everything from toothpaste to broccoli.

Furthermore, these attitudinal patterns are not consistent from one time to the next. They tend to alternate cyclically between rebellion and obedience. In other words, a time of intense conflict and defiance (if properly handled) gives way to a period of love and cooperation. Then when Mom and Dad relax and congratulate themselves for doing a super job of parenting, their little chameleon changes colors again.

Some might ask, "So what? Why should we be concerned about the attitudes of a boy or girl?" Indeed, there are many child-rearing specialists who suggest ignoring negative attitudes, including those that are unmistakably defiant in tone. Here is an example of what some of them say:

> This [recommendation that parents ignore disobedience] works best with annoying, but not harmful, behavior like bad language or tantrums. Effective ignoring involves not talking or looking at the child or using any body language that indicates attention.[4]

Another advocate of this naive approach was Dr. Luther Woodward, whose recommendations are paraphrased in a book that is now thankfully out of print, *Your Child from Two to Five*.[5] This was Dr. Woodward's ill-considered advice:

> What do you do when your preschooler calls you a "big stinker" or threatens to flush you down the toilet? Do you scold, punish . . . or sensibly take it in your stride?[6]

Dr. Woodward recommended a positive policy of understanding as the best and fastest way to help a child outgrow this verbal violence. He wrote, "When parents fully realize that all little tots feel angry and destructive at times, they are better able to minimize these outbursts. Once the preschooler gets rid of his hostility, the desire to destroy is gone and instinctive feelings of love and affection have a chance to sprout and grow. Once the child is six or seven, parents can rightly let the child know that he is expected to be outgrowing sassing his parents."[7]

Dr. Woodward then warned his readers that the permissive advice he was offering would not be popular with onlookers. He wrote: "But this policy takes a broad perspective and a lot of composure, especially when friends and relatives voice disapproval and warn you that you are bringing up a brat."[8]

In this case, your friends and relatives would probably be right. This suggestion (published during the permissive 1950s and typical of other writings from that era) is based on the erroneous notion that children will develop sweet and loving attitudes if adults will permit and encourage their emotional outbursts and their sassiness during childhood. It didn't work for Dr. Woodward's generation, and it won't be successful with your children. The child who has been calling his mother a big stinker (or worse) for six or seven years is unlikely to yield to parental leadership during the storms of adolescence. By then, the opportunity to shape the will of a strong-willed child is long gone, after which rebellious behavior will be a virtual certainty.

I expressed my divergent views on this subject in *The New Dare to Discipline* as follows:

> I believe that if it is desirable for children to be kind, appreciative, and pleasant, those qualities should be taught—not hoped for. If we want to see honesty, truthfulness, and unselfishness in our offspring, then these characteristics should be the conscious objectives of our early instructional process. If it is important to produce respectful, responsible young citizens, then we should set out to mold them accordingly. The point is obvious: *Heredity does not equip a child with proper attitudes; children will learn what they are taught.* We cannot expect the coveted behavior to appear magically if we have not done our early homework.[9]

I fear that many parents today are failing to teach attitudes in their children that will lead to successful and responsible lives.

But how does one shape the attitudes of children? Most parents find it easier to deal with outright disobedience than with unpleasant characteristics of temperament or personality. Let me restate two age-old suggestions, and then I'll offer a system that can be used with the especially disagreeable child.

There is no substitute for parental modeling of the attitudes we wish to teach. Someone wrote, "The footsteps a child follows are most likely to be the ones his parents thought they covered up." It is true. Our children are watching us carefully, and they instinctively imitate our behavior. Therefore, we can hardly expect them to be kind and giving if we are consistently grouchy and selfish. We will be unable to teach appreciativeness if we never say please or thank you at home or abroad. We will not produce honest children if we teach them to lie over the phone to someone trying to collect payment from us by saying, "Dad's not home." In these matters, our boys and girls quickly discern the gap between what we say and what we do. And of the two choices, they usually identify with our behavior and ignore our empty proclamations.

Most of the favorable attitudes that should be taught are actually extrapolations of the Judeo-Christian ethic, including honesty, respect, kindness, love, human dignity, obedience, responsibility, reverence, and so forth. And how are these time-honored principles conveyed to the next generation? The answer was provided by Moses in the words he wrote more than three thousand years ago in the book of Deuteronomy: "These commandments that I give you today are to be upon your hearts. Impress them on your children. Talk about them when you sit at home and when you walk along the road, when you lie down and when you get up. Tie them as symbols on your hands and bind them on your foreheads. Write them on the doorframes of your houses and on your gates" (Deuteronomy 6:6-9).

In other words, we can't instill these attitudes during a brief, two-minute bedtime prayer or during formal training sessions. We must *live* them from morning to night. They should be reinforced during our casual conversation, being punctuated with illustrations, demonstrations, compliments, and chastisement. Finally, let me suggest an approach for use with the strong-willed or negative child (age six or older) for whom other forms of instruction have been ineffective. I am referring specifically to the sour, complaining child who is making himself and the rest of his family miserable. The problem in disciplining such a child is the need to define the changes that are desired and then reinforce the improvements when they occur. Attitudes are abstractions that a six- or eight-year-old may not fully understand, and we need a system that will clarify the target in his mind.

Toward this end, I have developed an attitude chart (see illustration on the following page) that translates these subtle mannerisms into concrete, mathematical terms. Please note: The system that follows is *not* appropriate for the child who merely has a bad day or displays temporary unpleasantness associated with illness, fatigue, or environmental circumstances. Rather, it is a remedial tool to help change persistently negative and disrespectful attitudes by making the child conscious of her problem.

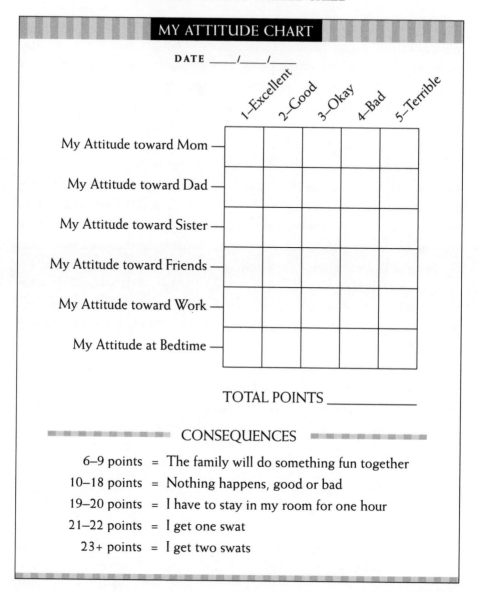

MY ATTITUDE CHART

DATE _____/_____/_____

	1–Excellent	2–Good	3–Okay	4–Bad	5–Terrible
My Attitude toward Mom —					
My Attitude toward Dad —					
My Attitude toward Sister —					
My Attitude toward Friends —					
My Attitude toward Work —					
My Attitude at Bedtime —					

TOTAL POINTS _____

CONSEQUENCES

6–9 points = The family will do something fun together
10–18 points = Nothing happens, good or bad
19–20 points = I have to stay in my room for one hour
21–22 points = I get one swat
23+ points = I get two swats

The attitude chart should be prepared and then reproduced, since a separate sheet will be needed each day. Place an *X* in the appropriate square for each category, and then add the total points "earned" by bedtime. Although this nightly evaluation process has the appearance of being objective to the child, it is obvious that the parents can influence the outcome by considering it in advance (it's called cheating). Mom and Dad may want Michael or Rebecca to receive eighteen points on the first night, barely missing the punishment but realizing he or she must stretch the following day. I must emphasize, however, that the system will fail miserably if a naughty child does not receive the punishment she deserves or if she hustles to improve but does not receive the family fun she was promised. This approach is nothing more than a method of applying reward and punishment to attitudes in a way that children can understand and remember.

For the child who does not fully comprehend the concept of numbers, it might be helpful to plot the daily totals on a cumulative graph, such as the one provided below.

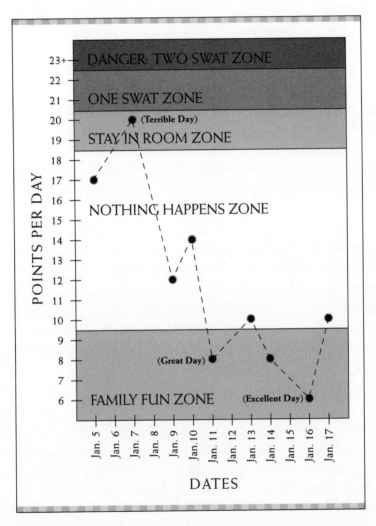

I don't expect everyone to appreciate this system or to apply it at home. In fact, parents of compliant, happy children will be puzzled as to why it would ever be needed. However, mothers and fathers of sullen, ill-tempered children will comprehend more quickly. Take it or leave it, as the situation warrants.

NINE TO TWELVE YEARS

Ideally, the foundation has been laid during the first nine years that will then permit a general loosening of the lines of authority. Every year that passes should bring fewer rules, less direct discipline, and more independence for the child. This does not mean that a ten-year-old is suddenly emancipated; it does mean that she is permitted to make more decisions about her daily living than when she was six. It also means that she should be carrying more responsibility each year of her life.

Physical punishment should be relatively infrequent during this period immediately prior to adolescence. Studies show that corporal punishment loses its effectiveness after the age of ten and should be discontinued. However, as is the case with all human beings, there are exceptions to the rules. Some strong-willed children absolutely demand to be spanked, and their wishes should be granted. However, compliant youngsters should have experienced their last round of corporal punishment by the end of their first decade (or even four years earlier). Some never need it at all.

The overall objective during this final preadolescent period is to teach the child that his actions have inevitable consequences. One of the most serious casualties in a permissive society is the failure to connect those two factors: behavior and consequences. Too often, a three-year-old child screams insults at her mother, but Mom stands blinking her eyes in confusion or simply ignores the behavior. A first-grader launches an attack on his teacher, but the school makes allowances for his age or is fearful of a lawsuit and takes no action. A ten-year-old is caught stealing candy in a store but is released with a reprimand. A fifteen-year-old sneaks the keys to the family car, but his father bails him out when he is arrested. A seventeen-year-old drives like a maniac, and her parents pay the higher insurance premiums after she wraps the family car around a telephone pole. You see, all through childhood some loving parents seem determined to intervene between behavior and consequences, breaking the connection and preventing the valuable learning that could have occurred.

Thus, it is possible for a young man or woman to enter adult life not really knowing that life can be harsh—that every move directly affects the future and that irresponsible behavior eventually produces sorrow and pain. One of the saddest sights is the adult who did not learn that behaviors have inevitable consequences and makes mistake after mistake that could easily have been avoided. Such a person applies for his first job and arrives late for work three times during the first week; then, when he is fired in a flurry of hot words, he becomes bitter and frustrated. It was the first time in his life that Mom and Dad couldn't come running to rescue him from unpleasant circumstances. Or an individual gets married and has children but bounces from job to job trying to "find himself" while his family struggles financially. (Unfortunately, many parents still try to bail out their grown children even when they are in their twenties, and sometimes even their thirties.) What is the result? This overprotection produces emotional cripples who often develop lasting characteristics of dependency and a kind of perpetual adolescence.

How does one connect behavior with consequences? Parents must be willing to let children experience a reasonable amount of pain when they behave irresponsibly. When Craig misses the school bus through his own dawdling, let him walk a mile or two and enter school in midmorning (unless safety factors prohibit this). If Caitlin carelessly loses her lunch money, let her skip a meal. Obviously, it is possible to carry this principle too far, being harsh and inflexible with an immature child. But the best approach is to expect boys and girls to carry the responsibility that is appropriate for their age and occasionally to taste the bitter fruit that irresponsibility bears.

Let me offer an illustration that may be read to an eleven- or twelve-year-old child. The following story was published a few days after an eclipse of the sun had occurred:

Tipton, Ind. (UPI)—Ann Turner, 15, is living proof of the danger of trying to watch a solar eclipse with the naked eye. Now she is blind.

On March 7, despite the warnings she had read, Ann "took a quick look through the window" at her home at the solar eclipse in progress.

"For some reason, I just kept staring out of the window," she told Pat Cline, a reporter for the *Tipton Daily Tribune*. "I was fascinated by what was taking place in the sky.

"There was no pain or feeling of discomfort as I watched. I stood there perhaps four or five minutes when Mom caught me and made me turn away from the window."

Ann said she "saw spots before my eyes but I didn't think much about it." Shortly afterward, she walked downtown and suddenly realized when she looked at a traffic signal that she could not read signs.

Frightened, Ann turned around and headed home. As she neared the porch, she said, she found she was "walking in darkness."

She was too scared to tell her family until the next day, although she "had an intuition or suspicion that something terrible was happening."

"I cried and cried," she said. "I didn't want to be blind. God knows I didn't want to live in darkness the rest of my life.

"I kept hoping the nightmare would end and I could see again but the darkness kept getting worse. I was scared. I had disobeyed my parents and the other warnings. I could not go back and change things. It was too late."

When Mr. and Mrs. Coy Turner learned what had happened, they took Ann to specialists. But the doctors shook their heads and said they could not help Ann regain her sight. They said she is 90 percent blind and can make out only faint lines of large objects on the periphery of what used to be her normal sight field.

With the help of a tutor, Ann is going ahead with her education. She is learning to adjust to the world of darkness.[10]

After reading this dramatic story to your boy or girl, it might be wise to say, "This terrible thing happened to Ann because she didn't believe what she was told by her parents and other adults. She trusted her own judgment instead. And the reason I read this to you is to help you understand that you might soon be in a situation that is similar to Ann's. As you go into your teen years, you will have many opportunities to do some things that we have told you are harmful. For example, someone may try to convince you to take illegal drugs that seem harmless at the time but end up resulting in all sorts of health problems later on. Someone else, perhaps even a teacher, may tell you that it is okay for you to experiment sexually with someone as long as you do it 'safely,' and you may end up with a disease that will ravage your body and cause numerous problems for you and the person you eventually marry. Just like Ann, you may not realize the consequences until it is too late. That is why it will be so important for you to believe the warnings that you've been taught rather than to trust your own judgment. Many young people make mistakes during the teenage years that will affect the rest of their life, and I want to help you avoid those problems. But the truth of the matter is, only you can set your course and choose your pathway. You can accept what your eyes tell you, like Ann did, or you can believe what your mother and I have said, and more important, what we read in God's Word. I have confidence that you will make the right decisions, and it's going to be fun watching you grow up."

There is so much that should be said about this late childhood era, but the limitations of time and space force me to move on. In conclusion, the period between ten and eleven years of age often represents the final time of closeness and unpretentious love between parent and child until the child reaches young adulthood. Enjoy it to the maximum, for believe me, there are more tumultuous days coming! (I have chosen to reserve the discussion of adolescent discipline for a separate chapter because of the significance of the topic.)

I'll end with a final illustration. I was once accompanied on a speaking trip by my wife, Shirley, requiring us to leave Danae and Ryan with their grandparents for a full week. Shirley's parents are dear people and loved our children very much. However, two bouncing, jumping, giggling little rascals can wear down the nerves of *any* adult, especially ones trying to enjoy their golden years. When we returned home from the trip I asked my father-in-law how the children behaved and whether or not they caused him any problems. He replied in his North Dakota accent, "Oh no! Dere good kids. But the important thing is, you jus' got to keep 'em out in da open."

That was probably the best disciplinary advice ever offered. Many behavioral problems can be prevented by simply avoiding the circumstances that create them. And especially for boys and girls growing up in congested cities, perhaps what we need most is to get 'em "out in da open." It's not a bad idea.

QUESTIONS AND ANSWERS

Q: My five-year-old is developing a problem with lying, and I don't know how to handle it. What can I do to get him to tell the truth?
A: Lying is a problem every parent must deal with. All children distort the truth from time to time, and some become inveterate liars. Responding appropriately is a task that requires an understanding of child development and the characteristics of a particular individual. I'll offer some general advice that will have to be modified to fit specific cases.

First, understand that a young child may or may not fully comprehend the difference between lies and the truth. There is a very thin line between fantasy and reality in the mind of a preschool boy or girl. So before you react in a heavy-handed manner, be sure you know what he understands and what his intent is.

For those children who are clearly lying to avoid unpleasant consequences or to gain an advantage of some sort, parents need to use that circumstance as a teachable moment. The greatest emphasis should be given to telling the truth in all situations. It is a virtue that should be taught—not just when a lie has occurred, but at other times as well. In your devotions with the children, read Proverbs 6:16-19 together: "There are six things the Lord hates, seven that are detestable to him: haughty eyes, a lying tongue, hands that shed innocent blood, a heart that devises wicked schemes, feet that are quick to rush into evil, a false witness who pours out lies and a man who stirs up dissension among brothers."

These are powerful verses around which to structure devotional periods with children. Explain who Solomon was, why his teachings are so important to us, and how Scripture helps us. It is like a flashlight on a dark night, guiding our footsteps and keeping us on the right path. It will even protect us while we are asleep, if we will bind it on our heart forever. Memorize Proverbs 6:16-19 together so it can be referred to in other contexts. Use it as a springboard to discussions of virtues and behavior that will please God. Each verse can be applied to everyday situations so that a child can begin to feel accountable for what he does and says.

Returning to the specific issue of lying, point out to the child that in a list of seven things the Lord hates most, two of them deal with dishonesty. Telling the truth is something God cares about, and therefore it should matter to us. This will explain why you are going to insist that your son or daughter learn to tell the truth even when it hurts to do so. Your goal is to lay a foundation that will help you underscore a commitment to honesty in the future.

The next time your child tells a blatant lie, you can return to this discussion and to the Scripture on which it was based. At some point, when you feel the maturity level of the youngster makes it appropriate, you should begin to insist that the truth be told and to impose mild punishment if it isn't. Gradually, over a period of years, you should be able to teach the virtue of truthfulness to your son or daughter.

Of course, you can undermine everything you're trying to establish if you are dishonest in front of your kids. Believe me, they will note it and behave likewise. If Daddy can twist the truth, he'll have little authority in preventing his kids from doing the same.

Q: I like your idea of balancing love with discipline, but I'm not sure I can do it. My parents were extremely rigid with us, and I'm determined not to make that mistake with my kids. But I don't want to be a pushover, either. Can you give me some help in finding the middle ground between extremes?

A: Maybe it would clarify the overall goal of your discipline to state it in the negative. It is not to produce perfect kids. Even if you implement a flawless system of discipline at home, which no one in history has done, your children will still be children. At times they will be silly, lazy, selfish, and, yes, disrespectful. Such is the nature of the human species. We as adults have the same weaknesses. Furthermore, when it comes to kids, that's the way they are wired. Boys and girls are like clocks; you have to let them run. My point is that the purpose of parental discipline is not to produce obedient little robots who can sit with their hands folded in the parlor thinking patriotic and noble thoughts! Even if we could pull that off, it wouldn't be wise to try.

The objective, as I see it, is to take the raw material our babies arrive with on this earth and gradually mold it, shaping them into mature, responsible, God-fearing adults. It is a twenty-year process that involves progress, setbacks, successes, and failures. When the child turns thirteen, you'll swear for a time that he's missed everything you thought you had taught—manners, kindness, grace, and style. But then maturity begins to take over, and the little green shoots from former plantings start to emerge. It is one of the richest experiences in life to watch that blossoming at the latter end of childhood.

Q: Do you think there is a relationship between permissive parenting and teen violence, especially at home?

A: Without question. Teen violence, at home and in public, has many causes, but permissive parenting is one of them. Many years ago, I came across an article on this subject and put it in my files. Though it is now old, it still answers the question you have posed. It is quoted below, in part:

> Two scientists at the Institute of Psychiatry and Human Behavior at the University of Maryland Medical School have identified what they call *a new syndrome of family violence: parent battering.*
>
> The term includes both physical assault and serious threats of physical harm by children and young people.
>
> Although the scientists do not know for sure, they suspect that the syndrome is not uncommon.

It seems to occur, they find, in families of all classes in which "one or both parents have abdicated the executive position" and no one, except possibly the battering child, is in charge.

An almost universal element in the families is that they deny the seriousness of the child's aggressive behavior.

For instance, a father who was almost killed when his son pushed him downstairs insisted that the boy had no problems with his temper.

Dr. Henry T. Harbin and Dr. Dennis Madden found that one of the most remarkable features of the cases they studied was the parents' tolerant response to the attack.

In one case, a youth of eighteen stabbed his mother, missing her heart by an inch, yet she was quite willing to let her son continue living at home.

Instead of asserting parental authority in the face of threats or attack, parents frequently gave in to their children's demands.

Even if their lives were in danger, they did not always call the police, and when questioned later they often lied to protect their children—and their self-image as effective parents.

Confronting the aberrant behavior of the child implies an admission of failure, the researchers said.

Another reason for denial was "to maintain an illusion, a myth of family harmony," to avoid thinking the unthinkable that the family was disintegrating.

"For parents to admit that their offspring have actually tried to kill them arouses massive anxiety and depression," the researchers believe.

When parents were asked who they would like to be in charge of a hypothetical family, few said that mothers or fathers should make the rules and some said that everyone in the family should be equal.

If battering children who were undergoing treatment at the violence clinic wanted to stop therapy or drop out of school, parents often answered, "Whatever you want to do."

Dr. Harbin said that, ideally, both parents should take a firm hand, but in any case, "someone needs to be in charge."[11]

Q: Isn't it our goal to produce children with self-discipline and self-reliance? If so, how does your approach to external discipline imposed by parents get translated into internal control?

A: Many authorities suggest that parents take a passive approach to their children for the reason implied by your question: They want their kids to discipline themselves. But since young people lack the maturity to generate self-control, they stumble through childhood without experiencing either internal or external discipline. Thus, they enter adult life having never completed an unpleasant assignment or accepted an order they disliked or yielded to the leadership of their elders. Can we expect such a person to exercise self-discipline in young adulthood? I think not. That individual doesn't even know the meaning of the word.

My belief is that parents should introduce their children to discipline and self-control by any reasonable means available, including the use of external influences, when they are young. By being required to behave responsibly, children gain valuable experience in controlling their impulses and resources. Year by year, responsibility is gradually transferred from the shoulders of the parents directly to the children. Eventually, they will act on what they learned in their earlier years—on their own initiative.

To illustrate, children should be required to keep their room relatively neat when they are young. Then somewhere during the midteens, their own self-discipline should take over and provide the motivation to continue the task. If it does not, the parents should close the door and let them live in a dump, if that is their choice.

In short, self-discipline does not come automatically to those who have never experienced it. Self-control must be learned, and it must be taught.

EIGHT

CORPORAL PUNISHMENT & THE STRONG-WILLED CHILD

BEHIND IN HIS READING

Junior bit the meter man,
Junior kicked the cook.
Junior's antisocial now
(According to the book).

Junior smashed the clock and lamp,
Junior hacked the tree.
(Destructive trends are treated
In chapters 2 and 3.)

Junior threw his milk at Mom,
Junior screamed for more.
(Notes of self-assertiveness
Are found in chapter 4.)

Junior tossed his shoes and socks
Out into the rain.
(Negation, that, and normal—
Disregard the stain).

Junior got in Grandpop's room,
Tore up his fishing line.
That's to gain attention
(See page 89).

Grandpop seized a slipper and
Yanked Junior 'cross his knee.
(Grandpop hasn't read a book
Since 1923).[1]

Dear ol' Grandpop. He may have been a little old-fashioned in his ideas, but he certainly knew how to handle Junior. So did most members of his generation. Moms and dads long before 1923 would never have put up with rebellious behavior from strong-willed children. Nor would they have been permitted to defy their elders or harass other members of the family. Drug usage and early sexual behavior would have brought the roof down on the kids who tried them. Unfortunately, in their zeal to make children behave properly, Victorian parents had a tendency to be *too* tough, *too* intimidating, and *too* punitive. Many of them were downright oppressive to vulnerable little kids who were doing nothing more than being childish.

I wish I could say that we in the twenty-first century are more enlightened and less likely to harm our children than our forebears, but it is not true. Growing up is a dangerous venture for millions of little people around the world who are suffering untold miseries at the hands of those who should be protecting and nurturing them.

No subject distresses me more than the tragedy of child abuse, which is depressingly common today. It is probable that a youngster living within a mile or two of your house is experiencing physical or emotional abuse in one form or another. It occurs in both poor and affluent homes, although the incidence is higher in inner-city neighborhoods. There and elsewhere, parents who are addicted to alcohol and illegal drugs are most likely to hurt or neglect kids.

During my years as a professor of pediatrics at a medical school, there was a steady stream of boys and girls who had been burned, bruised, and broken who were brought into our emergency hospital. Their little minds were warped by the awful circumstances of their lives. The incidence of abuse is even greater today. One of the common traumas seen in children's hospitals everywhere occurs when angry parents jerk boys and girls up by their arms, dislocating shoulders or elbows.

Diseased children sometimes suffer terribly, of course, but most of them experience some measure of emotional support to help them cope with their circumstances. For many of those boys and girls who have been beaten by a relative, however, there is no one to care, no one who understands. There is no one to whom he or she can go to express their longings and fears. They cannot escape. They cannot explain why they are hated. And many of them are too young to even call for help.

One such tragedy involved a six-year-old girl named Elisa Izquierdo, who was found dead in a lower Manhattan housing project in 1995.[2] Rescue workers discovered deep-red blotches, either welts or cigarette burns, over her entire body. There were enormous bruises near her kidney, on her face, and around her temples. Her genitals had been damaged severely, and the bone in her right pinkie finger jutted through the skin. Michael Brown, one of the fire fighters who tried to revive Elisa, said, "In my twenty-two years of service . . . this is the worst case of child abuse I have ever seen."[3] Elisa's mother, a crack-cocaine addict, admitted to making the little girl sleep in her own urine and feces and to hitting Elisa so hard that she flew headfirst into a concrete wall, permanently crippling her. In addition, she slid snakes down her daughter's throat to "exorcise" demons, held her upside down and used her curly hair as a mop, and used a hairbrush to damage the helpless little girl's genitals.[4]

In another case, a father killed his three-year-old son in order to win back his girlfriend. The man taped a garbage bag over the boy's head and sealed his mouth with duct tape. The father said the boy was crying when he left him, but he went ahead and drove away anyway.[5]

Obviously, these are extreme cases of physical abuse that horrify us all. But emotional neglect and rejection can also leave deep scars and wounds on the mind and body of children, sometimes resulting in physical symptoms decades later. In 1997, researchers at Harvard University, Drs. Linda Russek and Gary Schwartz, released a study revealing that children who perceive a lack of parental warmth and closeness early in life faced health problems later in life.[6] The forty-year study found that 91 percent of college men who reported a lack of closeness with their mothers had a greater risk of developing coronary heart disease, duodenal ulcers, high blood pressure, or alcoholism.[7] By contrast, the study found that only 45 percent of those surveyed who felt that they did have a close relationship with their mothers had suffered from one of these ailments.[8] Russek and Schwartz found a similar association between lack of closeness with a father and later health problems. They concluded:

> The effects of feelings of warmth and closeness appear to be addictive. . . . Since parents are usually the meaningful source of social support in early life, the perception of parental love and caring may have important biological and psychological health and illness implications throughout life.[9]

Other studies have also demonstrated a link between family stress and a number of physical problems. For example, an investigation reported in *Archives of Disease in Childhood* linked stress with slow growth in children.[10] The researchers found that "a total of 31.1 percent of children who had experienced family conflict were of short stature compared with 20.2 percent of those who had not."[11] They hypothesized that "stress reduces the release of growth hormones and increases the secretion of stress hormones (glucocorticoids), which can then damage the [brain] hippocampus" and interfere with the brain's learning and memory functions.[12]

These and other studies offer strong evidence that the foundation laid during childhood can affect a person throughout his or her adult life.

Given the delicate relationship between parents and their children and the rising incidence of physical and emotional assaults on boys and girls, the last thing I want to do is to provide a rationalization or justification for anything that could hurt them. Let me say it once more: I don't believe in harsh, oppressive, demeaning discipline, even when it is well-intentioned. Such destructive parenting is antithetical to everything I believe and stand for. At the risk of sounding self-serving, let me say that among the honors and awards I have received through the years, the one I value most is a bronze statue of a small boy and girl. The arm of one of the children is outstretched as though reaching for the loving hand of an adult. The inscription on the base of the statue, given by an organization dedicated to the prevention of child abuse, designated me as "The Children's Friend" in that year.

Considering this lifelong commitment to the welfare of children, why would I recommend corporal punishment as a management tool? It is a very good question, especially in view of the many articles and editorials appearing in the media these days that resoundingly condemn its use. Convincing the public that corporal punishment is universally harmful has become an unrelenting crusade within certain elements of the liberal media. I believe their efforts have been terribly misguided.

I would be quick to acknowledge that corporal punishment *can* be harmful when used wrongly. It *is* possible . . . even easy . . . to create an aggressive child who has observed violent episodes at home. If he is routinely beaten by parents, or if he witnesses physical violence between angry adults, the child will not fail to notice how the game is played. Thus, corporal punishment that is not administered according to very carefully thought-out guidelines has the potential to become dangerous. Parenthood does not give the right to slap and intimidate a child because Dad had a bad day or Mom is in a lousy mood. It is this kind of unjust discipline that causes some well-meaning authorities to reject corporal punishment altogether.

Just because a useful technique can be used wrongly, however, is no reason to reject it altogether. Many children desperately need this resolution to their disobedience. In those situations when the child fully understands what he is being asked to do or not to do but refuses to yield to adult leadership, an appropriate spanking is the shortest and most effective route to an attitude adjustment. When he lowers his head, clenches his fists, and makes it clear he is going for broke, justice must speak swiftly and eloquently. This response does not create aggression in children, but it does help them control their impulses and live in harmony with various forms of benevolent authority throughout life.

There is another reason I believe the proper use of corporal punishment is in the best interest of children. Strong-willed boys and girls can be terribly irritating to their parents, as we all know. Most of them have figured out how to press all the right (or wrong) buttons to make their moms and dads absolutely furious. One father said that nothing in his adult experience could make him more angry than the rebellious behavior of his ten-year-old son, day after day. Given that kind of volatile interaction, I am convinced that a determined, hard-nosed kid in the hands of an immature or emotionally unstable parent is a recipe for disaster. The likelihood of physical damage to that youngster is enormous, and it becomes even greater if the parents have been stripped of the ability to control challenging behavior before it gets out of hand.

When permissive advice-givers convince moms and dads that they can, and must, manage their children by talking and reasoning during nose-to-nose confrontations, the parents get more and more frustrated as the misbehavior intensifies. Eventually, too many of them blow up, and when they do, anything can happen. I am convinced that child abuse often emerges from that scenario in one way or another. How much better, and safer, it is for moms and dads to administer a judicious and carefully measured spanking to a child (or even a well-timed swat or two), before she and her parents are both out of control. It is even more advantageous for a savvy strong-willed child to know that spanking is an option, leading him to back off before he goes too far. By depriving parents of this possibility, the well-meaning counselors and psychologists inadvertently set up tough-minded kids for disaster at home.

The recommendations that I offer in this book, therefore, are intended not only to help moms and dads raise their children properly. I also seek to protect children from harm. Firm discipline, when administered with love, helps provide that protection.

Here's an example of corporal punishment administered correctly and with the desired result. It was relayed to me by a father, William Jarnagin, a certified public accountant, who wrote me the following letter. It speaks volumes about the proper approach to parent-child relationships:

Dear Dr. Dobson:

This is a note of thanks for your work in strengthening the American family. My wife and I have recently read four of your books and we have profited very much from them.

Please permit me to relate a recent experience with our six-year-old son, David. Last Friday night, my wife, Becky, told him to pick up some orange peelings he had left on the carpet, which he knows is a "no-no." He failed to respond, and as a result received one slap on his behind, whereupon he began an obviously defiant temper tantrum.

Since I had observed the whole episode, I then called for my paddle and applied it appropriately, saw to it that he picked up and properly disposed of the orange peelings, and sent him straight to bed, since it was already past his bedtime. After a few minutes, when his emotions had had a chance to settle down, I went to his room and explained that God had instructed all parents who truly love their children to properly discipline them, etc., and that we truly love him and therefore would not permit such defiant behavior.

The next morning, after I had gone to work, David presented his mother with the following letter, together with a little stack of ten pennies:

From David and Deborah
To Mom and Dad
Ross Dr. 3d house
Sellmer, Tennasse
39718
Dear Mom and Dad
here is 10 Cints for
Pattelling me when I
really neded and that
gos for Deborah to I
love you

Love yur son David
and yur Doter Deborah

Oh, incidentally, Deborah is our one-year-old daughter whose adoption should be final sometime in June.

Keep up your good work and may God bless you.

Sincerely,
William H. Jarnagin

Mr. William Jarnagin understands the appropriate response of a father to a child's defiance. It is neither harsh nor insulting nor dangerous nor whimsical. Rather, it represents the firm but loving discipline that is required for the best interest of the child. How fortunate is the boy or girl whose father and mother still comprehend that timeless concept.

If you have read my earlier books offering child-rearing advice, including *The New Dare to Discipline,* you may be aware that I have addressed this subject of corporal punishment extensively for many years.[13] Rather than repeating those other recommendations and explanations, I would like to devote the rest of this chapter to a very thorough article written by two noted physicians, Den A. Trumbull, M.D., and S. DuBose Ravenel, M.D. It was actually intended for physicians and was published in Focus on the Family's *Physician* magazine.[14] This informative review, provided below, summarizes current research and answers eight often-heard arguments against corporal punishment.

TO SPANK OR NOT TO SPANK
A look at an age-old question that baffles many physicians

BY DEN A. TRUMBULL, M.D., AND S. DUBOSE RAVENEL, M.D.

Primary-care physicians advise parents on many child-rearing issues. On the list of the most difficult is the issue of disciplinary spanking. Despite years of traditional acceptance, professional societies, including the American Academy of Pediatrics (AAP), have recently suggested that spanking can be harmful to children. In a surprising move recently, however, the AAP released a special report that suggests spanking may not be harmful to a child's health. In a supplement to the October 1996 *Pediatrics,* the cochairpersons, Drs. Stanford Friedman and Kenneth Schonberg of the Albert Einstein College of Medicine, summarized the findings of an AAP-sponsored conference last year that was devoted to reviewing the research on spanking. "Given a relatively 'healthy' family life in a supportive environment, spanking in and of itself is not detrimental to a child or predictive of later problems," they report.

The AAP's findings recognize what many physicians have believed for years and what John Lyons of the Northwestern University School of Medicine found in his research review: Studies demonstrate beneficial, not detrimental, effects of spanking. These findings, however, do not change the fact that opposition to parents spanking their children has been growing in elite circles of society over the past 15 years. No doubt much of this opposition springs from a sincere concern for the well-being of children. Child abuse is a reality, and stories of such abuse are horrifying. But while loving and effective discipline is not harsh and abusive, neither should it be weak and ineffectual. Indeed, disciplinary spanking can fall within the boundaries of loving discipline and need not be labeled abusive.

Or so most Americans seem to think. According to a recent Voter/Consumer Research poll commissioned by the Family Research Council, 76 percent of the more than 1,000 Americans surveyed said that spanking was an effective form of discipline in their home when they were children. These results are made more impressive by the fact that nearly half of those who answered otherwise grew up in homes in which they were never spanked. Taken together, more than four out of five Americans who as children were spanked by their parents say that it was effective discipline.

Some critics claim that spanking a child is abusive and contributes to adult dysfunction. These allegations arise from studies that fail to distinguish appropriate spanking from other forms of punishment.

Abusive forms of physical punishment such as kicking, punching, and beating are commonly grouped with mild spanking. Furthermore, the studies usually include, and even emphasize, corporal punishment of adolescents rather than focusing on preschool children, where spanking is more appropriate and effective. This blurring of distinctions between spanking and physical abuse, and between children of different ages, gives critics the illusion of having data condemning all disciplinary spanking.

There are several arguments commonly leveled against disciplinary spanking. Ironically, most of these arguments can be used against other forms of discipline. Any form of discipline (time-out, restriction, etc.), when used inappropriately and in anger, can distort a child's perception of justice and harm his emotional development. In light of this, let us examine some of the unfounded arguments promoted by spanking opponents.

ARGUMENT 1: Many psychological studies show that spanking is an improper form of discipline.
COUNTERPOINT: Researchers John Lyons, Rachel Anderson, and David Larson, M.D., of the National Institute of Healthcare Research in 1993 conducted a system-

atic review of the research literature on corporal punishment. They found that 83 percent of the 132 identified articles published in clinical and psychosocial journals were opinion-driven editorials, reviews, or commentaries devoid of new empirical findings. Moreover, most of the empirical studies were methodologically flawed by grouping the impact of abuse with spanking. The best studies demonstrated beneficial, not detrimental, effects of spanking in certain situations. Building upon this review, Dr. Robert E. Larzelere published an exhaustive review of the corporal punishment literature in the October 1996 supplement to *Pediatrics.* He also found insufficient data to condemn the use of spanking by parents.

ARGUMENT 2: Physical punishment establishes the moral righteousness of hitting other persons who do something that is wrong.

COUNTERPOINT: The "spanking teaches hitting" belief has gained in popularity over the past decade but is not supported by objective evidence. A distinction must be made between abusive hitting and nonabusive spanking. A child's ability to discriminate hitting from disciplinary spanking depends largely upon the parent's attitude toward spanking and the parent's procedure for spanking. There is no evidence in the medical literature that a mild spank to the buttocks of a disobedient child by a loving parent teaches the child aggressive behavior.

The critical issue is how spanking (or, in fact, any punishment) is used, more so than whether it is used. Physical abuse by an angry, uncontrolled parent will leave lasting emotional wounds and cultivate bitterness in a child. The balanced, prudent use of disciplinary spanking, however, is a deterrent to aggressive behavior with some children. Researchers at the Center for Family Research at Iowa State University studied 332 families to examine both the impact of corporal punishment and the quality of parental involvement on three adolescent outcomes—aggressiveness, delinquency, and psychological well-being. The researchers found a strong association between the quality of parenting and each of these three outcomes. Corporal punishment, however, was not adversely related to any of these outcomes. This study proves that quality of parenting is the chief determinant of favorable or unfavorable outcomes.

According to a study by Dan Olweus reported in *Developmental Psychology* in 1980, childhood aggressiveness is actually more closely linked to maternal permissiveness and negative criticism than to even abusive physical discipline.

It is unrealistic to expect that children would never hit others if their parents would only exclude spanking from their disciplinary options. Most toddlers (long before they are ever spanked) naturally attempt to hit others when conflict or frustration arises. The continuation of this behavior is largely determined by how the parent or caregiver responds. If correctly disciplined, the hitting will become less frequent. If ignored or ineffectively disciplined, the hitting will likely persist and even escalate. Thus, instead of contributing to greater violence, spanking can be a useful component in an overall plan to effectively teach a child to stop aggressive hitting.

ARGUMENT 3: Since parents often refrain from hitting until their anger or frustration reaches a certain point, the child learns that anger and frustration justify the use of physical force.

COUNTERPOINT: A 1995 study published in *Pediatrics* indicates that most parents who spank do not spank on impulse but purposefully spank their children with a belief in its effectiveness. Furthermore, the study revealed no significant correlation between the frequency of spanking and the anger reported by mothers. Actually, the mothers who reported being angry were not the same parents who spanked.

Reactive, impulsive hitting after losing control due to anger is unquestionably the wrong way for a parent to use corporal punishment. Eliminating all physical punishment in the home, however, would not remedy such explosive scenarios. It could even increase the problem.

When effective spanking is removed from a parent's disciplinary repertoire, he or she is left with nagging, begging, belittling, and yelling as soon as the primary disciplinary measures, such as time-out and logical consequences, have failed. By contrast, if proper spanking is proactively used in conjunction with other disciplinary measures, better control of the particularly defiant child can be achieved and moments of exasperation are less likely to occur.

ARGUMENT 4: Physical punishment is harmful to a child.

COUNTERPOINT: Any disciplinary measure—physical, verbal or emotional—can harm a child when carried to an extreme. Excessive scolding and berating of a child by a parent is emotionally harmful. Excessive use of isolation (time-out) for unreasonable periods of time can humiliate a child and ruin the measure's effectiveness.

Obviously, excessive or indiscriminate physical punishment is harmful and abusive. An appropriately administered spanking of a forewarned, disobedient child, however, is not harmful when administered in a loving, controlled manner.

Without the prudent use of spanking for the defiant child, a parent risks being inconsistent and rationalizing the child's behavior. This inconsistent manner of parenting is confusing and harmful to the child and is damaging to the parent-child relationship. There is insufficient evidence that proper disciplinary spanking is harmful to the child.

DISCIPLINE: Training that corrects, molds or perfects moral character.

Discipline (regardless of the method) is effective only when it involves

- truth brought forth in love;
- confession by the guilty party;
- forgiveness by the parent who is responsible for the discipline;
- resolution for the original problem; and
- assurance of continuity of love.

ARGUMENT 5: Spanking teaches a child that "might makes right," that power and strength are most important, and that the bigger can force their will upon the smaller.
COUNTERPOINT: Parental power is commonly exerted in routine child rearing, and spanking is only one example. Other situations where power and restraint are exercised by the average parent include:

- the young child who insists on running from his parent in a busy mall or parking lot
- the toddler who refuses to sit in his car seat
- the young patient who refuses to hold still as a vaccination is administered or as a laceration is repaired

Control over the child is necessary at times to ensure safety, health, and proper behavior. Classic child-rearing studies have shown that some degree of power assertion and control is essential for optimal child rearing. When power is exerted in the context of love and for the child's benefit, the child will not perceive it as bullying or demeaning.

ARGUMENT 6: Spanking is an ineffective solution to misbehavior.
COUNTERPOINT: Though the specific use of appropriate spanking has rarely been studied, there is evidence of its short-term and long-term effectiveness. When combined with reasoning, the use of negative consequences (including spanking) has been shown to decrease the recurrence of misbehavior with preschool children.

In clinical field trials where parental spanking has been studied, it has consistently been found to reduce the subsequent frequency of noncompliance with time-out. Spanking as an enforcement of time-out is a component of several well-researched parent-training programs and popular parenting texts.

Dr. Diana Baumrind of the Institute of Human Development at the University of California–Berkeley conducted a decade-long study of families with children three to nine years old. Baumrind found that parents employing a balanced disciplinary style of firm control (including spanking) and positive encouragement experienced the most favorable outcome in their children. Parents taking extreme approaches to discipline (authoritarian types using excessive punishment with less encouragement or permissive types using little punishment and no spanking) were less successful.

Baumrind concluded that evidence from this study "did not indicate that negative reinforcement or corporal punishment per se were harmful or ineffective procedures, but rather the total patterns of parental control determined the effects on the child of these procedures."

This approach of balanced, authoritative parenting employing the occasional use of spanking is advocated by several child-rearing experts. In the hands of loving parents, a spanking to the buttocks of a defiant toddler in appropriate settings is a powerful motivator to correct behavior and an effective deterrent to disobedience.

ARGUMENT 7: Spanking leads a parent to use harmful forms of corporal punishment that lead to physical child abuse.

COUNTERPOINT: The abuse potential when loving parents use appropriate disciplinary spanking is very low. Since parents have a natural affection for their children, they are more prone to underuse spanking than overuse it. Both empirical data and professional opinion oppose any causal relationship between spanking and child abuse.

Surveys indicate that 70 percent to 90 percent of parents of preschoolers use spanking, yet the incidence of physical child abuse in America is about 5 percent. Statistically, the two practices are far apart. Furthermore, according to the National Committee to Prevent Child Abuse, over the past decade reports of child abuse have steadily risen while approval for parental spanking has steadily declined.

Teaching parents appropriate spanking may actually reduce child abuse, according to Dr. Robert E. Larzelere in his review article on corporal punishment published in 1994 in *Debating Children's Lives.* Parents who are ill-equipped to control their child's behavior, or those who take a more permissive approach (refusing to use spanking), may be more prone to explosive attacks on their child, according to research.

Parental child abuse is an interactive process involving parental competence, parental and child temperaments, and situational demands. Abusive parents are more angry, depressed, and impulsive, and emphasize punishment as the predominant means of discipline. Abused children are more aggressive and less compliant than children from nonabusive families. There is less interaction between family members in abusive families, and an abusive mother displays more negative than positive behavior. The etiology of abusive parenting is multifactorial and cannot be simply explained by a parent's use of spanking.

In a reply to spanking opposition in a 1995 issue of *Pediatrics,* Drs. Lawrence S. Wissow and Debra Roter of the Johns Hopkins University's pediatrics department acknowledge that a definitive link between spanking and child abuse has yet to be established.

Finally, the Swedish experiment to reduce child abuse by banning spanking seems to be failing. In 1980, one year after this ban was adopted, the rate of child beatings was twice that of the United States. According to a 1995 report from the government organization Statistics Sweden, police reports of child abuse by family members rose fourfold from 1984 to 1994, while reports of teen violence increased nearly sixfold.

Most experts agree that spanking and child abuse are not on the same continuum but are very different entities. With parenting, it is the "user" and how a measure is used much more than the measure used that determine the outcome of the disciplinary effort. Clearly, spanking can be safely used in the discipline of young children with an excellent outcome. The proper use of spanking may actually reduce a parent's risk of abusing the child.

Argument 8: Spanking is never necessary.
COUNTERPOINT: All children need a combination of encouragement and correction as they are reared to become socially responsible individuals. In order for correction to deter disobedient behavior, the consequence imposed upon the child must outweigh the pleasure of the disobedient act. For very compliant children, milder forms of correction will suffice, and spanking may never be necessary. For more defiant children who refuse to comply with or be persuaded by milder consequences such as time-out, spanking is useful, effective, and appropriate.

Summary
Disciplinary spanking should be evaluated from a factual, objective perspective. It must be distinguished from abusive, harmful forms of corporal punishment. Appropriate disciplinary spanking can play an important role in optimal child development and has been found in prospective studies to be a part of the parenting style associated with the best outcomes. There is no convincing evidence that mild spanking is harmful. Indeed, spanking is supported by history, research and a majority of primary care physicians.[15]

Many thanks to Drs. Trumbull and Ravenel for allowing us to reprint this enlightening article. Both men are board-certified pediatricians in private practice and members of the Section on Developmental and Behavior Pediatrics of the American Academy of Pediatrics.

I'll conclude by sharing a related "Parent's Guide," also written by Dr. Trumbull. It offers nine specific guidelines on the use of disciplinary spanking.

PARENT'S GUIDE
Guidelines to Disciplinary Spanking

If your child is unruly, and you're at your wit's end, take a break and consider these guidelines before you spank your child.

1. Spanking should be used selectively for clear, deliberate misbehavior, particularly that which arises from a child's persistent defiance of a parent's instruction. It should be used only when the child receives at least as much encouragement and praise for good behavior as correction for problem behavior.

2. Milder forms of discipline, such as verbal correction, time-out and logical consequences, should be used initially, followed by spanking when non-compliance persists. Spanking has shown to be an effective method of enforcing time-out with the child who refuses to comply.

3. Only a parent (or in exceptional situations, someone else who has an intimate relationship of authority with the child) should administer a spanking.

4. Spanking should not be administered on impulse or when a parent is out of control. A spanking should always be motivated by love for the purpose of teaching and correcting, never for revenge.

5. Spanking is inappropriate before 15 months of age and is usually not necessary until after 18 months. It should be less necessary after 6 years, and rarely, if ever, used after 10 years of age.

6. After 10 months of age, one slap to the hand of a stubborn crawler or toddler may be necessary to stop serious misbehavior when distraction and removal have failed. This is particularly the case when the forbidden object is immovable and dangerous, such as a hot oven door or an electrical outlet.

7. Spanking should always be a planned action, not a reaction, by the parent and should follow a deliberate procedure.

- The child should be forewarned of the spanking for designated problem behaviors.
- Spanking should always be administered in private (bedroom or restroom) to avoid public humiliation or embarrassment.
- One or two spanks should be administered to the buttocks. This is followed by embracing the child and calmly reviewing the offense and the desired behavior in an effort to reestablish a warm relationship.

8. Spanking should leave only transient redness of the skin and should never cause physical injury.

9. If properly administered spankings are ineffective, other appropriate disciplinary responses should be tried, or the parent should seek professional help. A parent should never increase the intensity of spankings.[16]

QUESTIONS AND ANSWERS

Q: I have to fight with my nine-year-old daughter to get her to do *anything* she doesn't want to do. It's so unpleasant that I've about decided not to take her on. Why should I try to force her to work and help around the house?

What's the downside of my just going with the flow and letting her off the hook?

A: It is typical for nine-year-olds to not want to work, of course, but they still need to. If you permit a pattern of irresponsibility to prevail in your child's formative years, she may fall behind in her developmental timetable leading toward the full responsibilities of adult living. As a ten-year-old, she won't be able to do anything unpleasant since she has never been required to stay with a task until it is completed. She won't know how to give to anyone else because she's thought only of herself. She'll find it hard to make decisions or control her own impulses. A few years from now, she will steamroll into adolescence and then adulthood completely unprepared for the freedom and obligations she will find there. Your daughter will have had precious little training for those pressing responsibilities of maturity.

Obviously, I've painted a worst-case scenario with regard to your daughter. You still have plenty of opportunity to help her avoid such an outcome. I just hope your desire for harmony doesn't lead you to do what will be harmful to her in later years.

Q: We have an adopted girl who came to us when she was four years old. She is very difficult to handle and does pretty much what she pleases. For us to make her obey would be very unpleasant for her, and frankly we don't feel we have the right to do that. She has been through a lot in her short life. Besides, we're not her real parents. Do you think she'll be okay if we just give her a lot of love and attention?

A: I'm afraid what you have is a formula for serious problems with this girl later on. The danger is in seeing yourselves as substitute or stand-in parents who don't have the right to lead her. That is a mistake. Since you have legally adopted this child, you *are* her "real" parents, and your failure to see yourselves that way may be setting up the defiant behavior you mentioned. It is a common error made by parents of older adopted children. They pity their youngsters too much to confront them. They feel that life has already been too hard on them, and they must not make things worse by discipline and occasional punishment. As a result, they are tentative and permissive with a child who is crying out for leadership.

Transplanted children have the same need for guidance and discipline as those remaining with their biological parents. One of the surest ways to make them feel insecure is to treat them like they are different, unusual, or brittle. If the parents view such a child as an unfortunate waif to be shielded, he will tend to see himself that way too.

Parents of sick and disabled children often make this same mistake. They find discipline harder to implement because of the tenderness they feel for the child. Thus, a boy or girl with a heart condition or a terminal illness can become a little terror, simply because the usual behavioral boundaries are not established and defended. It must be remembered that the need to be led and governed is almost universal in childhood, and it isn't lessened by other problems and difficulties in life. In some cases, the desire for boundaries is actually increased by other troubles, for it is through loving control that parents build security and a sense of personal worth in a child.

Returning to the question, I advise you to love that little girl like crazy—and hold her to the same standards of behavior that you would your own flesh and blood. Remember, you *are* her parents!

Q: There is a child living near us who is not being harmed physically, but her parents are destroying her emotionally. You can't believe the screams and accusations that come from their house. So far, Child Protective Services has not intervened to rescue the little girl. Isn't it illegal to berate a child like this?

A: It is illegal in most states to abuse a child emotionally, but bad parenting can be difficult to define. Unfortunately, it is not illegal to raise a boy or girl without love unless neglect can be documented. It is usually not illegal to humiliate a child either. These forms of rejection may be even more harmful than some forms of physical abuse, but they are tougher to prove and are often not prosecutable. When emotional abuse occurs, as with the girl who lives near you, there may be no way to rescue her from this tragic situation. Nevertheless, I would report the incident to Child Protective Services and hope for intervention.

Q: What advice would you give parents who recognize a tendency within themselves to abuse their kids? Maybe they're afraid they'll get carried away when spanking a disobedient child. Do you think they should avoid corporal punishment as a form of discipline?

A: That's exactly what I think. Anyone who has ever abused a child—or has ever felt herself losing control during a spanking—should not put herself in such a situation. Anyone who has a violent temper that at times becomes unmanageable should not use that approach. Anyone who secretly enjoys the administration of corporal punishment should not be the one to implement it. And grandparents

("Grandpop" from the poem in chapter 8 included) probably should not spank their grandkids, unless the parents have given them permission to do so.

Q: Do you think you should spank a child for every act of disobedience or defiance?

A: Certainly not. Corporal punishment should be a rather infrequent occurrence. There is an appropriate time for a child to sit in a chair to think about his misbehavior, or he might be deprived of a privilege, sent to his room for a time-out, or made to work when he had planned to play. In other words, you should vary your response to misbehavior, always trying to stay one step ahead of the child. Your goal is to continually react in a way that benefits the child and is in accordance with his "crime." In this regard, there is no substitute for wisdom and tact in the parenting role.

Q: On what part of the body would you administer a spanking?

A: It should be confined to the buttocks area, where permanent damage is very unlikely. I don't believe you should slap a child on the face or jerk him around by the arm. If you spank a child only on the behind, you will be less likely to inflict any physical injury on him.

Q: How long do you think a child should be allowed to cry after being punished or spanked? Is there a limit?

A: Yes, I believe there should be a limit. As long as the tears represent a genuine release of emotion, they should be permitted to fall. But crying can quickly change from inner sobbing to an expression of protest aimed at punishing the enemy. Real crying usually lasts two minutes or less but may continue for five. After that point, the child is merely complaining, and the change can be recognized in the tone and intensity of his voice. I would require him to stop the protest crying, usually by offering him a little more of whatever caused the original tears. In younger children, crying can easily be stopped by getting them interested in something else.

Q: There is some controversy over whether a parent should spank with his or her hand or with some other object, such as a belt or a paddle. What do you recommend?

A: I recommend a neutral object of some type. For those who disagree on this point, I'd encourage them to do what seems right. It is not a critical issue to me.

The reason I suggest a switch (a small, flexible twig from a tree) or paddle is because the hand should be seen as an object of love—to hold, hug, pat, and caress. If you're used to suddenly disciplining with the hand, your child may not know when she's about to be swatted and can develop a pattern of flinching when you make an unexpected move. This is not a problem if you take the time to use a neutral object.

My mother always used a small switch, which could not do any permanent damage. But it stung enough to send a very clear message. One day when I had pushed her to the limit, she actually sent me to the backyard to cut my own instrument of punishment. I brought back a tiny little twig about seven inches long. She could not have generated anything more than a tickle with it. Mom never sent me on that fool's errand again.

Q: Is there an age when spankings can begin?
A: There is no excuse for spanking babies or children younger than fifteen to eighteen months of age. Shaking an infant can cause brain damage and even death! But midway through the second year (eighteen months), boys and girls become capable of understanding what you're telling them to do or not do. They can then very gently be held responsible for how they behave. Suppose a strong-willed child is reaching for an electric socket or something that will hurt him. You say, "No!" but he just looks at you and continues reaching toward it. You can see the mischievous smile on his face as he thinks, *I'm going to do it anyway!* I'd encourage you to speak firmly so that he knows he is pushing the limit. If he persists, slap his fingers just enough to sting. A small amount of pain goes a long way at that age and begins to introduce to the child the reality of the physical world and the importance of listening to what you say.

Through the next eighteen months, gradually establish yourself as a benevolent boss: mean what you say and say what you mean. Contrary to what you may have read in popular literature, this firm but loving approach to child rearing will *not* harm a toddler or make him violent. On the contrary, it is most likely to produce a healthy, confident child.

Q: I have spanked my children for their disobedience, and it didn't seem to help. Does this approach fail with some children?
A: Children are so tremendously variable that it is sometimes hard to believe that they are all members of the same human family. Some kids can be crushed with nothing more than a stern look; others seem to require strong and even

painful disciplinary measures to make a vivid impression. This difference usually results from the degree to which a child needs adult approval and acceptance. The primary parental task is to see things as the child perceives them, thereby tailoring the discipline to the child's unique needs. Accordingly, it is appropriate to punish a boy or girl when he or she knows it is deserved.

In a direct answer to your question, disciplinary measures usually fail because of fundamental errors in their application. It is possible for twice the amount of punishment to yield half the results. I have made a study of situations in which parents have told me that their children disregard punishment and continue to misbehave. There are four basic reasons for this lack of success:

1. The most common error is whimsical discipline. When the rules change every day and when punishment for misbehavior is capricious and inconsistent, the effort to change behavior is undermined. There is no inevitable consequence to be anticipated. This entices children to see if they can beat the system. In society at large, it also encourages criminal behavior among those who believe they will not face the bar of justice.

2. Sometimes a child is more strong-willed than his parent—and they both know it. He just might be tough enough to realize that a confrontation with his mom or dad is really a struggle of wills. If he can withstand the pressure and not buckle during a major battle, he can eliminate that form of punishment as a tool in the parent's repertoire. Does he think through this process on a conscious level? Usually not, but he understands it intuitively. He realizes that a spanking *must not* be allowed to succeed. Thus, he stiffens his little neck and guts it out. He may even refuse to cry and may say, "That didn't hurt." The parent concludes in exasperation, "Spanking doesn't work for my child."

3. The spanking may be too gentle. If it doesn't hurt, it doesn't motivate a child to avoid the consequence next time. A slap with the hand on the bottom of a diapered two-year-old is not a deterrent to anything. Be sure the child gets the message—while being careful not to go too far.

4. For a few children, spankings are simply not effective. A child who has attention deficit/hyperactivity disorder (ADHD), for example, may be even more wild and unmanageable after corporal punishment. Also, a child who has been abused may identify loving discipline with past abuse. Finally, the very sensitive child might need a different approach. Let me emphasize once more that children are unique. The only way to

raise them correctly is to understand each boy or girl as an individual and design parenting techniques to fit the needs and characteristics of that particular child.

Q: Do you think corporal punishment eventually will be outlawed?
A: I don't doubt that an effort will be made to end it. In fact, an attempt to outlaw corporal punishment was made in California in 1982, until the politicians were told by parents to back off.[17] The tragedy of child abuse has made it difficult for people to understand the difference between viciousness to kids and constructive, positive forms of punishment. Also, there are many "children's-rights advocates" in the Western world who will not rest until they have obtained the legal right to tell parents how to raise their children. In Sweden, corporal punishment and other forms of discipline are already prohibited by law.[18] Canadian courts have flirted with the same decision but ruled otherwise.[19] The American media has worked to convince the public that all spanking is tantamount to child abuse and therefore should be outlawed. If corporal punishment is banned, it will be a sad day for families, and especially for children!

NINE

BITTER BROTHERS
& SURLY SISTERS

I F PARENTS WERE ASKED to indicate the most irritating feature of child rearing, I'm convinced that sibling rivalry would win hands down. It has the capacity of driving otherwise sane and self-controlled adults a little crazy. Children are not content just to hate each other in private. They attack one another like miniature warriors, mobilizing their troops and probing for a weakness in the defensive line. They argue, hit, kick, scream, grab, taunt, tattle, and sabotage the opposing forces. I knew one child who deeply resented being sick with a cold while his older sibling was healthy, so he secretly blew his nose on the mouthpiece of his brother's clarinet! The big losers from such combat, of course, are the harassed parents who must listen to the noise of the battlefield and then try to patch up the wounded.

Sibling rivalry is not new, of course. It was responsible for the first murder on record (when Cain killed Abel) and has been present in virtually every home with more than one child from that time to this. The underlying source of this conflict is old-fashioned jealousy and competition between children. An excellent illustration of this irritating situation was written by Willard and Marguerite Beecher in their book *Parents on the Run*. They wrote:

> It was once believed that if parents would explain to a child that he was having a little brother or sister, he would not resent it. He was told that his parents had enjoyed him so much that they wanted to increase their happiness. This was supposed to avoid jealous competition and rivalry. It did not work. Why should it? Needless to say, if a man tells his wife he has loved her so much that he now plans to bring another wife into the home to "increase his happiness," she

would not be immune to jealousy. On the contrary, the fight would just begin—in exactly the same fashion as it does with children.[1]

We can learn some valuable lessons about siblings and how they interact with one another from an elementary principle of physics: A hotter object nearby will gradually raise the temperature of a cooler one. Do you get get the picture? A rebellious child usually makes the compliant youngster harder to handle. That is especially true if the strong-willed child is older. It is not unusual for parents to realize that their fun-loving, go-along-to-get-along boy or girl is starting to pick up the aggressive attitudes and behavior of the tougher brother or sister. In fact, every member of a family is influenced by a particularly difficult youngster, usually for the worse.

There is another factor that can be irritating and frustrating to moms and dads. Strong-willed and compliant kids often resent each other deeply. The tougher individuals dislike their prissy siblings who do everything right and are punished far less often. The easy children, on the other hand, get sick and tired of seeing the rebellious sib take on Mom or Dad and often come out the winner. The compliant children are also expected by them to "just take it" at times, because parents are weary of fighting with (and losing to) the rebellious youngster. The old adage that "the squeaky wheel gets the grease" applies here. Strong-willed kids tend to get away with more because they simply never give up and their parents become exasperated just trying to hang in there.

I described this interactive effect in my book *Parenting Isn't for Cowards*, especially as it relates to the health and well-being of the compliant child in the world of a strong-willed sibling. The compliant child "often has difficulties holding his own with his siblings, [and he] is more likely to internalize his anger and look for ways to reroute it."[2]

This represents a serious (but very quiet) threat to the well-being of the compliant child. My greatest concern for him is the ease with which he can be underestimated, ignored, exploited, or shortchanged at home. Haven't you seen two-child families where one youngster was a stick of dynamite who blew up regularly and the other was an all-star sweetheart? Under those circumstances it is not unusual for parents to take their cooperative sibling for granted. If there is an unpleasant job to be done, he will be expected to do it. Mom and Dad just don't have the energy to fight with the tiger.

If one child is to be chosen for a pleasant experience, it will probably go to the brattier of the two. He would scream bloody murder if excluded. When circumstances require one child to sacrifice or do without, you know who will be elected. Parents who favor the strong-willed child in this way are aware that they are being unfair, but their sense of justice has yielded to the pressures of practicality. They are simply too depleted and frustrated to risk irritating the tougher kid.

The consequences of such inequity should be obvious. Even though the compliant child goes along with the program and does not complain, he may accumulate a volume of resentment through the years. Isn't that what seems to have occurred to the brother of the Prodigal Son, as described by Jesus in Luke 15:11-32? He was the hardworking, responsible, compliant member of the family. Apparently, his kid brother was irresponsible, flighty, and very strong-willed. If we may be permitted to extrapolate a bit from the biblical account, it seems likely that there was little love lost between these brothers, even before the prodigal's impulsive departure.

The disciplined elder brother resented the spoiled brat who got everything he asked for. Nevertheless, the older brother kept his thoughts to himself. He would not want to upset his father, whom he respected enormously. Then came that incredible day when little brother demanded his entire inheritance in one lump sum. The compliant son overheard the conversation and gasped in shock. *What audacity!* he thought. Then, to his amazement he heard his father grant the playboy's request. He could hear the clink of numerous gold coins being counted. The elder brother was furious. We can only assume that the departure of this sibling meant Big Bud would have to handle double chores and work longer hours in the fields. It wasn't fair that the load should fall on him. Nevertheless, he said nothing. Compliant people are inclined to hold their feelings inside, but they are capable of harboring great resentment.

The years passed slowly as the elder brother labored to maintain the farm. The father had grown older by then, placing a heavier strain on this firstborn son. Every day he labored from dawn to dusk in the hot sun. Occasionally, he thought about his brother living it up in the far country, and he was briefly tempted. But, no. He would do what was right. Pleasing his father was the most important thing in his life.

Then, as we remember, the strong-willed goof-off ran out of money and became exceedingly hungry. He thought of his mom's cooking and the warmth of his father's fire. He clutched his rags around him and began the long journey home. When he was yet afar off, his father ran to meet him—embracing him and placing the royal robes around his shoulders. The fatted calf was killed and a great feast planned. That did it. The compliant brother could take no more.

The Prodigal Son had secured through his folly what the elder brother could not gain through his discipline: the approval and affection of his father. His spirit was wounded!

Whether my interpretation of this parable is faithful to the meaning of the Scripture will be left to the theologians. Of this I am certain, however: Strong-willed and compliant siblings have played out this drama since the days of Cain and Abel, and the responsible brother or sister often feels like the loser. He holds his feelings inside and then pays a price for storing them. He is more susceptible as an adult to ulcers, hypertension, colitis, migraine headaches, and a wide range of other psychosomatic illnesses. Furthermore, his sense of utter powerlessness can drive his anger underground. It may emerge in less obvious quests for control.

It is not necessary or healthy to allow children to destroy each other and make life miserable for the adults around them. Sibling rivalry is difficult to cure, but it certainly can be treated. Toward that end, let me offer three suggestions that should be helpful in achieving at least a state of armed neutrality at home.

1. Don't inflame the natural jealousy of children

Sibling rivalry is a virtual inevitability, especially between strong-willed kids, but at least Mom and Dad should seek to avoid the situations that make it worse. One of these red flags is comparing children unfavorably with each other, since they are always looking for a competitive edge. The question in a child's mind is not, "How am I doing?" it is, "How am I doing compared with Mike [or Blake or Sarah]?" The issue is not how fast a child can run, but who crosses the finish line first. A boy does not care how tall he is; he is vitally interested in who is tallest. Children systematically measure themselves against their peers on everything from skateboarding ability to who has the most friends. Both sexes are especially sensitive to any failure that occurs and is talked about openly within their own family. Accordingly, parents who want a little peace at home should guard against comparative comments that routinely favor one child over another. To violate this principle is to set up even greater rivalry between them.

Perhaps an illustration will help make the case. When I was about ten years old, I loved to play with a couple of dogs that belonged to two families in the neighborhood. One was a pug bulldog mix with a very bad attitude and a low dog IQ. His one big trick was that he was crazy about chasing and retrieving tennis balls. The other dog was a sweet, passive Scottie named Baby. He didn't have any tricks at all, except to bark from morning to night. One day as I was tossing the ball for the bulldog, it occurred to me that it might be interesting to throw it in the direction of Baby. That turned out to be a very dumb idea. The ball rolled under the Scottie with the grouch in hot pursuit. The bulldog went straight for Baby's throat and hung on. It was an awful scene. Neighbors came running from everywhere as the Scottie screamed in terror. It took ten minutes and a garden hose for the adults to pry loose the bulldog's grip. By then Baby was almost dead. He spent two weeks in the animal hospital, and I spent two weeks in the doghouse. I was hated by the entire town.

I have thought about that experience many times and have since recognized its application to most human relationships. Indeed, it is just as simple to precipitate a fight between people as it is between dogs. All that is necessary is to toss a ball, symbolically, in the direction of one of the rivals and then step back and watch the brawl. It can be done by repeating negative comments made by one about the other or by baiting the first in the presence of the second. It can be accomplished in business by assigning similar territory to two managers. They will tear each other to pieces in the places where their responsibilities overlap. Alas, it happens every day.

This principle is especially applicable to siblings. It is remarkably easy to make them mortal enemies. All a parent must do is toss a ball in the wrong direction. The natural antagonism and competitiveness of kids will do the rest.

Children and teens are particularly uptight about the matter of physical attractiveness and body characteristics. It is highly inflammatory to commend one child at the expense of the other. Suppose, for example, that Rachel is permitted to hear this casual remark about her sister: "Becky sure is going to be a gorgeous girl." The very fact that Rachel was not mentioned will probably establish the two girls as rivals. If there is a significant difference in beauty between the two, you can be sure that Rachel has already concluded, *Yeah, I'm the ugly one.* When her fears are then confirmed by her peers, resentment and jealousy are generated.

Beauty is the most significant factor in the self-esteem of children and teenagers. Anything that parents utter on this subject within the hearing of children should be screened carefully. It has the power to make siblings hate one another.

Intelligence is another hot button for children. It is not uncommon to hear parents say in front of their children, "I think Alissa is actually brighter than Mark." Bang! Here comes another battle. Adults sometimes find it difficult to comprehend how powerful that kind of comparison can be in a child's mind. Even when the comments are unplanned and spoken offhandedly, they convey how a child is seen within the family. We are all vulnerable to the power of that bit of information.

Children (especially teens) are also extremely competitive with regard to physical attributes and athletic abilities. Those who are slower, weaker, and less coordinated than their brothers or sisters are rarely able to accept "second best" with grace and dignity. Consider, for example, the following note given to me by the mother of two boys. It was written by her nine-year-old son to his eight-year-old brother the evening after the younger child had beaten him in a race.

Dear Jim:
I am the greatest and your the badest. And I can beat everybody in a race and you can't beat anybody in a race. I'm the smartest and your the dumb-est. I'm the best sport player and your the badest sport player. And your also a hog. I can beat anybody up. And that's the truth. And that's the end of this story.

Yours truly,
Richard

This note is humorous to me because Richard's motive was so poorly disguised. He had been badly stung by his humiliation on the field of honor, so he came home and raised the battle flags. He probably spent the next eight weeks looking for opportunities to fire torpedoes into Jim's soft underbelly. Such is the nature of humankind.

Here is another example: One of my assistants at Focus on the Family has an older brother who was a child prodigy at music. The elder sibling was playing Mozart sonatas on the piano at age six, while his younger brother and sister were lucky to plunk out "Chopsticks." At recital after recital, they would hear acclamation for their brother's abilities and then the offhand remark, "Oh, you did okay too."

After seven years of pleading and begging, the younger brother finally convinced his mother that he would never rival his brother at the piano and that he needed to find his own identity by playing the saxophone. A few weeks later, he brought home his saxophone and started to practice. Of course, since he was just learning the notes, he was not quite ready to solo with a band. His older brother, with whom he had always had a good relationship (and does to this day), came over, picked up the saxophone, and at the drop of a hat, played like someone who had been practicing for fifteen years. The younger brother, totally humiliated, started a knock-down-drag-out fight. Eventually, the younger brother became quite good at the saxophone—and developed a healthy identity of his own. But a less confident child might have pulled into a shell of resentment and refused to try anything perceived as risky. So much of human behavior turns on these rather straightforward principles.

Am I suggesting, then, that parents eliminate all aspects of individuality within family life or that healthy competition should be discouraged? Of course not. Competition drives us to reach for the best that is within. I am saying, however, that in matters of beauty, brains, athletic ability, and anything else valued in the family or neighborhood, children should know that in their parents' eyes, they are respected and have equal worth with their siblings. Praise and criticism *at home* should be distributed as evenly as possible, although some children will inevitably be more successful in the outside world. Finally, we should remember that children do not build fortresses around strengths—they construct them to protect weakness. Thus, when a child begins to brag and boast and attack her siblings, she is revealing the threats she feels at that point. Our sensitivity to those signals will help minimize the potential for jealousy within our children.

2. Establish a workable system of justice at home

Sibling rivalry is also at its worst when there are inadequate or inconsistently applied rules that govern the interaction between kids—when the "lawbreakers" do not get caught, or, if apprehended, are set free without standing trial. It is important to understand that laws in a society are established and enforced for the purpose of protecting people from each other. Likewise, a family is a minisociety with the same requirements for property rights and physical protection.

For purposes of illustration, suppose that I live in a community where there is no established law. Police officers do not exist and there are no courts to whom disagreements can be appealed. Under those circumstances, my neighbor and I can abuse each other with impunity. He can take my lawn mower and throw rocks through my windows, while I steal the peaches from his favorite tree and dump my leaves over his fence. This kind of mutual antagonism has a way of escalating day by day, becoming ever more violent with the passage of time. When permitted to run its natural course, as in early American history, the end result can be feudal hatred and murder.

Individual families are similar to societies in their need for law and order. In the absence of justice, "neighboring" siblings begin to assault one another. The older child is bigger and tougher, which allows her to oppress her younger brothers and sisters. But the junior member of the family is not without weapons of his own. He can strike back by breaking the toys and prized possessions of the older sibling and interfering when friends are visiting. Mutual hatred then erupts like an angry volcano, spewing its destructive contents on everyone in its path.

Too often, however, children who appeal to their parents for intervention are left to fight it out among themselves. Mom or Dad may not have sufficient disciplinary control to enforce their judgments. In other families, they are so exasperated with constant bickering among siblings that they refuse to get involved. In still others, they require an older child to live with an admitted injustice "because your sister is smaller than you." Thus, they tie the older child's hands and render him utterly defenseless against the mischief of his younger sibling. And in the many families today in which both parents work, the children may be busily disassembling each other at home with no supervision whatsoever.

I will say it again: One of the most important responsibilities of parents is to establish an equitable system of justice and a balance of power at home. There should be reasonable rules that are enforced fairly for each member of the family. For purposes of illustration, let me list the beginnings of a set of "laws" on which to build a protective shield around each child. They can never be implemented perfectly, but this is a place to start:

- A child is *never* allowed to make fun of the other in a destructive way. Period! This must be an inflexible rule with no exceptions.
- Each child's room is his or her private territory. There must be locks on both doors, and permission to enter is a revocable privilege. (Families with more than one child in each bedroom can allocate available living space for each youngster.)
- As much as possible, the older child is not permitted to tease the younger child.
- The younger child is forbidden from harassing the older child.
- The children are not required to play with each other when they prefer to be alone or with other friends.
- Parents mediate any genuine conflict as quickly as possible, being careful to show impartiality and extreme fairness.

As with any system of justice, this plan requires (1) respect for leadership of the parents, (2) willingness of the parents to mediate, (3) reasonable consistency over time, and (4) occasional enforcement or punishment. When this approach is accomplished with love, the emotional tone of the home can be changed from one of hatred to (at least) tolerance.

3. Recognize that the hidden "target" of sibling rivalry is you

The third general principle is a matter of understanding how kids think. Their conflict often becomes a way of manipulating parents. Quarreling and fighting provide an opportunity for both children to capture adult attention. It has been written, "Some children had rather be wanted for murder than not wanted at all." Toward this end, a pair of obnoxious kids can tacitly agree to bug their parents until they get a response—even if it is an angry reaction.

One father told me about the time his son and his nephew began to argue and then beat each other with their fists. Both fathers were nearby and decided to let the fight run its natural course. During the first lull in the action, one of the boys glanced sideways toward the passive men and said, "Isn't anybody going to stop us before we get hurt?!" The fight, you see, was something neither boy wanted. Their violent combat was directly related to the presence of the two adults and would have taken a different form if the boys had been alone. Children will "hook" their parents' attention and intervention in this way.

Believe it or not, this form of sibling rivalry is easiest to control. The parents must simply render the behavior unprofitable to each participant. I would recommend that you review the problem (for example, a morning full of bickering) with the children and then say, "Now, listen carefully. If the two of you want to pick on each other and make yourselves miserable, then be my guests [assuming there is a fairly equal balance of power between them]. Go outside and argue until you're exhausted. But it's not going to occur under my feet anymore. It's over! And you know that I mean business when I make that kind of statement. Do we understand each other?"

Having made the boundaries clear, I would act decisively the instant either child returned to his bickering in my presence. If the children had separate bedrooms, I would confine one child to each room for at least thirty minutes of complete boredom without radio, computer, or television. Or I would assign one to clean the garage and the other to mow the lawn. Or I would make them both take an unscheduled nap. My purpose would be to make them believe me the next time I asked for peace and tranquility.

It is simply not necessary to permit children to destroy the joy of living. And what is most surprising, children are the happiest when their parents enforce reasonable limits with love and dignity. But there is nothing simple when it comes to raising children. Obviously, it is no job for cowards.

QUESTIONS AND ANSWERS

Q: We are planning our family very carefully and want to space the children properly. Is there an ideal age span that will bring greater harmony between them?

A: Children who are two years apart and of the same sex are more likely to be competitive with one another. On the other hand, they are also more likely to enjoy mutual companionship. If your babies are four or more years apart, there will be less camaraderie between them, but you'll at least have only one child in college at a time. My evasive reply to your question reflects my personal bias: There are many more important reasons for planning a baby at a particular time than the age of those already born. Of greater significance are the health of the mother, the parents' desire for another child, financial considerations, and the stability of the marriage. The relative age of the siblings is not one of the major determiners, in my opinion.

Q: My older child is a great student and earns straight As year after year. Her younger sister, now in the sixth grade, is completely bored in school and won't even try. The frustrating thing is that the younger girl is probably brighter than her older sister. Why would she refuse to apply her abilities like this?

A: There could be many reasons for your younger daughter's academic disinterest, but let me suggest the most probable explanation. Children will often refuse to compete when they think they are likely to place second instead of first. Therefore, a younger child may avoid challenging an older sibling in her area of greatest strength. If Son Number One is a great athlete, then Son Number Two may be more interested in collecting butterflies. If Daughter Number One is an accomplished pianist, then Daughter Number Two may scorn music and take up tennis. This is the exact scenario that I described in the story about my assistant and his older brother. The younger sibling did not have the desire (or the ability) to compete against his older sibling at the piano and desperately wanted to do something else in which he would not be compared unfavorably.

This rule does not always hold true, of course, depending on the child's fear of failure and the way he estimates his chances of competing successfully. If his confidence is high, he may blatantly wade into the territory owned by his big brother, determined to do even better. However, the more typical response is to seek a new area of compensation that is not yet dominated by a family superstar.

If this explanation fits the behavior of your younger daughter, then it would be wise to accept something less than perfection from her school performance. Siblings need not fit the same mold—nor can we force them to do so.

Q: I am a single parent with two strong-willed young boys who are just tearing each other apart. I think I could deal with their sibling rivalry if only I had some encouragement and practical help in dealing with everyday life. The pressure of working, cooking dinner, and doing the job of two parents leaves me sapped and unable to deal with their constant bickering. What encouragement can you offer to those of us who are single parents? Each day seems more difficult than the one before it. Can you help plead our case to those who don't understand what we're facing?

A: According to the *Statistical Abstract of the United States,* there are now over 12 million single-parent homes in the United States.[3] In my view, single parents have the toughest job in the universe! Hercules himself would tremble at the range of responsibilities people like you must handle every day. It's difficult enough for two parents with a solid marriage and stable finances to satisfy the demands of parenting. For a single mother or father to do that task excellently over a period of years is evidence of heroism.

The greatest problem faced by single parents, especially a young mother like yourself, is the overwhelming amount of work to be done. Earning a living, fixing meals, caring for kids, helping with homework, cleaning the house, paying bills, repairing the car, handling insurance, doing the banking, preparing the income tax returns, shopping, etc., can require twelve hours or more a day. She must continue that schedule seven days a week all year long, sometimes with no support from family or anyone else. It's enough to exhaust the strongest and healthiest woman. Then where does she find time and energy to meet her own social and emotional needs—and how does she develop the friendships on which that part of her life depends? Single parenting is no easier for fathers, who may find themselves trying to comb their daughter's hair and explain menstruation to their preteen girls.

There is only one answer to the pressures single parents face. It is for the rest of us to give these moms and dads a helping hand. They need highly practical assistance, including the friendship of two-parent families who will take their children on occasion to free up some time. Single moms need the help of young men who will play catch with their fatherless boys and take them to the school soccer game. They need men who will fix the brakes on the minivan and patch the leaky roof. On the other hand, single dads need someone who can help them nurture their children, and if they have a daughter, teach her how to be a lady.

Single parents need prayer partners who will hold them accountable in their walk with the Lord and bear their burdens with them. They need an extended family of believers to care for them, lift them up, and remind them of their priorities. Perhaps most important, single parents need to know that the Lord is mindful of their circumstances.

Clearly, I believe it is the responsibility of those of us in the church to assist you with your parenting responsibilities. This requirement is implicit in Jesus' commandment that we love and support the needy in all walks of life. He said, "I tell you the truth, whatever you did for one of the least of these brothers of mine, you did for me" (Matthew 25:40). That puts things in perspective. Our efforts on behalf of a fatherless or motherless child are seen by Jesus Christ as a direct service to Himself!

This biblical assignment is even more explicitly stated in James 1:27: "Religion that God our Father accepts as pure and faultless is this: to look after orphans and widows in their distress."

Thankfully, churches today are becoming more sensitive to the needs of single parents. More congregations are offering programs and ministries geared to the unique concerns of those with particular needs. I'd advise all single parents to find such a church or fellowship group and make themselves at home there. Christian fellowship and support can be the key to survival.

TEN

THE STRONG-WILLED ADOLESCENT
(IS THERE ANY OTHER KIND?)

ALAS, WE ARRIVE NOW at the door of adolescence, that dynamic time of life that comes in with a pimple and goes out with a beard—or to put it another way, it comes in with a bicycle and ends with a car. It's an exciting time of life, but to be honest, I wouldn't want to stumble through it again. I doubt if you would either. We adults remember all too clearly the fears and jeers and tears of our tumultuous youth. Perhaps that is why many parents begin to tremble and quake when their children approach the adolescent years, especially if one or more of them have been the fireball of the family.

One of the curious aspects of the teen experience today, which wasn't true thirty years ago, is its largely homogenized nature around the world. For example, adults who have traveled internationally may have recognized a certain kind of graffiti spray painted on buildings, bridges, and trains wherever they go. It looks about the same in Sydney, Chicago, London, Moscow, or Berlin. Somehow kids around the world know how to duplicate those scrawled block letters that mark gang territories. Teens in far-flung places are busily imitating each other in almost every other regard too. They are determined to look alike, dress alike, and "be" alike wherever they are found. Kids even have their own international language of sorts that adapts to the ever-changing jargon of the moment.

What is the common bond that links young people together? It is the worldwide pop culture, which knows no geographical boundaries. MTV, the most watched television cable network in the world, is the primary vehicle driving this conformity. Its wretched twenty-four–hour programming is seen now in more than 377 million households every day, mostly by impressionable teens or young adults.[1] The corporate conglomerate makes billions of dollars marketing pop culture—and rebellion—to a generation. Its executives are not only keenly aware of the influence they are having around the world—that is precisely what they are striving for. One of their corporate ads pictures the back of a teenager's head with *MTV* shaved in his hair. The copy reads, "MTV is not a channel. It's a cultural force. People don't watch it, they love it. MTV has affected the way an entire generation thinks, talks, dresses, and buys."[2] The amazing thing about this ad is that MTV not only admits they are trying to manipulate the young and immature; they spend big bucks bragging about it.

MTV is not the only degrading cultural force that is operating on the international scene. The American entertainment industry also shapes the world-wide community negatively through its distribution of movies, television, videos, and the Internet. This is why the kids in Kenya and Fiji and Santiago and Budapest tend to pant after the same Hollywood starlets, dance with the same rock musicians, and model themselves, unfortunately, after the same immoral antiheroes such as Madonna and Britney Spears and Eminem. It is why tattooing, body piercing, strange multicolored hairstyles, and scantily clad girls have a similar look wherever one goes.

One of the most disgusting and disturbing examples of debauchery within the pop culture was seen at Super Bowl XXXVIII, held in February 2004. It included a halftime show that was pure filth, complete with crotch-grabbing antics, explicit sexual and violent lyrics, bumping and grinding movements, and girls who looked like prostitutes wearing garter belts and little else. The show, if it can be called that, featured pop singers Janet Jackson and Justin Timberlake. At the concluding moment of the performance, Timberlake pulled off the top of her outfit, revealing a bare breast. Millions of people around the world, many of them wide-eyed children and impressionable teens, were watching this disgraceful performance.[3] The program was produced and sponsored by—who else?—MTV and its coconspirators at CBS and the NFL. With this program these money-grubbing executives contributed once more to the degenerate morals of a generation of young people in every country on earth. No wonder decent people in other nations hate the United States and consider it a wicked influence for their children. At least with regard to Hollywood and the pop culture industry, they are absolutely right!

Even more disturbing is that MTV airs this kind of immorality day after day on cable television, though most parents are too busy doing their own thing to notice.

What this means is that the job of raising kids, especially those seething with rebellion, has become much more difficult. A hundred years ago, when fourteen-year-old Billy Bob Brown, the strong-willed son of Farmer Brown, began to get snippy around the house, his dad could take him out to the back forty acres and "get his mind straight." There they were, just the two of them, working through their conflict. And usually, Billy Bob quickly figured out that he had better shape up—or else. Now, teen pop culture imposes on parent-child relationships a vast and enormously influential network of ideas, enticements, sexuality, profanity, support, and, mostly, an articulation of anger that compounds the difficulties of growing up.

According to environmentalist and author Bill McKibben, "If you had set out to create a culture purposefully damaging to children, you couldn't do better than America at the end of the twentieth century [and well into the next]."[4] Columnist, author, and radio talk-show host Michael Medved put it this way: "There has been a shift from a supportive culture . . . to a deliberately assaultive culture."[5] Western culture is increasingly radical, sexual, and revolutionary. It is determined to take your kids to hell, and your greatest wisdom and experience will be required to stop it.

A good place to begin is by monitoring your child's access to the mass media. According to a recent survey, children ages two through eighteen spend on average five hours and twenty-nine minutes every day watching television, listening to music, or playing computer and video games. That total increases for children over eight, who spend nearly forty hours a week engaged in some sort of media-related activity. The survey also found that 53 percent of children have a television in their bedroom, which includes 32 percent of two- to seven-year-olds and 65 percent of eight- to eighteen-year-olds. Seventy percent of all children have a radio in their room, and 16 percent have a computer.[6]

What an ominous description this report provides of American children (and those around the world) in the twenty-first century! It is all related to the frantic pace of living. We adults are too exhausted and harried to care for those we love most. We hardly know what they are doing at home, much less when they are away. What a shame! Yankelovich Partners, Inc., said the image of families gathered around a single TV set in the family room is fading. Instead, many kids are off by themselves, where they can choose anything that they want to see. Ann Clurman, a partner at Yankelovich, said, "Almost everything children are seeing is essentially going into their minds in some sort of uncensored or unfiltered way."[7]

I strongly urge you to get those devices, whether they are television sets, computers, DVDs, or VCRs *out of the bedroom*. Locate them in the family room, where they can be monitored and where the amount of time spent on them is regulated. How can you do less for your children? It is also our responsibility to watch various forms of entertainment *with* our boys and girls when they are young. Otherwise, our kids are sitting ducks for the con men of our time who want to control their hearts and minds.

I wrote in greater detail about these and other adolescent dangers in my book *Bringing Up Boys*. Those who are looking for greater help at this point can consult that source. For now, here is a summary of that discussion:

> Well, dear parents, I know that what I have shared in this chapter has been upsetting. It is no wonder that many of you feel caught in the backwash of a postmodern culture whose only god is self-gratification and whose only value is radical individualism. Nevertheless, you do need to know the truth and what you can do to protect those you love. . . . Here are some things to consider:
>
> First, let's give priority to our children. In days gone by, the culture acted to shield them from harmful images and exploitation. Now it's open season for even the youngest among us. Let's put the welfare of our boys [and girls] ahead of our own convenience and teach them the difference between right and wrong. They need to hear that God is the author of their rights and liberties. Let's teach them that He loves them and holds them to a high level of moral accountability.
>
> Second, let's do everything in our power to reverse the blight of violence and lust that has become so pervasive across this land. Let's demand that the entertainment moguls stop producing moral pollutants. Let's recapture from the courts that system of self-rule that traditionally allowed Americans to debate their deepest differences openly and reach workable solutions together. Radical individualism is destroying us! Postmodernism is a cancer that rots the soul of humanity. The creed that proclaims, "If it feels good, do it!" has filled too many hospitals with drug-overdosed teenagers, too many prison cells with fatherless youth, too many caskets with slain young people, and caused too many tears for bewildered parents.
>
> Finally, let's vow together today to set for our children the highest standards of ethics and morality and to protect them, as

much as possible, from evil and death. Our families can't be perfect, but they *can* be better—much better.[8]

With that, I'll offer some other ideas and suggestions that relate to all adolescents, including those who are harder to handle.

1. Give teenagers the gifts they hunger for most—respect and dignity!

As we all know, the period of early adolescence is typically a painful time of life, marked by rapid physical and emotional changes. This characteristic difficulty was expressed by a seventh-grade boy who had been asked to recite Patrick Henry's historic speech at a special program commemorating the birth of the United States. But when the young man stood nervously before an audience of parents, he became confused and blurted out: "Give me puberty or give me death!" His statement is not as ridiculous as it sounds. Many teens sincerely believe they must choose between these dubious alternatives.

The thirteenth and fourteenth years commonly are the most difficult twenty-four months in life. A preadolescent child of ten or twelve suddenly awakens to a brand-new world around him, as though his eyes were opening for the first time. That world is populated by agemates who scare him out of his wits. His greatest anxiety, even exceeding the fear of death, which is remote and unthinkable, is the possibility of rejection or humiliation in the eyes of his peers. This ominous threat will lurk in the background for years, motivating kids to do things that make absolutely no sense to the adults who watch. It is impossible to comprehend the adolescent mind without understanding this terror of the peer group.

Related to this social vulnerability are the doubt and feelings of inferiority that reach an all-time high at this age. An adolescent's worth as a human being hangs precariously on peer-group acceptance, which is notoriously fickle. Thus, relatively minor evidences of rejection or ridicule are of major significance to those who already see themselves as fools and failures. It is difficult to overestimate the impact of having no one to sit with on the school-sponsored field trip, not being invited to an important event, being laughed at by the "in" group, waking up in the morning to find seven shiny new pimples on your oily forehead, or being humiliated by the boy or girl you thought had liked you. Some adolescents consistently face these kinds of social catastrophes throughout their teen years. It makes some of the most strong-willed among them downright mean at home.

Dr. Urie Bronfenbrenner, now retired from Cornell University, identified early adolescence as the most destructive period of life. Bronfenbrenner recalls being asked during a U.S. Senate hearing to indicate the most critical years in a child's development. He knew the senators expected him to emphasize the importance of preschool experience, reflecting the popular notion that all significant learning takes place during the first six years of life. However, Bronfenbrenner said he had never been able to validate that assumption. He agreed that the preschool years are vital, but so is every other phase of childhood. In fact, he told the Senate committee that the middle school years are probably the most critical to the development of a child's mental health. It is during this period of self-doubt that the personality is often assaulted and damaged beyond repair. Consequently, said Bronfenbrenner, it is not unusual for students to enter junior high school as happy, healthy children—and then emerge two years later as broken, discouraged teenagers.[9]

I couldn't agree more emphatically. Both physical and emotional dangers lurk everywhere at this time. I'll never forget a vulnerable girl named Diane who was a student when I was in high school. She attended modern-dance classes and was asked to perform during an all-school assembly program. Diane was in the ninth grade and had not yet begun to develop sexually. As she spun around the stage that day, the unthinkable happened! The top of her strapless blouse suddenly let go (it had nothing to grip) and dropped to her waist. The student body gasped and then roared with laughter. It was terrible! Diane stood clutching frantically at her bare body for a split second and then fled from the stage in tears. She never fully recovered from the tragedy during her high school years. And you can bet that her "friends" made sure she didn't.

Middle school students are typically brutal to each other, attacking and slashing a weak victim in much the same way a pack of wolves kills and devours a deformed caribou. They act this way because they are afraid of being bullied themselves, according to Dorothy Espelage, the author of a study of 558 students at a Midwestern middle school. "Kids don't have the skills to stop [bullying]," Espelage said. "They also fear that if they try, attention will turn to them. They also have a sense that it's all in fun—but to the victims, it's not funny." Espelage and her colleagues found that 80 percent of the students in their study said they had engaged in physical aggression, social ridicule, teasing, name-calling, and threats within the last thirty days.[10]

Another study, done by researchers at the University of Georgia and the University of Minnesota, found that bullying peaks when youngsters make the move from elementary to middle school. Their findings suggest that teasing and threatening are just part of the search for status. "Once the dominance is established and their place with their new friends is secure, the aggression subsides," the study's authors wrote.[11]

I have witnessed firsthand the brutality of the young. When I was in my twenties, I had the privilege of teaching in a public middle school. For two years, I taught science and math to 225 rambunctious troops each day, although I learned much more from them than they did from me. There on the firing line, my concepts of discipline and child development began to solidify. The workable, practical solutions were validated, while the lofty theories dreamed up by academics exploded like so much TNT when tested on the battlefield each day.

One of the most important lessons I learned in those years was the linkage between self-worth (or self-hatred) and rebellious behavior. I observed very quickly during my teaching career that I could impose all manner of discipline and classroom rules for my students, provided I treated each young person with genuine dignity and respect. I earned my students' friendship before and after school, during lunch, and through classroom encounters. I was tough, especially when challenged, but never discourteous, mean, or insulting. I defended the underdog and tenaciously tried to build each child's confidence and self-respect. However, I never compromised my standards of deportment. Students entered my classroom without talking each day. They did not behave disrespectfully, curse, or stab one another with ballpoint pens. I was clearly the captain of the ship, and I sailed it with military zeal.

The result of this combination of kindness and firm discipline stands as one of the most pleasant memories of my professional life. I loved my students and had every reason to believe that I was loved in return. I actually missed them on weekends (a fact my wife never quite understood). At the end of the final year when I was packing my books and saying good-bye, twenty-five or thirty teary-eyed kids hung around my gloomy room for several hours and finally stood sobbing in the parking lot as I drove away. And, yes, this twenty-six-year-old teacher also shed a few tears of his own that day. It is no wonder that one of my favorite movies, released in 1996, is *Mr. Holland's Opus,* which portrays a teacher who embodies the characteristics I have described. (Please forgive this self-congratulatory paragraph. I haven't bothered to tell you about my failures, which are far less interesting.)

If you can communicate kindness to your oppressed and harassed teenagers, even to those who are sullen and difficult, then many of the usual disciplinary problems of adolescence can be circumvented. That is, after all, the best way to deal with people of any age.

Let's look now at the second suggestion, which can be, in effect, a means of implementing the first.

2. The key to the puzzle

There is often an irrationality associated with adolescence that can be terribly frustrating to parents. It is difficult at that time to reason your way out of conflict. Let me offer an illustration that may explain the problem.

In graduate school I was told a story about a medical student who was required as part of his training to spend a few weeks working in a psychiatric hospital. Unfortunately, he was given little orientation to the nature of mental illness, and he mistakenly thought he could reason his patients back to a world of reality. One schizophrenic inmate was of particular interest to him, because the man believed himself to be dead.

"Yeah, it's true," the patient would tell anyone who asked. "I'm dead. Been dead for years."

The intern couldn't resist trying to talk the schizophrenic out of his delusion. He sat down with the patient and said, "I understand you think you're dead. Is that right?"

"Sure is," replied the man. "I'm deader than a doornail."

The intern continued, "Well, answer me this: Do dead people bleed?"

"No, of course not," replied the schizophrenic, sounding perfectly sane.

The intern then took the patient's hand in his own and stuck a needle into the fleshy part of his thumb. As the blood oozed from the puncture, the schizophrenic gasped and exclaimed, "Well, what do you know! Dead people do bleed!"

There may be times when you may find yourself holding similar conversations with your uncomprehending adolescent. These moments will likely occur while you are trying to explain why he must be home by a certain hour, why she should keep her room straight, why he can't have the car on Friday night, or why it doesn't really matter that she wasn't invited to the cool party given by the most popular kid in the senior class. These issues defy reason, and teens are more likely to respond instead to the dynamic emotional, social, and chemical forces that propel them. I can also assure you, from the survey of thirty-five thousand parents mentioned earlier, that the strong-willed child is especially susceptible to these internal and sometimes irrational forces. Whatever testiness was there in the past twelve years is most likely to get worse before it gets better.

Let me quote from a *US News & World Report* article that helps articulate this phenomenon:

> One day, your child [if naturally compliant] is a beautiful, charming 12-year-old, a kid who pops out of bed full of good cheer, clears the table without being asked, and brings home good grades from school. The next day, your child bursts into tears when you ask for the salt and listens to electronic music at maximum volume for hours on end. Chores? Forget it. Homework? There's little time, after talking to friends on the phone for five hours every night. Mornings? Your bluebird of happiness is flown, replaced by a groaning lump that can scarcely be roused out of bed. Welcome to adolescence.[12]

What is going on here? Why the sudden volatility and irrationality? The answer is straightforward. It's the mischievous hormones that have begun to surge! They are the key to understanding nearly everything that doesn't add up in the teen years. The emotional characteristics of a suddenly rebellious teenager, or the worsening of them, are rather like premenstrual syndrome (PMS) or severe menopause in women. Obviously, dramatic changes are going on inside! If the upheaval was caused entirely by environmental factors, its onset in puberty would not be so predictable. The emotional changes I have described arrive right on schedule, timed to coincide precisely with the onset of physical maturation. Both changes, I contend, are driven by a common hormonal assault. Human chemistry apparently goes haywire for a few years, affecting mind as much as body.

Does this understanding make it easier for parents to tolerate and cope with the reverberations of puberty? Probably not, but it should. For several years, a teenager may not interpret his world accurately. His social judgment is impaired. His fear of danger is muted, and his view of responsibility is warped. Therefore, it is a good idea not to despair when it looks as though everything you have tried to teach your kid seems to have been forgotten—or never learned. He is going through a metamorphosis that has turned everything upside down. But stick around. He'll regain his equilibrium in due time and your relationship will stabilize—providing *you're* not the one who is insane by that point.

And now a word of advice for parents of a strong-willed girl whose personality becomes downright nasty every month. I strongly recommend that you encourage your daughter to plot the particulars of her menstrual cycle on a graph. Talk to her about PMS and how it influences behavior, self-esteem, and moods.

Ask her to record when her period begins and ends each month, as well as how she feels before, during, and after her cycle. (Don't bring up the subject until she is in midcycle.) I think you and she will see that the emotional blowups that tear the family apart are predictable and recurring. Premenstrual tension during adolescence can produce a flurry of tornadoes every twenty-eight days. If you know they are coming, you can retreat to the storm cellar when the wind begins to blow. Unfortunately, many parents never seem to notice the regularity and predictability of depression, agitation, and conflict with their daughter. Watch the calendar. It will tell you so much about your girl.

Emotional balance in teenage boys is not as cyclical as it is in girls, but boys' behavior is equally influenced by hormones. Everything from sexual passion to aggressiveness is motivated by the new chemicals that surge through their veins.

Having made the case for hormonal influences, now let me add that nothing is as simple as it sounds.

Recent studies reveal that hormones are not the only culprits in the mix. Immaturity is also caused by incomplete brain development during early adolescence. These findings were summarized in the same *US News & World Report* article I quoted from earlier. Here is what was written:

> And just as a teenager is all legs one day and all nose and ears the next, different regions of the brain are developing on different timetables. For instance, one of the last parts to mature is in charge of making sound judgments and calming unruly emotions. And the emotional centers in the teenage brain have already been revving up, probably under the influence of sex hormones. This imbalance may explain why your intelligent 16-year-old doesn't think twice about getting into a car driven by a friend who is drunk, or why your formerly equable 13-year-old can be hugging you one minute and then flying off the handle the next.[13]

Researchers have also discovered that a teenager's brain goes through an experience called pruning, in which the brain purges itself of neurons and synapses it no longer finds useful. These neurons and synapses are developed between the ages of nine and ten and then are eliminated as the brain decides which to retain. Thus, until the prefrontal cortex of the brain has gone through this pruning process, most young teenagers do not have all of their brainpower at their disposal, especially the power to make good judgments. This can also result in teenagers having difficulty managing multiple tasks.[14]

Isn't that interesting? These findings should be helpful when the kid you brought into the world in love, and for whom you would give your very life, accuses you of being Attila the Hun and hisses like a snake when told no. This negativism isn't entirely your fault. And this individual, when grown, will look back and talk with you about how cantankerous she was during this time.

Remember the mother named Joy, who appeared with a panel on a Focus on the Family radio broadcast and told us how her impossibly rebellious, strong-willed daughter wrote an emotional letter from college, apologizing and saying her mother was her best friend? That is not an unusual outcome. I will say more about this optimistic prognosis in the final chapter.

The bottom line is that the adolescent years represent a transition period that will soon pass. Don't be too discouraged when the storms are raging. Keep your confidence when under fire, and do the best you can to work your way through these conflicts. And by all means stay in touch with your kids, even when you and they are having trouble understanding each other. Remember that your formerly pleasant and happy child, who seemingly degenerated overnight into a sour and critical anarchist, may also be worried about what is happening to her. She may be confused by the resentment and anger that have become so much a part of her personality. She clearly needs the patient reassurance of loving parents who can explain the normality of this agitation and help her ventilate the inner tension. It's a job for Superparent!

3. Pry open the door of communication

But how can you talk to someone who won't talk—someone whose language consists of seven phrases: I dunno. I don't care. Leave me alone. I need money. Can I have the car? My friends think you're unfair. And, I didn't do it. Prying open the door of communication with an angry adolescent can require more tact and skill than any other parenting assignment. Often, mothers and fathers act like adolescents, shouting and screaming and engaging in endless battles that leave them exhausted but without strategic advantage. There has to be a better way of communicating than shouting at one another. Let me propose an alternative.

For purposes of illustration, suppose that Brian is now fourteen years old and has entered a period of remarkable defiance. He is breaking rules right and left and seems to hate the entire family. He becomes angry when his parents discipline him, of course, but even during tranquil times he seems to resent them for merely being there. Last Friday night he arrived home an hour beyond his curfew but refused to explain where he was or why he was late. What course of action would be best for his parents to take?

Let's assume that you are Brian's father. I would recommend that you invite him out to breakfast on a Saturday morning, leaving the rest of the family at home. It would be best if this event occurred during a relatively tranquil time, certainly not in the midst of a hassle or intergenerational battle. Admit that you have some important matters to discuss with him that can't be communicated adequately at home, but don't tip your hand before Saturday morning.

Then at the appropriate moment during breakfast, convey the following messages (or an adaptation thereof):

A. Brian, I wanted to talk to you this morning because of the changes that are taking place in you and in our home. We both know that the past few weeks have not been very pleasant. You have been angry most of the time and have become disobedient and rude. And your mother and I haven't done so well either. We've become irritable, and we've said things that we've regretted later. This is not what God wants of us as parents or of you as our son. There has to be a better way of solving our problems. That's why we're here.

B. As a place to begin, Brian, I want you to understand what is happening. You have gone into a new period of life known as adolescence. This is the final phase of childhood, and it is often a very stormy and difficult few years. Nearly everyone goes through these rough times during their early teens, and you are right on schedule. Many of the problems you face today were predictable from the day you were born, simply because growing up has never been an easy thing to do. There are even greater pressures on kids today than when we were young. I've said that to let you know this: We love you as much as we ever did, even though the past few months have been difficult in our home.

C. What is actually taking place, you see, is that you have had a taste of freedom. You are tired of being told what to do. Within certain limits, that is healthy evidence that you are growing up and becoming your own man. However, you want to be your own boss and make your own decisions without interference from anyone. Brian, you will get what you want in a very short time. You are fourteen now, and you'll soon be fifteen and seventeen and nineteen. You will be grown before we know it, and your mom and I will no longer have any responsibility for you. The day is coming when you will marry whomever you wish, go to whatever school you choose, and select the profession or job that suits you. Your mother and I will not seek to make those decisions for you. We will respect your adulthood. Furthermore, Brian, the closer you get to that day, the more freedom we plan to give you. You have more privileges now than you had last year, and that trend will continue. We will soon set you free, and you will be accountable only to God and yourself.

D. But, Brian, you must understand this message: You are not grown yet. During the past few weeks, you have wanted your mother and me to leave you alone—to let you stay out half the night if you choose, to fail in school, to carry no responsibility at home. And you have blown up whenever we have denied even your most extreme demands. The truth of the matter is, you have wanted us to grant you a twenty-year-old's freedom during your fourteenth year, although you still expect to have your shirts ironed and your meals fixed and your bills paid. You have wanted the best of both worlds with none of the responsibilities or limitations of either. It doesn't work that way. So what are we to do? The easiest thing would be for us to let you have your way. There would be no hassles and no conflict and no more frustration. Many parents of fourteen-year-olds have done just that. But we must not yield to this temptation. You are not ready for complete independence, and we would be showing hatred (instead of love) for you if we surrendered at this time. We would regret our mistake for the rest of our life, and you would soon blame us too. And as you know, you have two younger sisters who are watching you very closely, who must be protected from the things you are teaching them.

E. Besides, Brian, God has given us a responsibility as parents to do what is right for you, and He is holding us accountable for the way we do that job. I want to read you an important passage from the Bible that describes a father named Eli, a priest in the temple, who did not discipline and correct his two unruly teenage sons. [Read the dramatic story from 1 Samuel 2:12-17, 22-25, 27-34; 3:11-14; 4:1-4 and 10-22.] It is very clear that God was angry with Eli for permitting his sons to be disrespectful and disobedient. Not only did He allow the sons to be killed in battle, but He also punished their father for not accepting his parental responsibilities.

This assignment to parents can be found throughout the Bible: Mothers and fathers are expected to train their children and discipline them when required. What I'm saying is that God will not hold us blameless if we let you behave in ways that are harmful to yourself and others. The Bible also tells parents not to overcorrect and demoralize their children. We're going to try harder to conform to that Scripture too.

F. That brings us to the question of where we go from this moment. I want to make a pledge to you, here and now: Your mother and I intend to be more sensitive to your needs and feelings than we've been in the past. We're not perfect, as you well know, and it is possible that you will feel we have been unfair at one time or another. If that occurs, you can express your views and we will listen to you. We want to keep the door of communication wide open between us. When you seek a new privilege, I'm going to ask myself this question, "Is there any way I can grant this request without harming Brian or other people?" If I can permit what you want in good conscience, I will do so. I will compromise and bend as far as my best judgment will let me.

G. But hear this, Brian. There will be some matters that cannot be compromised. There will be occasions when I will have to say no. And when those times come, you can expect me to stand like the Rock of Gibraltar. No amount of violence and temper tantrums and door slamming will change a thing. In fact, if you choose to fight me in those remaining areas, then I promise that you will lose big-time. Admittedly, you're too big and grown up to spank, but I can still make you uncomfortable. And that will be my goal. Believe me, Brian, I'll lie awake nights figuring out how to make you miserable. I have the courage and the determination to do my job during these last few years you are at home, and I intend to use all of my resources for this purpose, if necessary. So it's up to you. We can have a peaceful time of cooperation at home, or we can spend this last part of your childhood in unpleasantness and struggle. Either way, you will arrive home when you are told, you will carry your share of responsibility in the family, and you will continue to respect your mother and me.

H. Finally, Brian, let me emphasize the message I gave you in the beginning. We love you more than you can imagine, and we're going to remain friends during this difficult time. There is so much pain in the world today. Life involves disappointment and loss and rejection and aging and sickness and ultimately death. You haven't felt much of that discomfort yet, but you'll taste it soon enough. So with all that heartache outside our door, let's not bring more of it on ourselves. We need each other. We need you, and believe it or not, you still need us occasionally. We're going to be praying for you every day and asking the Lord to lead and guide you. I know He will answer that prayer. And that, I suppose, is what I wanted to convey to you this morning. Let's make it better from now on.

Do you have things that need to be said to me?

The content of this message should be modified to fit individual circumstances and the needs of particular adolescents. And the response from the teenager will vary tremendously from person to person. An open boy or girl may reveal deep feelings at such a moment of communication, permitting a priceless time of catharsis and ventilation. On the other hand, a stubborn, defiant, proud adolescent may sit immobile with head downward. But even if your teenager remains stoic or hostile, at least the cards have been laid on the table and parental intentions have been explained.

4. Keep them moving

And now a word of practical advice for the parents of very strong-willed adolescents. They simply must not be allowed to get bored. Giving them large quantities of unstructured time is asking for trouble. The hormones that surge through their youthful bodies, especially testosterone in boys, will often lead them in the direction of danger or trouble. That's why unsupervised time after school, when parents are at work, can lead to harmful behavior. This is hardly new advice. The old adage warns, "An idle mind is the devil's workshop." True enough. My advice is to get these energetic, mischievous teenagers occupied in constructive activities (without overdoing it). See that they get into a good youth program (a Bible-believing church would be the best place to start, from my perspective) and/or become involved in athletic pursuits, music, hobbies, animal care, part-time jobs, or an academic interest such as electronics or agriculture. Obviously, implementing this suggestion is not as urgent for the parents of compliant kids, but the idea is still relevant. By whatever means, you must find a way to keep their gangly legs churning.

One way to help accomplish that is to direct your teenagers to positive messages that are relevant to their lives. I strongly recommend, for example, Focus on the Family's teen magazines, *Breakaway* (for boys) and *Brio* (for girls), which attempt to address teen issues in a language adolescents can understand. For information about these resources, feel free to contact Focus on the Family at 1-800-A-FAMILY or log on to www.family.org for more information.

Not only should adolescents be busy doing constructive things, but they desperately need personal connectedness to their family. Every available study draws this conclusion. When parents are involved intimately with their kids during the teen years and when their relationship leads to an active family life, rebellious and destructive behavior is less likely to occur. Drs. Blake Bowden and Jennie Zeisz studied 527 teenagers at Cincinnati Children's Hospital to learn what family and lifestyle characteristics were related to mental health and adjustment. Their findings were significant.

Adolescents whose parents ate dinner with them five times a week or more were the least likely to be on drugs, depressed, or in trouble with the law. They were more likely to be doing well in school and surrounded by a supportive circle of friends. By contrast, the more poorly adjusted teens ate with their parents only three evenings a week or less. What Bowden's study shows is that children do far better in school and in life when they spend time with their parents, and specifically when they get together almost every day for conversation and interaction.[15]

This is one of *the* most effective tools for helping your teen through the dangerous years of adolescence. And, yes, it works with strong-willed children, too.

5. Use incentives and privileges to advantage

As I pointed out previously, one of the most common mistakes parents of rebellious kids make is allowing themselves to be drawn into endless verbal battles that leave them exhausted but without strategic advantage. Don't subject your daughter to perpetual threats and finger-wagging accusations and insulting indictments. And most important, don't nag her endlessly. Adolescents hate to be nagged by Mommy and Daddy! When that occurs, they typically protect themselves by appearing deaf. Thus, the quickest way to terminate all communication between generations is to follow a young person around the house, repeating the same monotonous messages of disapproval with the regularity of a cuckoo clock.

What, then, is the proper response to slovenliness, disobedience, defiance, and irresponsibility? That question takes us back to the threat, implied to Brian, that his father would make him miserable if he did not cooperate. Don't let the news leak out, but the tools available to implement that promise are relatively weak. Since it is unwise (and unproductive) to spank a teenager, parents can only manipulate environmental circumstances when discipline is required. They have the keys to the family automobile (unless the teen has her own car, taking away a prize bargaining chip) and can allow their teenager to use it. They may grant permission to go to the beach or to the mountains or to a friend's house or to a party. They control the family purse and can choose to share it or loan it or dole it or close it. They can ground their adolescent or deny use of the telephone, stereo, or television and VCR for a while.

Now, obviously, these are not very influential motivators and are at times totally inadequate for the situation. After we have appealed to reason, cooperation, and family loyalty, all that remain are relatively ineffective methods of punishment. We can only link our kids' behavior with desirable and undesirable consequences and hope the connection will be enough to elicit their cooperation.

If that sounds pretty weak, let me admit what I am implying: A willful, angry sixteen-year-old boy or girl *can* win a confrontation with his or her parents today if worst comes to worst. The law has totally shifted in teenagers' favor. For example, they can have sex, conceive a child, and, in many states, abort a child without their parents' knowledge. Drugs and alcohol are easy to obtain. Very few adult privileges and vices can be denied a teenager who has a passion for independence and the will to fight. Under some circumstances in certain states, a sixteen-year-old can be legally emancipated and freed from all parental supervision. Sometimes in cases of extreme rebellion, your reaction in a crisis has to be based on bluster and intimidation. It isn't enough, but you run with what is available to you.

As I said earlier, the culture is not on your side. Every spark of adolescent discontent is fanned into a smoldering flame. The grab for the buying power of children and teens has become intense, and marketers are after them almost from the time they leave the womb. Often, teenagers are given money by guilt-ridden parents who neglect them as they pursue their careers. In fact, in 1998, teenagers spent a record $141 billion—an average of $4,548 each![16] In addition, many teens have free rein in shopping malls, charge cards in hand. One teenage girl, when asked if her parents trusted her with a credit card, laughed out loud and said, "I max out my gas card every month. My parents pay for it," adding that she was not sure of her credit limit. She went on to say that she spent several hundred dollars a month on gas, cigarettes, and food and only stopped when her card was rejected. "I know I can't handle my own credit card. I can't even handle my checking account," she concluded.[17]

Our culture assaults teens with every antisocial message imaginable and appeals to their weaknesses and lack of adult judgment. Parents must step into the gap. If parents are absent during this crucial time, the results can be disastrous. We need look no further than the example of Eric Harris and Dylan Klebold, the two young men involved in the Columbine High School tragedy in 1999. Left alone for hours by their parents, they turned to the Internet and violent video games, eventually carrying out their aggression in a murderous spree in the halls of their school. When teens are isolated from their parents, they are more vulnerable to serious emotional problems, including suicide.[18] I think the need for parental involvement is best expressed by Patricia Hersch, author of *A Tribe Apart: A Journey into the Heart of American Adolescence,* who said, "Every kid I talked to at length eventually came around to saying without my asking that they had wished they had more adults in their lives, especially their parents."[19]

So what is the answer? That takes us back to the importance of laying a foundation of respect for parental authority during the early years of a child's development. Without that foundation—without a touch of awe in a child's perception of his mother or father—the balance of power and control is definitely shifted toward the younger combatant.

As Patricia Hersch stated, and despite what the perception may be, teenagers desperately want to be connected to their parents during the tumultuous years of adolescence. In 1999, the National Longitudinal Study on Adolescent Health found that teenagers who feel more connected and comfortable with their parents, teachers, and other adults are less likely to commit violence, use illegal drugs, or become sexually active.[20]

Another national survey of teens done by the Horatio Alger Foundation found that a majority of adolescents felt that the decline of the family, along with "sagging moral and social values," was one of the biggest problems they face. In fact, they rated family to be more important to personal success than making a contribution to society. Jennifer Park, who helped prepare the report on the survey, said, "Family is very important. This is something that is really constant throughout the whole generation."[21]

Let me share an experience from my own life that I included in my book *Bringing Up Boys*. When I was sixteen years old, I began to play some games that my mother viewed with alarm. I had not yet crossed the line into all-out rebellion, but I was definitely leaning in that direction. My father was a minister who traveled constantly during that time, and Mom was in charge. One night, we had an argument over a dance I wanted to go to, and she objected. I openly defied her that night. I said, in effect, that I was going and if she didn't like it, that was just too bad. Mom became very quiet, and I turned in a huff to go into my bedroom. I paused in the hall when I heard her pick up the phone and call my dad, who was out of town. She simply said, "I need you." What happened in the next few days shocked me down to my toes. My dad canceled his four-year speaking schedule and put our house up for sale. Then he accepted a pastoral assignment seven hundred miles south. The next thing I knew, I was on a train heading for Texas and a new home in the Rio Grande Valley. That permitted my dad to be at home with me for my last two years of high school. During these years we hunted and fished together and bonded for a lifetime. There in a fresh environment, I made new friends and worked my way through the conflict that was brewing with my mom. I didn't fully understand until later the price my parents paid to do what was best for me. It was a very costly move for them, personally and professionally, but they loved me enough to sacrifice at a critically important time. In essence, they saved me. I was moving in the wrong direction, and they pulled me back from the cliff. I will always appreciate these good people for what they did.

There is more to the story, of course. It was difficult making new friends in a strange high school at the beginning of my junior year. I was lonely and felt out of place in a town that failed to acknowledge my arrival. My mother sensed this feeling of friendlessness and, in her characteristic way, was hurting with me. One day, after we had been in the community for about two weeks, she took me by the hand and pressed a piece of paper into the palm. She looked in my eyes and said, "This is for you. Don't tell anybody. Just take it and use it for anything you want. It isn't much, but I want you to get something that looks good to you."

I unfolded the paper, which turned out to be a twenty-dollar bill. It was money that my mother and father didn't have, considering the cost of the move and my dad's small salary. But no matter, I stood at the top of their priorities during these stormy days. We all know that money won't buy friends, and twenty dollars (even then) did not change my life significantly. Nevertheless, my mother used that method of saying to me: "I feel what you feel; I know it's difficult right now, but I'm your friend and I want to help." All troubled teens should be so fortunate as to have parents who are pulling for them and praying for them and feeling for them, even when they are at their most unlovable.

I have been suggesting that parents be willing to take whatever corrective action is required during the adolescent years, but to do it without nagging, moaning, groaning, and growling. Let love be your guide! Even though it often doesn't seem like it, your teen desperately wants to be loved and to feel connected to you. Anger does not motivate teenagers. That is why the parent or teacher who can find the delicate balance between love and firm discipline is the one who ends up winning the heart of teenagers. The adult who screams and threatens but does not love is only going to fuel teenage rebellion.

There is hope. Laurence Steinberg, a psychology professor at Temple University, observed: "Parents are caught by surprise [by adolescence]. They discover that the tricks they've used in raising their kids effectively during childhood stopped working." However, he advised parents that if they stick it out, things will improve. "I have a 14-year-old son," Steinberg said, "and when we moved out of the transition phase into middle adolescence, we saw a dramatic change. All of a sudden, he's our best friend again."[22]

This brings us to another important understanding of adolescence and the strong-willed kids who live there.

6. Hold on with an open hand

Another serious mistake made by parents of older teenagers (sixteen to nineteen years of age) is refusing to grant them the independence and maturity they require. Our inclination as loving guardians is to hold our kids too tightly, despite their attempts to squirm free. We try to make all their decisions, keep them snugly beneath our wings, and prevent even the possibility of failure. And in so doing, we force our young adults into one of two destructive patterns: Either they passively accept our overprotection and remain dependent "children" into adult life or they rise up in great wrath to reject our bondage and interference. They lose on both counts. On the one hand they become emotional cripples who are incapable of independent thought, and on the other they grow into angry, guilt-ridden adults who have severed ties with the family they need. Indeed, parents who refuse to grant appropriate independence to their older adolescents are courting disaster not only for their children but also for themselves.

Let me state it more strongly: I believe American parents are not very good at letting go of their grown children. This observation was powerfully illustrated in a book written years ago, *What Really Happened to the Class of '65?* [23] The book's narrative begins in the midsixties when *Time* magazine selected the senior class of Palisades High School in southern California as the focus for its cover story on "Today's Teenager." The editors had clearly chosen the cream of the crop for their report. These graduating young men and women lived in one of the wealthiest school districts in America, with an average income in 1965 of $42,000 per family (which would perhaps exceed $400,000 today). Listed among the members of their class were the children of many famous people, including James Arness, Henry Miller, Karl Malden, Betty Hutton, Sterling Hayden, and Irving Wallace. [24] These students were part of the most beautiful, healthiest, best educated, and most affluent generation in history, and they knew it. Little wonder that *Time* perceived them to be standing "on the fringe of a golden era" as they left high school and headed for college. [25] Their future sparkled like the California sunrise on a summer day.

But that was in 1965. Ten years later, two members of that class, Michael Medved and David Wallechinsky, became interested in investigating what really *did* happen to the optimistic young graduates of Palisades High School. Had they achieved the anticipated promise of glory and accomplishment? It was a fascinating (although profane and vulgar) commentary on a generation of over-indulged kids, not only from Pacific Palisades, but from all across the United States. It focused on the major stereotypes populating American secondary schools, including the gorgeous cheerleader, the cool quarterback, the intellectual, the goof-off, the nerd, the dreamboat, the flirt, the underachiever, and the wild girl (who reportedly made love to 425 boys before losing count). One by one, their private lives and personal histories were revealed. [26]

As it turned out, the class of 1965, far from entering a "golden era," was plagued by personal tragedy and emotional unrest. In fact, the students who graduated from American high schools in that year may be the most unstable and lost generation of young men and women ever produced in our country. A few weeks after they received their diplomas, our cities began to burn during the long, hot summer of racial strife. That signaled the start of the chaos to come. They entered college at a time when drug abuse was not only prevalent but almost universal for students and teachers alike. Intellectual pursuits were the first casualty in this narcotic climate. The Vietnam War soon heated campus passions to an incendiary level, generating anger and disdain for the government, the president, the military, both political parties, and, indeed, the American way of life. That hostility gave rise to bombings, riots, and the burning of "establishment" edifices.

This generation of college students had already witnessed the brutal assassination of their idol, John F. Kennedy, when they were barely sixteen years old. Then at a critical point in their season of passion, they lost two more beloved heroes, Robert Kennedy and Martin Luther King Jr. Those murders were followed by the street wars that punctuated the 1968 Democratic Convention and the killing of students at Kent State University. These violent convulsions reached their overt culmination in the wake of President Nixon's military foray into Cambodia, which virtually closed down American campuses. As our population ages, fewer and fewer people lived through and remember those tumultuous days. Nevertheless, they represented a knife edge in Western culture, separating what came before with what we have known since.

Accompanying the social upheaval of that era was a sudden disintegration of moral and ethical principles, such as has never occurred in the history of humankind. All at once, there were no definite values. There were no standards. No absolutes. No rules. No traditional beliefs on which to lean. Nor could anyone over thirty even be trusted. And some bright-eyed theologians chose that moment of confusion to announce the death of God. It was a distressing time to be young—to be groping aimlessly in search of personal identity and a place in the sun. That was the social setting for the students who entered college or went into the workforce during the late 1960s.

The class of '65 caught that cultural revolution right between the eyes, and their personal lives thereafter have reflected the changes of the times. In case after case, they tasted the sordid and seamy offerings of a valueless society. They became hooked on heroin, LSD, barbiturates, and alcohol. They experienced broken marriages and sexual extravaganzas and experimental lifestyles. They produced unwanted children who hadn't the slightest chance of being raised properly. By 1978, the year I wrote the first edition of *The Strong-Willed Child*, 11 percent of the Palisades class had served time in jail, and one individual (the school's most popular "dreamboat") had committed suicide. At least eighteen members of the class had been hospitalized for psychiatric treatment. A former teacher at Palisades High School characterized the decade from 1965 to 1975 as "the saddest years of the century."[27] I certainly agree.

My reason for describing this depressing era in such detail is to point out the mistakes made during that period. Unfortunately, the conditions that produced it are still evident today! The errors lumbered into by those parents were not only powered by disruptive social forces, they were also caused by parental failure to allow the class of 1965 to grow up. Although the older generation exercised very little influence over their sons and daughters after graduation, they nevertheless failed to emancipate them. An amazingly consistent pattern is evident throughout the book, with moms and dads bailing their kid out of jail, paying their bills, making it unnecessary for them to work, and encouraging them to live at home again. They offered volumes of unsolicited advice to accompany their undeserved and unappreciated material gifts. The result was disastrous.

Let me personalize the issues before us. How can you avoid making similar mistakes with your child, and especially with your strong-willed son or daughter? It is a very important question, because the more rebellious and frustrating your kid is, the more likely you are to give too much, tolerate too much, advise too much, and rescue too much. These blunders come down to a common thread—one that results from hanging on too tightly when you should be letting go. In so doing, you run the risk of making emotional cripples out of your recently minted adults. This is what the parents in Palisades did in the late sixties. But you can do better.

Here's how not to fall into the same pattern: Begin preparing a child for their ultimate release during the toddler years, before a relationship of dependence is established. Unfortunately, the natural inclination of parents is to do the opposite. As Domeena Renshaw wrote:

> It may be messier for the child to feed himself; more untidy for him to dress himself; less clean when he attempts to bathe himself; less perfect for him to comb his hair; but unless his mother learns to sit on her hands and allow the child to cry and to try, she will overdo for the child, and independence will be delayed.[28]

This process of granting appropriate independence must continue throughout the elementary school years. Parents should permit their kids to go to summer camp even though it might be safer to keep them at home. They should allow them to spend the night with their friend when invited. The kids should make their own bed, take care of their animals, and do their homework. In short, the parental purpose should be to grant increasing freedom and responsibility year by year, so that when the child gets beyond adult control, he or she will no longer need it.

When this assignment is handled properly, a high school senior should be largely emancipated, even though he still lives with his parents. If I may share another personal example, this was the case during my last year at home. When I was seventeen years of age, my parents tested my independence by going on a two-week trip and leaving me behind. They loaned me the family car, and gave me permission to invite my (male) friends to spend the fourteen nights at our home. I remember being surprised by this move and the obvious risks they were taking. I could have thrown fourteen wild parties, wrecked the car and destroyed our house. Frankly, I wondered if they were wise to give me that much latitude. I did behave responsibly (although our house suffered the effects of some typical adolescent horseplay). After I was grown and married, I asked my mother why she took those risks—why she left me unsupervised for two weeks. She smiled and replied, "Because I knew in approximately one year you would be leaving for college, where you would have complete freedom with no one to tell you how to behave. And I wanted to expose you to that independence while you were still under my influence." Her intuitive wisdom was apparent once more. She was preparing me for the ultimate release, which often causes an overprotected young person to behave foolishly the moment she escapes the heavy hand of authority.

Our objective as parents, then, is to do nothing for boys and girls that they can profit from doing for themselves. I admit the difficulty of implementing this policy. Our deep love for our children makes us tremendously vulnerable to their needs. Life inevitably brings pain and sorrow to little people, and we hurt when they hurt. When others ridicule them or laugh at them, when they feel lonely and rejected, when they fail at something important, when they cry in the midnight hours, when physical harm threatens their existence—these are the trials that seem unbearable to those of us who watch from the sidelines. We want to rise like a mighty shield to protect them from life's sting—to hold them snugly within the safety of our embrace. Yet there are times when we must let them struggle. Children can't grow without taking risks. Toddlers can't walk initially without falling down. Students can't learn without facing some hardships. And ultimately, an adolescent can't enter young adulthood until we release him from our protective custody. But as I have indicated, parents in the Western world find it difficult to let their offspring face and conquer the routine challenges of everyday living. This was typical for members of the class of 1965, whose parents prevented them from solving their problems by always doing the job for them. These same parents also failed to provide a moral and spiritual foundation for them.

Let me offer three guidelines for our parenting efforts during the final era of childhood. The first is simply: *Hold on with an open hand.* This implies that we still care about the outcome during early adulthood, but we must not clutch our children too tightly. Our grip must be relaxed. We should pray for them, love them, and even offer advice to them when it is sought. But the responsibility to make personal decisions must be borne by the next generation, and they must also accept the consequences of those choices.

Another phrase expressing a similar concept is *Hold them close and let them go.* This seven-word suggestion could almost represent the theme of my book. Parents should be deeply involved in the lives of their young children, providing love, protection, and authority. But when those children reach their late teens and early twenties, the cage door must be opened to the world outside. That is the most frightening time of parenthood, particularly for Christian mothers and fathers who care so deeply about the spiritual welfare of their family. How difficult it is to await an answer to the question, "Did I train them properly?" The tendency is to retain control in an attempt to avoid hearing the wrong reply to that all-important question. Nevertheless, our sons and daughters are more likely to make proper choices when they do not have to rebel against our meddling interference to gain their independence.

The third guideline could easily have been one of King Solomon's proverbs, although it does not appear in the Bible. It states, *If you love something, set it free. If it comes back to you, then it's yours. If it doesn't return, then it never was yours in the first place.* This little aphorism contains great wisdom. It reminds me of a day a number of years ago when a wild coyote pup trotted in front of our house in southern California. He had strayed into our residential area from the nearby mountains. I managed to chase him into our backyard, where I trapped him in a corner. After fifteen or twenty minutes, I succeeded in placing a collar and leash around his neck. He fought the noose with all his strength, jumping, diving, gnawing, and straining at the tether. Finally, in exhaustion, he submitted to his servitude. He was my captive, to the delight of the neighborhood children. I kept the little rascal for an entire day and considered trying to make a pet of him. However, I contacted an authority on coyotes, who told me the chances were very slim that I could tame his wild streak. Obviously, I could have kept him chained or caged, but he would never really have belonged to me. I asked a game warden to return the lop-eared creature to his native territory in the canyons above Los Angeles. You see, his friendship meant nothing to me unless I could set him free and retain him by his own choice.

My point is that love demands freedom. This is true not only of relationships between animals and humans, but also in all interpersonal interactions. For example, the quickest way to destroy romantic love between a husband and wife is for one partner to clamp a steel cage around the other. I've seen hundreds of women trying unsuccessfully to demand love and fidelity from their husband. It doesn't work. Think back to your dating experiences before marriage. Do you recall that any romantic relationship was doomed the moment one partner began to worry about losing the other, phoning six or eight times a day and hiding behind trees to see who was competing for the lover's attention? That hand-wringing performance will devastate a perfectly good love relationship in a matter of days. To repeat: *Love demands freedom.*

Why else did God give us the choice of either serving Him or rejecting His companionship? Why did He give Adam and Eve the option of eating forbidden fruit in the Garden of Eden, instead of forcing their obedience? Why didn't He just make men and women slaves who were programmed to worship at His feet? The answers are found in the meaning of love. God gave us a free choice because there is no significance to love that knows no alternative. It is only when we come to Him because we hungrily seek His fellowship and communion that the relationship has any validity. Isn't this the meaning of Proverbs 8:17: "I love them that love me; and those that seek me early shall find me" (KJV)? That is the love that only freedom can produce. It cannot be demanded or coerced or required or programmed against our will. It can only be the product of a free choice, a concept that is honored even by the Almighty.

The application of this perspective to older adolescents and those in their early twenties should be obvious. There comes a point where our record as parents is in the books, our training has been completed, and the moment of release has arrived. As I did with the young coyote, we must unsnap the leash and remove the collar. If our child runs, he runs. If she marries the wrong person, she marries the wrong person. If he takes drugs, he takes drugs. If our children go to the wrong school, reject their faith, refuse to work, or squander their resources on liquor and prostitutes, then they must be permitted to make these destructive choices. But it is not our task to pay the bills, ameliorate the consequences, or support their folly.

Adolescence is not an easy time of life for either generation. In fact, it can be downright terrifying. But the key to surviving this emotional experience is to lay the proper foundation and then face this time with courage. Even the rebellion of the teen years can be a healthy factor. This conflict contributes to the process by which an individual changes from a dependent child to a mature adult, taking his place as a coequal with his parents. Without that friction, the relationship could continue to be an unhealthy mommy-daddy-child triad late into adult life, with serious implications for future marital harmony. If the strain between generations was not part of the divine plan of human development, it would not be so universally prevalent, even in homes where love and authority have been maintained in proper balance. And remember that billions of other parents have trod the same journey from childhood to adolescence and beyond. Most of them survived it. And you will too!

7. Above all else, introduce your kids to Jesus Christ and then ground them thoroughly in the principles of your faith. This is job #1.

This word of advice is relevant to Christian parents of both strong-willed and compliant children. Everything of value depends on one primary responsibility—that of providing your kids with an unshakable faith in Jesus Christ. How can anything else compare in significance to this goal of keeping the family circle unbroken in the life to come? What an incredible objective to work toward!

If the salvation of our children is really that vital to us, then our spiritual training should begin before children can even comprehend what it is all about. They should grow up seeing their parents on their knees before God, talking to Him. They will learn quickly at that age and will never forget what they've seen and heard. Even if they reject their faith later, the seeds planted during that time will be with them for the rest of their lives. This is why we are instructed to "bring them up in the nurture and admonition of the Lord" (Ephesians 6:4, KJV).

Again, I was fortunate to have had parents who understood this principle. After I was grown they told me that I attempted to pray before I learned to talk. I watched them talk to God and tried to imitate the sounds I had heard. At three years of age, I made a conscious decision to become a Christian. You may think it impossible at such an age, but it happened. I remember the occasion clearly today. I was attending a Sunday evening church service and was sitting near the back with my mother. My father was the pastor, and he invited those who wished to do so to come pray at the altar. Fifteen or twenty people went forward, and I joined them spontaneously. I recall crying and asking Jesus to forgive my sins. I know that sounds strange, but that's the way it occurred. It is overwhelming for me to think about that event today. Imagine the King of the universe, Creator of all heaven and earth, caring about an insignificant kid barely out of toddlerhood! It may not make sense, but I know He met me at that altar.

Not every child will respond that early or dramatically, of course, nor should he. Some are more sensitive to spiritual matters than others, and they must be allowed to progress at their own pace. But in no sense should we as parents be casual or neutral about our children's training. Their world should sparkle with references to Jesus and to our faith. That is the meaning of Deuteronomy 6:6-9: "These commandments that I give you today are to be upon your hearts. Impress them on your children. Talk about them when you sit at home and when you walk along the road, when you lie down and when you get up. Tie them as symbols on your hands and bind them on your foreheads. Write them on the doorframes of your houses and on your gates."

I believe this commandment from the Lord is one of the most crucial passages for parents in the entire Bible. It instructs us to surround our children with godly teaching. References to spiritual things are not to be reserved just for Sunday morning or even for a bedtime prayer. They should permeate our conversation and the fabric of our lives. Why? Because our children are watching our every move during those early years. They want to know what is most important to us. If we hope to instill within them a faith that will last for a lifetime, then they must see and feel our passion for God.

As a corollary to that principle, I must remind you that children miss nothing in sizing up their parents. If you are only half convinced of your beliefs, they will quickly discern that fact. Any ethical weak spot—any indecision on your part—will be incorporated and then magnified in your sons and daughters. Like it or not, we are on the hook. Their faith or their faithlessness is usually a reflection of our own. As I've said, our children will eventually make their own choices and set the course of their life, but those decisions will be influenced by the foundation we have laid.

That brings me to another extremely important point, even though it is controversial. I firmly believe in acquainting children with God's judgment and wrath while they are young. Nowhere in the Bible are we instructed to skip over the unpleasant Scriptures in our teaching. The wages of sin is death, and children have a right to understand that fact.

I remember my mother reading the story of Samson to me when I was about nine years old. After this mighty warrior fell into sin, you will recall, the Philistines put out his eyes and held him as a common slave. Some time later, Samson repented before God, and he was forgiven. He was even given back his awesome strength. But my mother pointed out that he never regained his eyesight, nor did he ever live in freedom again. He and his enemies died together as the temple collapsed upon them.

"There are terrible consequences to sin," she told me solemnly. "Even if you repent and are forgiven, you will still suffer for breaking the laws of God. They are there to protect you. If you defy them, you will pay the price for your disobedience."

Then she talked to me about gravity, one of God's physical laws. "If you jump from a ten-story building, you can be certain that you will crash when you hit the ground. It is inevitable. You must also know that God's moral laws are just as real as His physical laws. You can't break them without crashing sooner or later."

Finally, she taught me about heaven and hell and the great Judgment Day when those who have been covered by the blood of Jesus will be separated eternally from those who have not. It made a profound impression on me.

Many parents would not agree with my mother's decision to acquaint me with the nature of sin and its consequences. They have said to me, "Oh, I wouldn't want to paint such a negative picture for my kids. I want them to think of God as a loving Father, not as a wrathful judge who punishes us." In so doing, they withhold a portion of the truth from their children. He is both a God of love and a God of judgment. There are 116 places in the Bible where we are told to "fear the Lord." By what authority do we eliminate these references in describing who God is to our children?

I am thankful that my parents and my church had the courage to acquaint me with the warning notes in Scripture. This awareness of sin and its consequences has kept me moral at times when I could have fallen into sexual sin. Biblical faith was a governor—a checkpoint beyond which I was unwilling to go. By that time I was not afraid of my parents. I could have fooled them. But I could not get away from the all-seeing eye of the Lord. I knew I would stand accountable before Him someday, and that fact gave me the extra motivation to make responsible decisions.

I can't overstate the importance of teaching divine accountability, especially to your strong-willed children. Since their tendency is to test the limits and break the rules, they will need this internal standard to guide their behavior. Not all will listen to it, but some will. But while doing that, be careful to balance the themes of love and justice as you teach your children about God. To tip the scales in either direction is to distort the truth and create confusion in a realm where understanding is of utmost significance.

QUESTIONS AND ANSWERS

Q: Which year is most challenging when raising a strong-willed child?
A: Based on our survey of thirty-five thousand parents, the most rebellious year of childhood is eighteen. That is because a boy or girl in late adolescence feels he or she is "grown" and therefore resents anything that even resembles parental leadership or authority. It makes no difference that the young person is still living under Mom and Dad's roof and eating at their table. Teens have an intense desire to say, "Get off my back!" The second most challenging year is sixteen, and the third is fourteen. These findings vary from one individual to another, but those three years typically produce the most conflict and resentment. Then, if the young adult moves out, things get much better quickly.

Q: Generally speaking, what kind of discipline do you recommend for a teenager who is habitually miserable to live with?
A: That takes us back to what I wrote about using action to get action, rather than using anger to get action. The action approach offers one of the few tools available to very heady teenagers. Any time you can get them to do what is necessary without becoming furious, you are ahead of the game. Let me provide a few examples of how this might be accomplished.

1. I've been told that years ago in Russia, teenagers convicted of using drugs were denied their driver's license for years. Here in the United States, Michigan lawmakers recently passed a law prohibiting students from getting their license if they were caught calling in a prank bomb threat.[29] Both tactics have proved effective.
2. When my daughter was a teenager, she used to slip into my bathroom and confiscate my razor, my shaving cream, my toothpaste, or my comb. Of course, she never brought them back. Then after she had gone to school, I would discover that something was missing. There I was with wet hair or "fuzzy" teeth, trying to locate the confiscated item in her bathroom. It was not a big deal, but it was irritating at the time. Can you identify?

   I asked Danae a dozen times not to do this, but to no avail. Thus, the phantom (that would be me) struck without warning one cold morning. I hid everything she needed to put on her "face" and then left for the office. My wife told me she had never heard such wails and moans as were uttered that day. Our daughter plunged desperately through bathroom drawers looking for her toothbrush, comb, and hair dryer. My problem never resurfaced.

3. A family living in a house with a small hot-water tank was continually frustrated by their teenager's endless showers. Everyone who followed him had to take a cold bath. Screaming at him did no good. Once he was locked behind the bathroom door, he stayed in the steamy stall until the last drop of warm water had been drained. Solution? In midstream, Dad stopped the flow of hot water by turning a valve at the tank. Cold water suddenly poured from the nozzle. Junior popped out of the shower in seconds.

4. A single mother couldn't get her daughter out of bed in the morning until she announced a new policy: The hot water would be shut off promptly at 6:30 A.M. The girl could either get up on time or bathe in ice water. Another mother had trouble getting her eight-year-old out of bed each morning. She then began pouring bowls of frozen marbles under the covers with him each morning. The marbles ran to the center of the bed, precisely where his body lay. The sleepy boy arose quite quickly.

5. Instead of standing in the parking lot and screaming at students who drive too fast, school officials now put huge bumps in the road that jar the teeth of those who ignore them. They do the job quite nicely.

6. You as the parent have the car that a teenager needs, the money that he covets, and the authority to grant or withhold privileges. If push comes to shove, these chips can be exchanged for commitments to live responsibly, share the workload at home, and stay off little brother's back. This bargaining process works for younger kids too. I like the one-to-one trade-off for television viewing time. It permits a child to watch one minute of television for every minute spent reading.

The possibilities are endless.

Q: My sixteen-year-old daughter is driving me crazy. She is disrespectful, noisy, and selfish. Her room looks like a pigpen, and she won't work any harder in school than absolutely necessary to get by. Everything I taught her, from manners to faith, seems to have sailed through her ears. What in the world should my husband and I do now?
A: I'm going to offer you some patented advice that may not make sense or seem

responsive to the problem you've described. But stay with me. The most important thing you can do for your daughter is to just get her through it. The concept is a bit obscure, so let me make an effort to explain it.

Imagine your daughter is riding in a small canoe called *Puberty* on the Adolescent River. She soon comes to a turbulent stretch of white water that rocks her little boat violently. There is a very real danger that she will capsize and drown. Even if she survives today's rapids, it seems inevitable that she will be caught in swirling currents downstream and plunge over the falls. That is the apprehension harbored by millions of parents with kids bouncing along on the wild river. It's the falls that worry them most.

Actually, the typical journey down the river is much safer than believed. Instead of the water becoming more violent downstream, it eventually transitions from frightening rapids to tranquility once more. What I'm saying is that I believe your daughter is going to be okay even though she is now splashing and thrashing and gasping for air. Her little boat is more buoyant than you might think. Yes, a few individuals do go over the falls, usually because of drug abuse or another addictive behavior. But even some of those kids climb back in the canoe and paddle on down the river. Most will regain their equilibrium in a few years. In fact, the greatest danger of sinking a boat could come from parents!

The philosophy we applied with our teenagers (and you might try with yours) can be called "loosen and tighten." By this I mean we tried to loosen our grip on everything that had no lasting significance and tighten down on everything that did. We said yes whenever we possibly could to give support to the occasional no. And most important, we tried never to get too far away from our kids emotionally.

It is simply not prudent to write off a son or daughter, no matter how foolish, irritating, selfish, or insane a child may seem to be. You need to be there, not only while his or her canoe is bouncing precariously, but also after the river runs smooth again. You have the remainder of your life to reconstruct the relationship that is now in jeopardy. Don't let anger fester for too long. Make the first move toward reconciliation. And, finally, be respectful, even when punishment or restrictions are necessary.

Then wait for the placid water in the early twenties.

Q: Give me a straightforward answer to the question: How can I best survive the tumultuous years of my three strong-willed teenagers?
A: I have long recommended that parents whose kids are in the middle of a tumultuous adolescent experience must maintain a "reserve army." Let me ex-

plain: A good military general will never commit all his troops to combat at the same time. He maintains a reserve force that can relieve the exhausted soldiers when they falter on the front lines. I wish parents of adolescents would implement the same strategy. Instead, they commit every ounce of their energy and every second of their time to the business of living, holding nothing in reserve for the challenge of the century. It is a classic mistake that can be disastrous for parents of strong-willed adolescents.

The problem begins with a basic misunderstanding during the preschool years. I hear mothers say, "I don't plan to work until the kids are in kindergarten. Then I'll get a job." They appear to believe that the heavy demands on them will end magically when they get their youngest in school. In reality, the teen years will generate as much pressure on them as the preschool era did. An adolescent turns a house upside down . . . literally and figuratively. Not only is the typical rebellion of those years an extremely stressful experience, but the chauffeuring, supervising, cooking, and cleaning required to support an adolescent can be exhausting. Someone within the family must reserve the energy to cope with those new challenges. Mom is usually the candidate of choice. Remember, too, that menopause and a man's midlife crisis are scheduled to coincide with adolescence, which makes a wicked soup! It is a wise mother who doesn't exhaust herself at a time when so much is going on at home.

I know it is easier to talk about maintaining a lighter schedule than it is to secure one. It is also impractical to recommend that all mothers not seek formal employment during this era. Millions of women have to work for economic reasons, including the rising number of single parents in our world. Others choose to pursue busy careers. That is a decision to be made by a woman and her husband, and I would not presume to tell them what to do.

But decisions have inevitable consequences. In this case, there are biophysical forces at work that simply must be reckoned with. If, for example, 80 percent of a woman's available energy in a given day is expended in getting dressed, driving to work, doing her job for eight or ten hours, and stopping by the grocery store on the way home—then there is only 20 percent left for everything else. Maintaining the family, cooking meals, cleaning the kitchen, relating to her husband, and engaging in all other personal activities must be powered by that diminishing resource. It is no wonder that her batteries are spent by the end of the day. Weekends should be restful, but they usually are not. Thus, she plods through the years on her way to burnout.

This is my point: A woman in this situation has thrown all her troops into frontline combat. She has no reserve to call on. In that weakened condition, the routine stresses of raising an adolescent can be overwhelming. Let me say it again. Raising boisterous teenagers is an exciting and rewarding, but also frustrating, experience. Teens' radical highs and lows affect our mood. The noise, the messes, the complaints, the arguments, the sibling rivalry, the missed curfews, the paced floors, the wrecked cars, the failed tests, the jilted lovers, the wrong friends, the busy telephone, the pizza on the carpet, the ripped new shirt, the rebellion, the slammed doors, the mean words, the tears—it's enough to drive a rested mother crazy. But what about a career woman who already gave at the office, then came home to this chaos? Any unexpected crisis or even a minor irritant can set off a torrent of emotion. There is no reserve on which to draw. In short, the parents of adolescents should save some energy with which to cope with aggravation!

Whether or not you are able to accept and implement any of this advice is your business. It is mine to offer, and this is my best shot. To help you get through the turbulence of adolescence, you should:

1. Keep the schedule simple.
2. Get plenty of rest.
3. Eat nutritious meals.
4. Stay on your knees.

When fatigue leads adults to act like hot-tempered teenagers, anything can happen at home.

Q: My son is now sixteen years old. We wish that we had instilled in him earlier many of the principles that you have talked about. He throws his clothes around the house, refuses to help with routine tasks, and generally makes life miserable for everyone else. Is there any hope for shaping his will at this rather late age?
A: If any approach will succeed in charging his sluggish batteries or motivating him to live within the rules, it will probably involve an incentive-and-disincentive program of some variety. The following three steps might be helpful in initiating such a system:

1. Decide what is important to the youngster for use as a motivator. Two hours with the family car on date night is worth the world to a sixteen-year-old who has just gotten his or her license. (This could be the most

expensive incentive in history if the young driver is a bit shaky behind the wheel.) An allowance is another easily available source of inspiration. Teenagers have a great need for cold cash today. A routine date with Helen Highschool might cost twenty dollars or more—in some cases far more. Yet another incentive may involve a fashionable article of clothing that would not ordinarily be within your teen's budget. Offering him or her a means of obtaining such luxuries is a happy alternative to the whining, crying, begging, complaining, and pestering that might occur otherwise. Mom says, "Sure, you can have the ski sweater, but you'll have to earn it." Once an acceptable motivator is agreed upon, the second step can be implemented.

2. Formalize the agreement. A contract is an excellent means of settling on a common goal. Once an agreement has been written, it is signed by the parent and the teen. The contract may include a point system that enables your teenager to meet the goal in a reasonable time period. If you can't agree on the point values, you could allow for binding arbitration from an outside party. Let's examine a sample agreement in which Marshall wants a CD player, but his birthday is ten months away and he's flat broke. The cost of the player is approximately $150. His father agrees to buy the device if Marshall earns ten thousand points over the next six to ten weeks doing various tasks. Many of these opportunities are outlined in advance, but the list can be lengthened as other possibilities become apparent:

   a. For making bed and straightening room each morning. . 50 points
   b. For each hour of studying . . . . 150 points
   c. For each hour of housecleaning or yard work. . . . . 300 points
   d. For being on time to breakfast and dinner . . . . 40 points
   e. For babysitting siblings (without conflict) . . . 150 points per hour
   f. For washing the car each week . . . . 250 points
   g. For arising by 8:00 A.M. Saturday morning . . . . 100 points

While the principles are almost universally effective, the method will vary. With a little imagination, you can create a list of chores and point values that works in your family. It's important to note that points can be gained for cooperation and lost for resistance. Disagreeable and unreasonable behavior can be penalized fifty points or more. (However, penalties must be imposed fairly and rarely or the entire system will crumble.) Also, bonus points can be awarded for behavior that is particularly commendable.

3. Finally, establish a method to provide immediate rewards. Remember that prompt reinforcement achieves the best results. This is necessary to sustain teens' interest as they move toward the ultimate goal. A thermometer-type chart can be constructed, with the point scale listed down the side. At the top is the ten-thousand-points mark, beside a picture of a CD player or other prize. Each evening, the daily points are totaled and the red portion of the thermometer is extended upward. Steady, short-term progress might earn Marshall a bonus of some sort— perhaps a CD of his favorite musician or a special privilege. If he changes his mind about what he wishes to buy, the points can be diverted to another purchase. For example, five thousand points is 50 percent of ten thousand and would be worth $75 toward another purchase. However, do not give your child the reward if he does not earn it. That would eliminate future uses of reinforcement. Likewise, do not deny or postpone the goal once it is earned.

The system described above is not set in concrete. It should be adapted to the age and maturity of the adolescent. One youngster would be insulted by an approach that would thrill another. Use your imagination and work out the details with your son or daughter. This suggestion won't work with every teenager, but some will find it exciting. Lots of luck to you.

ELEVEN

DEALING WITH THE ADHD CHILD

W E COME NOW TO A SUBJECT of great relevance to the parents of strong-willed children who also happen to have a condition known as attention deficit/hyperactivity disorder, or ADHD. Any physical problem that increases the level of activity and reduces self-control in a youngster is almost certain to create management problems. It is worse when that boy or girl is also inclined to resist parental authority. The conjunction of those characteristics is likely to make life difficult, and in some cases highly stressful for his mother, his father, his siblings, and his teacher.

This connection between hyperactivity and defiance has been documented clinically. Dr. Bill Maier, psychologist in residence at Focus on the Family, indicated that between 40 and 60 percent of kids with ADHD may have a condition known as Oppositional Defiant Disorder, or ODD, which manifests itself with a pattern of persistent arguing with adults; losing one's temper frequently; refusing to follow orders; deliberately annoying others; and showing recurrent anger, resentfulness, spitefulness, and vindictiveness.[1] ODD and ADHD is a volatile cocktail, to be sure.

Given this understanding, ADHD is a condition that we should consider carefully in our discussion of the strong-willed child. Thankfully, much definitive research has already been done. Many books on the subject of ADHD have been published in recent years; they've been written by researchers and clinicians who have spent their professional life working with and on behalf of affected children. Therefore, it is unnecessary for me to go into great detail here when other sources are so readily available. Instead, I will provide an overview of ADHD and address some of the disciplinary issues that are typically encountered with a tough-minded, hyperactive boy or girl.

First, let me speak to the controversy surrounding ADHD. Talk-show hosts, lay columnists, and many parents have strong opinions about this disorder, and some of the most vocal among them are simply wrong. The uninformed culture would tell us today that ADHD is a fad diagnosis without scientific support and that the problem would go away if parents simply knew how to discipline their kids better. It is not true. Certainly, many parents do need to learn better ways of managing their children, but that is another issue. ADHD is a physical and emotional disorder that has not been dreamed up by aggressive health professionals who claim to see it popping up everywhere. It may be overdiagnosed because there are no simple lab tests to confirm the condition; nevertheless, no evidence exists to indicate that parents and their doctors are routinely "drugging" kids unnecessarily or that a large number of teachers want to medicate students because they don't have the skills to control them in the classroom. While some abuses may occur, those generalizations are unfair and inaccurate.

I can tell you from personal experience that when a boy or girl does have the disorder and when it is pronounced, it certainly doesn't have to be concocted by somebody. I have seen ADHD kids—even preschoolers—who were all afterburner and no rudder. They could not hold still for more than a few seconds and seemed to be frantically driven from within. I remember one little two-year-old girl whose parents brought her to see me at Children's Hospital. This toddler was virtually climbing on my head and shoulders within moments of entering my office. There was fatigue and frustration on the faces of her parents, who were worn out from chasing their little dynamo from morning to night. Try telling exhausted moms and dads like this couple that their child's condition was imaginary. You'll quickly learn how strongly they feel about your mistaken hypothesis.

With that, I'll provide a primer for parents who suspect that their strong-willed child has ADHD. First, we'll review a comprehensive cover story published about this subject in *Time* (1994), which is still accurate today.*

Fifteen years ago, no one had ever heard of attention deficit/hyperactivity disorder. Today it is the most common behavioral disorder in American children, the subject of thousands of studies and symposiums and no small degree of controversy. Experts on ADHD say it afflicts as many as 3.5 million youngsters, or up to 5 percent of those under 18. It is two or three times as likely to be diagnosed in boys as in girls. The disorder has replaced what used to be popularly called "hyperactivity," and it includes a broader collection of symptoms. ADHD has three

---

*©1994 TIME Inc., reprinted with permission

main hallmarks: extreme distractibility, an almost reckless impulsiveness, and in some but not all cases, a knee-jiggling, toe-tapping hyperactivity that makes sitting still all but impossible.

For children with ADHD, a ticking clock or sounds and sights caught through a window can drown out a teacher's voice, although an intriguing project can absorb them for hours. Such children act before thinking; they blurt out answers in class. They enrage peers with an inability to wait their turn or play by the rules. These are the kids no one wants at a birthday party.

For kids who are hyperactive, the pattern is unmistakable, says Dr. Bruce Roseman, a pediatric neurologist with several offices in the New York City area, who has ADHD himself. "You say to the mother, 'What kind of personality did the child have as a baby? Was he active, alert? Was he colicky?' She'll say, 'He wouldn't stop—waaah, waaah, waaah!' You ask, 'When did he start to walk?' One mother said to me, 'Walk? My son didn't walk. He got his pilot's license at one year of age. His feet haven't touched the ground since.' You ask, 'Mrs. Smith, how about the terrible twos?' She'll start to cry, 'You mean the terrible twos, threes, fours, the awful fives, the horrendous sixes, the awful eights, the divorced nines, the I-want-to-die tens!'"

There is no question that ADHD can disrupt lives. Kids with the disorder frequently have few friends. Their parents may be ostracized by neighbors and relatives, who blame them for failing to control the child. "I've gotten criticism of my parenting skills from strangers," says the mother of a hyperactive boy in New Jersey. "When you're out in public, you're always on guard. Whenever I'd hear a child cry, I'd turn to see if it was because of Jeremy."

School can be a shattering experience for such kids. Frequently reprimanded and tuned out, they lose any sense of self-worth and fall ever further behind in their work. More than a quarter are held back a grade; about a third fail to graduate from high school. ADHD kids are also prone to accidents, says neurologist Roseman. "These are the kids I'm going to see in the emergency room this summer. They rode their bicycle right into the street and didn't look. They jumped off the deck and forgot it was high."

But the psychological injuries are often greater. By ages five to seven, says Dr. Russell Barkley, author of *Taking Charge of ADHD,* half to two-thirds are hostile and defiant. By ages 10 to 12, they run the risk of developing what psychologists call "conduct disorder"—lying, stealing, running away from home and ultimately getting into trouble with the law. As adults, says Barkley, 25 percent to 30 percent will experience substance-abuse problems, mostly with depressants like marijuana and alcohol. One study of hyperactive boys found that 40 percent had been arrested at least once by age 18—and these were kids who had been treated with stimulant medication; among those who had been treated with the drug plus other measures, the rate was 20 percent— still very high.

It is an article of faith among ADHD researchers that the right interventions can prevent such dreadful outcomes. "If you can have an impact with these kids, you can change whether they go to jail or to Harvard Law School," says psychologist Judith Swanson at the University of California Irvine. . . .

Whether ADHD is a brain disorder or simply a personality type, the degree to which it is a handicap depends not only on the severity of the traits but also on one's environment. The right school, job or home situation can make all the difference. The lessons of ADHD are truisms. All kids do not learn in the same way. Nor are all adults suitable for the same line of work. Unfortunately, American society seems to have evolved into a one-size-fits-all system. Schools can resemble factories: put the kids on the assembly line, plug in the right components and send 'em out the door. Everyone is supposed to go to college; there is virtually no other route to success. In other times and in other places, there have been alternatives: apprenticeships, settling a new land, starting a business out of the garage, going to sea. In a conformist society, it becomes necessary to medicate some people to make them fit in.

Surely an epidemic of attention deficit/hyperactivity disorder is a warning to us all. Children need individual supervision. Many of them need more structure than the average helter-skelter household provides. They need a more consistent approach to discipline and schools that tailor teaching to their individual learning styles. Adults too could use a society that's more flexible in its expectations, more accommodating to differences. Most of all, we all need to slow down. And pay attention.[2]

This article provides us with a basic understanding of ADHD in graphic terms. Sounds pretty scary, doesn't it? However, before concluding that the disorder will condemn your child to a life of misery and failure, I have much more positive news for you. An excellent book, entitled *Why A.D.H.D. Doesn't Mean Disaster,* published in 2004, was written by three of my professional colleagues.[3] They are Dr. Walt Larimore, vice president of medical outreach at Focus on the Family; Mrs. Diane Passno, one of Focus on the Family's executive vice presidents; and Dr. Dennis Swanberg, a minister, speaker, and beloved humorist. Dr. Swanberg and his son both have pronounced ADHD. Diane has a brilliant daughter, Danielle, who graduated from Dartmouth with a degree in engineering. She was high school valedictorian and homecoming queen, a state-champion athlete, and an all-around great kid. And, yes, she has ADHD too.

These authors are well-qualified to tell us how to live successfully with the disorder and to explain why it can actually be an asset. It will provide encouragement to every parent of a rip-snortin', rootin'-tootin', go-get-'em kid who is affected by ADHD.

The following quotation sets the tone for the book. It was written by Paul Elliott, M.D., who said:

In my opinion, the ADD brain structure is not truly an abnormality. In fact, I believe a very good case can be made that it is not only normal, though in the minority, but may well be a superior brain structure. However, the talents of the person with ADD brain structure are not those rewarded by our society in its current stage of development. In other words, the problems of the person with ADD are caused as much by the way we have our society, educational system, and the business methods organized as by other factors more directly related to the ADD itself.[4]

Mrs. Passno laid out her thesis:

Many parents need a new perspective about their kids who have been diagnosed with attention deficit/hyperactivity disorder. ADHD is a buzzword for our generation of parents and kids. The last thing in the world a parent wants to learn is that their beloved little bundle of joy has a prognosis that might limit his opportunities, particularly when he's just starting out. The stereotype ADHD has given to these kids is simply awful. And most parents lack either the understanding or the confidence to challenge the conventional thinking.

Stereotyping kids is deceptive and dangerous. It can do unseen damage to a child's understanding of who he is and what he is able to accomplish in life. As early as kindergarten, what most kids do when they are told they are destined to fail is they begin to live up to the expectation. They become classic underachievers.

[We] have a goldfish that will probably outlive everyone in our family. This twenty-nine–cent prize had been in a bowl on the kitchen sink for the past six years, swimming around and around in a tight little circle. One day, I moved Sgt. Pepper to a huge tank, six times the size of his old domain. For the first several days, he continued to swim in the same tight little circles the size of his old bowl. He didn't understand that his world had expanded. In the same way, a child who becomes "that ADHD kid who drives everyone nuts" may never understand what he can accomplish with his unique set of gifts. And if he is never given permission to be anything different, most likely, he never will.[5]

Dennis Swanberg, who holds an earned Ph.D., weighed in on the subject, sharing his perspective as a person who has learned to cope very successfully with his own and his son's ADHD. He wrote:

> This book has been a particular passion of mine for years. It has been my privilege, first in the pulpit, and later as a public speaker with my own television program, to overcome the barriers ADHD poses and find the benefits. None of these successes were even on my radar screen when I was young and struggled simply to get through another day at school. But if I can make it, anyone can. I hope to encourage those of you who are having similar difficulties with raising a kid like I was.
>
> Even so, our main purpose for writing this book is to encourage you and help you consider that attention deficit/hyperactivity disorder can be a *dividend* rather than a disorder or mental disability. It can be turned into a blessing rather than a curse, an asset rather than a handicap. Sure, there will always be challenges and frustrations associated with something out of the ordinary like ADHD. But by the time you finish this book, we hope and pray that no matter whether you have ADHD yourself, or are the parent of an ADHD child, you will see your future from a hopeful new perspective.[6]

I think you get the flavor of the book and why I hope those of you who have an affected child will read it. It is filled with many success stories about kids and parents who overcame ADHD.

We'll devote the balance of this chapter to a question-and-answer format. I'll share the podium with my friend, Dr. Walt Larimore.

QUESTIONS AND ANSWERS

Q: I know that I can't diagnose my own son, but it would be helpful if you would list the kinds of behavior to look for in him. What are the typical characteristics of someone with ADHD?

A: Dobson: Psychiatrists Edward M. Hallowell and John J. Ratey are authors of an excellent book entitled *Driven to Distraction*.[7] In it they list twenty symptoms that are often seen in a person with ADHD. These are among the criteria used by doctors to make the diagnosis:

1. A sense of underachievement, of not meeting one's goals (regardless of how much one has accomplished)
2. Difficulty getting organized
3. Chronic procrastination or trouble getting started
4. Many projects going simultaneously; trouble with follow-through
5. Tendency to say what comes to mind without necessarily considering the timing or appropriateness of the remark
6. An ongoing search for high stimulation
7. A tendency to be easily bored
8. Easy distractibility, trouble focusing attention, tendency to tune out or drift away in the middle of a page or a conversation, often coupled with an ability to focus at times
9. Often creative, intuitive, highly intelligent
10. Trouble going through established channels, following proper procedure
11. Impatient; low tolerance for frustration
12. Impulsive, either verbally or in action, as in impulsive spending of money, changing plans, enacting new schemes or career plans, and the like
13. Tendency to worry needlessly, endlessly; tendency to scan the horizon looking for something to worry about alternating with inattention to or disregard for actual dangers
14. Sense of impending doom, insecurity, alternating with high risk-taking
15. Depression, especially when disengaged from a project
16. Restlessness
17. Tendency toward addictive behavior
18. Chronic problems with self-esteem
19. Inaccurate self-observation
20. Family history of ADD, manic-depressive illness, depression, substance abuse, or other disorders of impulse control or mood

Q: Does ADHD go away as children grow up? If not, what are the implications for the adult years?

A: **Dobson:** We used to believe the problem typically disappeared with the onset of puberty. That's what I was taught in graduate school. Now it is known that ADHD is a lifelong condition for about two-thirds of those affected, influencing behavior from the cradle to the grave. The symptoms may lessen in time for some, but not for the majority. Some ADHD adults learn to be less disorganized and impulsive as they get older. They channel their energy into sports activities or professions in which they function very well. Others have trouble settling on a career or holding a job. Follow-through remains a problem as they flit from one task to another. They are particularly unsuited for desk jobs, such as accounting positions or other assignments that demand attention to detail, long hours of sitting, and the ability to juggle many balls at once.

Another characteristic of ADHD in adolescence and adulthood is the thirst for high-risk activity. Even as children, they are accident-prone, and their parents get well acquainted with the local emergency room personnel. As they get older, rock climbing, bungee jumping, car racing, motorcycle riding, white-water rafting, and related activities are among their favorite pursuits. Adults with ADHD are sometimes called "adrenaline junkies" because they are hooked on the high produced by the high octane adrenaline rush associated with dangerous behavior. Others are more susceptible to drug use, alcoholism, and other addictive behaviors. One study revealed that approximately 40 percent will have been arrested by eighteen years of age.[8]

Some of those who have ADHD are at higher risk for marital conflict too. It can be very irritating to a compulsive, highly ordered husband or wife to be married to a "messie"—someone whose life is chaotic and who forgets to pay the bills, fix the car, or keep records for income-tax reports. Such a couple may need professional counseling to help them learn to work together and capitalize on each other's strengths.

Q: How common is ADHD?
A: **Larimore:** Here is what we know about the incidence of the disorder. The *Journal of the American Medical Association (JAMA)* stated that ADHD "is among the most common neurodevelopmental disorders in children."[9] The *British Medical Journal* estimated that approximately 7 percent of school-age children have ADHD—and that boys are affected three times as often as girls.[10] A 1995 Virginia study showed that 8 percent to 10 percent of young school children were taking medication for ADHD.[11] Boys are twice as likely to have ADHD and a

learning disability. Rates of diagnosis of ADHD are twice as high in Caucasian children as in Latinos and African-Americans.[12]

Q: Are the brains of people with ADHD different?

A: Larimore: Although the cause of ADHD is unknown, the theories abound. Some believe it is associated with subtle differences in brain structure. Brain scans reveal a number of subtle changes in the brain of those diagnosed with ADHD. In fact, one of the former names for ADHD was "minimal brain disorder."

Others say it's related to neural pathways, neurotransmitters, or brain chemistry—particularly abnormalities in the brain chemical dopamine. Still other researchers believe ADHD is related to the brain's blood supply or electrical system. Recent research has raised the question of whether frequent exposure in early childhood to rapid electronic stimuli (such as television and computers) might contribute to this problem.

Richard DeGrandpre, Ph.D., in his book *Ritalin Nation: Rapid-Fire Culture and the Transformation of Human Consciousness* theorizes about what he called a "sensory addiction phenomenon."[13] Dr. DeGrandpre believes that early exposure to electronic sensory bombardment, especially at a time when the brain is just forming connections and synapses, may result in biological or neurological effects, including, but not limited to, ADHD.

DeGrandpre believes that these effects can be exaggerated in the absence of parental structure. He points out that people in Western nations live in an incredibly stimulating world; there are constant stimuli experienced by even a very young child. I don't know that we can really get rid of it all, but we can encourage parents to provide a structured environment so children can learn to deal with and perhaps limit these stimuli.

One source of information that may support DeGrandpre's theory is the experience of the Amish, who typically forgo modern conveniences such as computers and television. Among these children who are protected from this stimulation, ADHD appears to be very uncommon. Researchers have reported that out of two hundred Amish children followed prospectively and compared with the non-Amish population, symptoms of ADHD were unusual.[14]

Q: What about prescription stimulant medications?

A: Larimore: Many parents call or write us at Focus on the Family to ask about using prescription medications for ADHD. They've heard the controversies and they are worried that starting a child on medication might be a bad decision. On the other hand, many worry that not prescribing it may also be harmful. They ask, "What should we do?"

Without doubt, the use of prescription drugs for both children and adults can be very successful as a short-term treatment of ADHD. There is a virtual mountain of evidence supporting the safety and effectiveness of using medications, although none of these studies extended for more than two years. According to these studies, 70 percent to 95 percent of ADHD patients benefit from appropriate medication.[15] These medications seem to reduce disruptive behavior dramatically, improve school performance, and even raise IQ test scores. The medications seem to be equally effective for both boys and girls.

The most commonly prescribed drugs are Ritalin, Concerta, Strattera, Dexedrine, and Adderall. In most instances, these substances have a remarkably positive effect—at least for the short term.[16]

Q: There are so many options. Which is best?

A: Larimore: The treatment for ADHD should be individualized and tailored for each child and each family. So, while there is no "best" course of treatment, there are a number of excellent options. Learning more about them can assist you in working with your child's physician in choosing among these alternatives.

One problem with some of the older ADHD medications was that their effects didn't last more than a few hours at most. This meant that extra doses would have to be given at school or later in the afternoon once the child was home. Worse yet, when the short-acting medications wore off, a rebound effect sometimes occurred, during which the child's symptoms and behaviors actually worsened! This not only created difficulty for the school, it also caused embarrassment for the child and led to noncompliance.

Other side effects of the stimulant medications included anxiety, nervousness, palpitations (irregular heartbeat), sweating, and insomnia (difficulty going to sleep). More rare side effects included irritability, mood swings, depression, withdrawal, hallucinations, and loss of spontaneity. The friends of one of my young patients told her, "Carla, please don't take your medication before you come to our party. You'll be no fun!"

But I have good news. Newer medications are now available to solve this problem for many patients. Every medication has undesirable side effects and should be administered only when indicated and appropriate. Ritalin, for example, has a number of potential side effects. It can reduce the appetite and cause insomnia in some patients. Nevertheless, for the vast majority of ADHD patients, newer prescription treatments are remarkably effective and safe.

Let me offer one caution, however. The main danger of drug abuse from stimulants is from your child's friends or classmates who do not have ADHD and want to use the stimulant to get high. In one study, 16 percent of ADHD children had been approached to sell, give, or trade their medication.[17] As shocking as those numbers are, the problem of Ritalin abuse seems to be worsening.

So to protect your ADHD child's friends, be sure to carefully supervise their use of stimulants.

Q: My six-year-old son is not only hyperactive, but he wets the bed as well. Can you offer advice for dealing with that recurring problem?
A: Dobson: Your child probably suffers from enuresis, which usually occurs in children who are developmentally immature. It is more common in children with ADHD. Each child has his own timetable of maturation, and some are in no great hurry. However, enuresis can cause both emotional and social distress for the older child. Thus, it is wise that this problem be conquered during the early childhood years, if possible.

There have been some promising developments in recent years. In April 1999, Japanese researchers produced an electronic alarm that is effective in stopping kids from bed-wetting. The machine, which was devised by a urologist and a telephone maker, measures a child's brain waves and monitors the bladder. When a child has to urinate, the alarm goes off and tells the child it is time to go to the toilet.[18]

An alarm works well with children because bed-wetting often occurs during very deep sleep, making it difficult for them to learn nighttime control on their own. Their mind does not respond to the signal or reflex action that ordinarily awakens light sleepers. The alarm is loud enough to awaken most deep sleepers and get them to the bathroom.

Consult your family physician or a urologist for the best course of treatment for your child. There is a range of options now available for you, including a drug called Desmopressin, which helps regulate urine production.

Q: I am not sure if my son has ADHD, but he *is* hyperactive and drives everyone crazy. He simply does not fit in with his peers. He always seems to be left out when other kids play, and he has trouble making friends. He

just won't, or can't, carry on a sustained conversation with other children and usually winds up acting silly and driving them away. Does this sound like ADHD? Do you have any advice on how we can make him fit in better with the group?

A: **Dobson:** There are many disorders that could account for the characteristics you describe. ADHD is only one of them. Another is Asperger syndrome, which is a neurological problem related to autism. Yet another is called Rett syndrome. And still another is called Tourette syndrome. In some cases, there is no defined diagnosis. In other cases, the unique personality of a particular child without an abnormality may simply irritate other children and bring on rejection and ridicule.

We now know that an individual's success in life, along with his personal happiness, depends greatly on his emotional intelligence—his ability to function well in a group and develop strong relationships. Psychologist Willard Hartup of the University of Minnesota said, "Children who are generally disliked, who are aggressive and disruptive, who are unable to sustain close relationships with other children and who cannot establish a place for themselves in the peer culture, are seriously at risk in the years ahead." Intervention for these youngsters is obviously needed and can be very beneficial.[19]

Once more, let me emphasize that it is extremely important for parents to recognize the complexity of children and seek professional help when needed. Assistance for a child with specialized needs is available in most cities today, but you as a parent have to find it. University child-development centers might be a good place to begin your search.

Q: Is ADHD inherited?

A: **Larimore:** There is increasing evidence from medical studies that genetic factors play a role in ADHD. Jacquelyn Gillis and her team, then at the University of Colorado, reported in 1992 that the risk of ADHD in a child whose identical twin has the disorder is between eleven and eighteen times greater than that of a nontwin sibling of a child with ADHD. She showed that between 55 percent and 92 percent of the identical twins of children with ADHD eventually develop the condition.[20]

A large study in Norway of 526 identical twins (who inherit exactly the same genes) and 389 fraternal twins (who are no more alike genetically than siblings born years apart) found that these children had nearly an 80 percent chance of inheriting ADHD. They concluded that up to 80 percent of the differences in attention, hyperactivity, and impulsivity between people with ADHD and those without the disorder can be explained by genetic factors.[21]

What does this mean for your family? Simply that if one or both of the parents have ADHD, their child is more likely to have ADHD as well. If that is the case, dealing with an affected child may remind Mom or Dad of some painful memories from their own childhood or teenage years. This can make it even more difficult to deal with the child. Furthermore, the unaffected siblings may be more likely to have children of their own with ADHD. These are just a few of the reasons why many therapists recommend counseling for the entire family.

Q: What are some of the ways that ADHD affects the family?
A: ADHD is not a problem that affects only the affected individual. The time and effort required to deal with ADHD can significantly disrupt the entire family.

In most families, the mother has the greatest emotional, relational, and spiritual risk in caring for an ADHD child. Although these kids can be intensely loving, they can also turn on their moms in a second. They can be verbally or emotionally abusive to their parents, which can wound parents deeply. They can be wonderful one day and horrible the next—or they can change from hour to hour.

Moms of ADHD kids need to quickly give up the delusion that their homes will be immaculate or that every meal will be a joyous family affair. ADHD parents have to learn that they are not perfect and that they may need help. Not only can they be rejected and hurt by their child, these parents may have to face the rejection, hostility, or animosity of children, other adults, or neighbors.

The ADHD child is often physically aggressive and must be taught to convert physical aggression into verbal expression (a skill some adults need to learn!). He or she may be verbally abusive. Once again, learning how to teach your child to redirect this harmful behavior into constructive behavior is essential. Parents of ADHD kids quickly learn that they cannot force or coerce their kids to be like "normal" kids—many of them will never adhere to that ideal. They are wired differently, and their parents need to learn a wide variety of parenting skills to cope with, teach, train, and creatively discipline these unique kids.

Let's not forget the siblings. They also have to live with the ADHD child—who can make life miserable for his unaffected brothers and sisters. Medical studies are beginning to show that siblings can also be at risk for emotional problems. These siblings can be chronically victimized by the ADHD child, who may bully them; verbally or physically abuse them; and be intense, demanding, and obnoxious.

Further, if siblings do not receive the attention and time that they need and deserve—because of the time and effort diverted to the ADHD child—they may feel alienated, rejected, or unloved. These feelings can lead to a range of behavioral problems, especially in adolescence. Therefore, many ADHD care providers recommend that siblings be part of the family counseling. The good news is that the skills these siblings gain will be helpful to them for life.

Q: What about homeschooling for ADHD youngsters?
A: Larimore: For many kids with learning difficulties, homeschooling can be an educational alternative—especially for the parents who are dedicated to doing this and are willing to do what is required. I have talked to many doctors of ADHD patients who relate encouraging examples of kids who have done much better when they've entered a homeschool environment.

Q: We have a five-year-old son who has been diagnosed with ADHD. He is really difficult to handle, and I have no idea how to manage him. I know he has a neurological problem, so I don't feel right about making him obey like we do our other children. It is a big problem for us. What do you suggest?
A: Dobson: I understand your dilemma, but I urge you to discipline your son. Every youngster needs the security of defined limits, and the ADHD boy or girl is no exception. Such a child should be held responsible for his or her behavior, although the approach may be a little different. For example, most children can be required to sit on a chair for disciplinary reasons, whereas some very hyperactive children would not be able to remain there. Similarly, corporal punishment is sometimes ineffective with a highly excitable little bundle of electricity. As with every aspect of parenthood, disciplinary measures for the ADHD child must be suited to his or her unique characteristics and needs.

Q: How, then, should I discipline my ADHD child?
A: Dobson: Let me offer some guidelines for how to train and guide your youngster. The following eighteen suggestions were included in an excellent book by Dr. Domeena Renshaw, *The Hyperactive Child.*[22] Regrettably, her book is now out of print, but her advice is still valid.

1. Be consistent in rules and discipline.
2. Keep your own voice quiet and slow. Anger is normal. Anger can be controlled. Anger does not mean you do not love a child.

3. Try hard to keep your emotions cool by bracing for expected turmoil. Recognize and respond to any positive behavior, however small. If you search for good things, you will find a few.

4. Avoid a ceaselessly negative approach: "Stop"—"Don't"—"No."

5. Separate behavior, which you may not like, from the child's person, whom you like, e.g., "I like you. I don't like your tracking mud through the house."

6. Have a very clear routine for this child. Construct a timetable for waking, eating, playing, watching TV, studying, doing chores, and going to bed. Follow it flexibly when he disrupts it. Slowly your structure will reassure him until he develops his own.

7. Demonstrate new or difficult tasks using action accompanied by short, clear, quiet explanations. Repeat the demonstration until learned. This uses audiovisual-sensory perceptions to reinforce the learning. The memory traces of a hyperactive child take longer to form. Be patient and repeat.

8. Designate a separate room or a part of a room that is his own special area. Avoid brilliant colors or complex patterns in decor. Simplicity, solid colors, minimal clutter, and a worktable facing a blank wall away from distractions assist concentration. A hyperactive child cannot filter out overstimulation himself yet.

9. Do one thing at a time: Give him one toy from a closed box; clear the table of everything else when he's coloring; turn off the radio/TV when he is doing homework. Multiple stimuli prevent him from concentrating on his primary task.

10. Give him responsibility, which is essential for growth. The task should be within his capacity, although the assignment may need much supervision. Acceptance and recognition of his efforts (even when imperfect) should not be forgotten.

11. Read his pre-explosive warning signals. Quietly intervene to avoid explosions by distracting him or discussing the conflict calmly. Removal from the battle zone to the sanctuary of his room for a few minutes is useful.

12. Restrict playmates to one or at most two at one time, because he is so excitable. Your home is most suitable so you can provide structure and supervision. Explain your rules to the playmate and briefly tell the other parent your reasons.

13. Do not pity, tease, be frightened by, or overindulge this child. He has a special condition of the nervous system that is manageable.

14. Know the name and dose of his medication. Give it regularly. Watch and remember the effects to report back to your physician.

15. Openly discuss with your physician any fears you have about the use of medications.

16. Lock up all medications to avoid accidental misuse.

17. Always supervise the taking of medication, even if it is routine over a long period of years. Responsibility remains with the parents! One day's supply at a time can be put in a regular place and checked routinely as he becomes older and more self-reliant.

18. Share your successful "helps" with his teacher. The outlined ways to help your hyperactive child are as important to him as diet and insulin are to a diabetic child.

Q: What else would you recommend to parents?

A: **Larimore:** Learn as much as you can about the disorder. Successful management of ADHD involves a range of options, and you need to become acquainted with them. They begin with the diagnosis.

People living with ADHD are usually greatly relieved to learn that they have an identifiable, treatable condition. They are gratified (as are their parents) to learn that they've done nothing wrong. This condition is not caused; people are born with it. It's part of their design and makeup. Best of all, God can and does use ADHD in His particular plan for their life.

One organization that may be able to help is CHADD (Children and Adults with Attention-Deficit/Hyperactivity Disorder). It has an exceptional amount of evidence-based and trustworthy information available and can identify some parent support groups. However, let me share a caution here. Parent support groups, if not carefully organized, can turn into "gripe-and-whine" sessions. That is not helpful and is sometimes discouraging. All of us need someone to gripe to on occasion, no doubt, but there should be some direction to the group. Someone needs to say, "Okay, now that we've heard everyone's complaints, what can we do about them?" I've known parents who came home from such a group and reacted negatively to their child because of what they talked about at the support group. That's not helpful for the parent or the child.

Second, commit to giving your child unconditional love. The most important treatment for children with ADHD is abundant affection and affirmation.

They are frequently accused of not trying, of being lazy, of not being a good kid. Teachers get angry at them. Some classmates get upset with them because they often don't do well in school, and they begin to treat them disrespectfully. My heart goes out to these youngsters.

Let's face it, these ADHD kids don't always make us feel or look good. Love, to me, is being committed to doing what this individual kid needs, regardless of the circumstances. These children often have greater needs than those who are not affected.

Many times they feel like they are second-class individuals. I've had kids in my practice tell me, "There's something wrong with me." I've had ADHD children actually say, "God made a mistake when He put me together. That's why I'm here."

Part of loving these special kids is to help them discover the great giftedness that God has given them—to show them that God didn't make a mistake when He made them.

Children simply do not all have to fit the same mold, even in school. For many of these youngsters, parents may need to de-emphasize academics. Simply put, for many ADHD kids, there are things that are more important than academics, such as being loved and accepted by family and friends just the way that God made them. Your child needs to understand that God has a place for her and has given her a special gift, and that she does have specialized abilities. She needs to know that you are going to work with her to discover and develop those special gifts and skills, and that you can't wait to see what God's going to do with her. This may be far more important to your ADHD child than getting too excited over the fact that she is not doing quite as well in the classroom as others.

Loving these kids unconditionally does *not* mean expecting them to do less than their best—the best that *they* can do. It does mean directing and encouraging them to overcome challenges and achieve those things that they are uniquely gifted in doing.

The important point to make to your child is that a diagnosis of ADHD is not a handicap. He is in the same boat as some famous people, who, if not officially diagnosed with the disorder, had symptoms and behaviors remarkably akin to those with ADHD: Albert Einstein, Tom Cruise, Henry Winkler (the Fonz!), John Lennon, Winston Churchill, Henry Ford, Stephen Hawking, Alexander Graham Bell, Presidents Woodrow Wilson, John F. Kennedy, and Dwight D. Eisenhower, Generals George Patton and William Westmoreland . . . and the list goes on. What a remarkable group of which to be a part!

TWELVE

A FINAL WORD OF ENCOURAGEMENT

I T'S TIME NOW to put a ribbon on this pleasant foray into the life of strong-willed children and those who have the responsibility of raising them. I'll close by sharing a few thoughts that come straight from my heart.

Many wonderful emotions accompany the exhilarating privilege of bringing a baby into the world and then watching that little tyke begin to grow and learn and develop. How well I remember our son and daughter taking their first step, saying their first word, riding their first tricycle, praying their first prayer, and progressing rapidly through the many other exciting milestones of childhood. The first day of kindergarten was a highly emotional morning for me, when I placed our precious little girl on the steps of the bus, moved back to take her picture, and watched as she and the other children rode slowly down the street. Then I wiped away a tear as I walked back to the house. Our baby was growing up.

There would be many other joyful and bittersweet experiences along the way, as Shirley and I gradually realized the breathtaking brevity of the parenting years. Even when our kids were in elementary school, we were already starting to dread the day when our parenting responsibilities would be over. Predictably, in what seemed like a moment of time, a cold wind of change blew through our home, leaving an empty nest that took some getting used to.

Yes, being a mom or dad is one of the most marvelous experiences in living, and I feel compassion for infertile couples who have been denied the privilege of procreation. But men and women who are granted that precious gift know that a measure of pain and sorrow comes with it. Kids often struggle with a variety of learning problems, physical disabilities, accidents, diseases, and/or social difficulties. Then come the tumultuous years of adolescence when, for some teens more than others, every day can be a challenge. All of these stress points are exacerbated when a child has a willful temperament and a tendency to fuss and argue and disobey. Parents raising such a youngster sometimes feel as though they live every day on a battlefield.

It is on behalf of those frustrated, discouraged, and confused parents that I have written this book. I have wanted, especially, to put an arm around moms and dads who feel like an utter failure in this most important responsibility in life. They (perhaps *you*) wanted to be a perfect parent, doing that job with greater success than any other. Instead, it now looks as though every good intention has been misinterpreted, resented, and resisted. Is that where you are today?

At times do you find yourself thinking, *I love this kid more than anything in the world, but I don't really like him or her very much? We can't get along for more than ten minutes without clashing over relatively insignificant matters. Why does this child make me so angry, when what I want most is harmony and love? Why is our relationship so unsatisfying and disturbing? What did I do to mess up something that began with such promise and hope? Not only have I failed my child, I have failed God, too.*

Let's talk about those feelings for a moment, which are common at one time or another within almost all caring moms and dads. Parenthood can be a very guilt-inducing proposition. Babies come into our life when we are young and immature, and there are no instruction manuals to guide our first halting steps. There is no manufacturing tag on a newborn's wrist that says, "Some assembly required." So we take these tiny human beings home with us, not yet knowing who they are, and then proceed to bumble along as best we can. As a consequence, many of the day-by-day decisions we make on their behalf are the result of sheer guesswork, as we hope against hope that we are doing the right thing. Our own inadequacies also get in the way. We become tired and frustrated and selfish, which sometimes affects our judgment. In those moments, we react without thinking and realize the next morning that we handled things all wrong.

In short, children are so maddeningly complex that it is impossible to raise them without making many blunders and mistakes. After about twenty years of on-the-job training, we begin to figure out what parenting is all about. By then it is time to let go and pretend we don't care anymore.

Added to these difficulties are our own personal problems, which can include marital conflict or divorce, physical illness, financial pressures, and the other cares of living. Our unmet needs, such as those experienced by single parents, also can lead us into behavior that will later seem terribly foolish. Do I sound as though I'm whining here? I hope not. I'm simply attempting to articulate the discomfort that occurs for parents of strong-willed children when they begin to feel that they have botched the assignment. (The parents of compliant children may not fully understand this emotional reaction, although there is usually enough stress in child rearing to affect everybody.)

Despite these discouraging moments, it is my firm conviction that bearing and raising children is worth everything it costs us. Along with the difficulties come the greatest joys and rewards life has to offer. How could that be true? How can the very thing that brings us anxiety and frustration be the source of such happiness and fulfillment? There is an obvious contradiction here that bears consideration.

Christian writer C. S. Lewis tried to express the palpable pain that he experienced when he lost his wife to cancer. He would not have been so devastated by her passing, he said, if he had not allowed himself to love her with all his heart. In the movie *Shadowlands,* based on this period of Lewis's life, he wondered if it would have been better never to have loved at all and avoided the risk of losing the woman he adored. It would certainly have been safer to live in a fortress, protecting himself from disappointment and grief by remaining emotionally detached and uncaring. Lewis considered these responses to sorrow and concluded that, in the end, love is worth the risk. This is the way he penned it:

> To love at all is to be vulnerable. Love anything and your heart will certainly be wrung and possibly broken. If you want to make sure of keeping it intact, you must give your heart to no one, not even to an animal. Wrap it carefully around with hobbies and little luxuries . . . lock it up safe in the casket or coffin of your selfishness. But in that casket—safe, dark, motionless, airless—it will change. It will not be broken; it will become unbreakable, impenetrable, irredeemable. . . . The only place outside heaven where you can be perfectly safe from all the dangers of love is hell![1]

Then Lewis concluded: "We love to know that we are not alone."

Doesn't this insight speak eloquently of the pain associated with parenthood? It certainly does to me. This is what bearing and raising children comes down to. Loving those we have borne is a risky business, but one that also brings great joy and happiness. Even though there are often trials and tears associated with the challenge, it is a noble journey. We as parents are given the privilege of taking the raw materials that comprise a brand-new human being and then molding him or her day-by-day into a mature, disciplined, productive, and God-fearing adult who will someday live in eternity. Doing that job right, despite its setbacks and disappointments, is one of the greatest achievements in living.

I want to offer hope to those moms and dads today who are demoralized at this stage of the journey. First, you must recognize that strong-willed children are *not* a liability, and you should never let yourself feel victimized or cheated by having borne one of them. DO NOT compare your child with the "perfect" children of your relatives or friends. They will have their share of problems too in time. Admittedly, a tough-minded kid is tougher to raise and at times may push you right to the edge. But that wonderful assertiveness and determination will be an asset when your child is grown. That irritating temperament was a gift from God, and He makes no mistakes.

You should also recognize that these kids often possess a certain strength of character that will help them grab the opportunities that come their way. When they make up their minds to reach for something, they are likely to stay with it until the goal is achieved. They are also less susceptible to peer pressure, maybe not during early adolescence, but as maturity begins to set in. What I said before bears repeating. Though they typically argue and fight and complain throughout their years at home, the majority will turn around when they reach young adulthood and do what their parents most desire. Better days are around the corner.

However, the realization of that potential appears to depend on the provision of a structured early home environment led by loving, fair-minded mothers and fathers who are clearly tougher and wiser than their children. Those who are reasonably effective in shaping the will without breaking the spirit are going to appreciate the person their child eventually becomes.

That is what we found when we surveyed thirty-five thousand parents. More than 85 percent of adult strong-willed children who rebelled significantly during their teenage years came back to what they had been taught—entirely or at least somewhat. Only 15 percent were so headstrong that they rejected their family's core values in their midtwenties. These findings tell us that you, too, are probably doing a better job with your kids than you think. Future years will confirm that the guilt that haunted your thoughts and invaded your dreams was unjustified and self-imposed.

In short, the youngster who sometimes exasperates you today probably has little green buds growing all over his tree, even if all you see now are the barren twigs of winter. It will take time for him or her to flower, of course, but springtime is on its way. Trust me on this one.

It is always encouraging for me to hear from parents who have lived through the stresses of parenting and discovered that the principles of good parenting are valid. They work because they came from the Creator of children. One mother of a very strong-willed child sent me a letter some years ago after concluding, much too early, that my advice *didn't* work and that I must not have understood hardnosed youngsters like her own. This is what she wrote:

Dear Dr. Dobson:

After purchasing your book, The Strong-Willed Child, *I must tell you I was disappointed. The beginning was encouraging, but then the rest was devoted to general child-rearing techniques. I thought the entire book would be written about the strong-willed child. Are you sure you know what one is? Nearly every child is strong-willed, but not every child is "strong-willed!"*

Our third (and last) daughter is "strong-willed!" She is twenty-one months old now, and there have been times when I thought she must be abnormal. If she had been my firstborn child there would have been no more in this family. She had colic day and night for six months, then we just quit calling it that. She was simply unhappy all the time. She began walking at eight months and she became a merciless bully with her sisters. She pulled hair, bit, hit, pinched, and pushed with all her might. She yanked out a handful of her sister's long black hair.

This mother went on to describe the characteristics of her tyrannical daughter, which I have heard thousands of times. She then closed, advising me to give greater emphasis to the importance of corporal punishment for this kind of youngster.

I wrote her a cordial letter in reply and told her I understood the frustration. I attempted to encourage her and offer hope for the future. Five years later, she wrote me again:

Dear Dr. Dobson,

This letter is long overdue, but thank you! Thank you for a caring reply to what was probably not a very nice letter from a discouraged mom. Thank you for your positive remarks, the first I had had in a long time.

Perhaps you would be interested in an update on our Sally Ann. Back when I wrote to you, she was probably a perfect "10" when it came to strong-willedness. "Difficult" hardly scratches the surface of descriptive words for her babyhood. As Christian parents, we tried every scriptural method we could find for dealing with her. I had decided she was abnormal. Something so innocent as offering her morning juice (which she loved) in the wrong glass threw her into thirty minutes of tantrums—and this was before she could really talk! Family dinners were a nightmare.

Before she turned two, Sally Ann would regularly brutalize her older sisters, ages four, eight, and twelve, even bringing the twelve-year-old to tears many times. A spanking from me did not deter her in the least. Finally, in prayer one day the Lord plainly showed me that her sisters must be allowed to retaliate—something I was strictly against (and still am!). However, in this case, all I can say is that it worked. I carefully and clearly told my three girls (with little Sally Ann in my lap) what they were to do the next time they were attacked by their littlest sister: they were to give her a good smack on the top of her chubby little leg, next to her diaper. Sally got the point: within two days the attacks ceased.

Disciplining our youngest was never easy, but with God's help, we persevered. When she had to be spanked, we could expect up to an hour of tantrums. It would have been so easy to give in and ignore the misbehavior, but I am convinced that, without it, our Sally would have become at best a holy terror, and at worst, mentally ill. Tell your listeners that discipline does pay off, when administered according to the Word of God.

Sally today is a precious seven-year-old and a joy to her family. She is still rather strong-willed, but it is well within normal limits now! She is very bright and has a gentle, creative, and sympathetic nature unusual in one so young. I know the Lord has great plans for her. She has already asked Jesus into her life and knows how to call upon Him when she has a need (like fear from a nightmare, etc.).

In conclusion, though I still don't think you went far enough in your book, loving discipline certainly is the key. With perseverance!

Thank you and may God's continued blessing be upon you and your household and your ministry, through Jesus Christ our Lord.

In His love,
Mrs. W. W.

A Final Word of Encouragement

Once again, I wrote to this mother and concluded with these words:

Thank you too, Mrs. W., for your original letter and for this update. It was a special treat to hear from you again. You're obviously on the right track with Sally Ann. Hang in there during the adolescent challenges that still lie before you.

James Dobson

If Mrs. W. reads this revised edition of *The New Strong-Willed Child,* I want her to know that I had her in mind when I set out to rewrite it. I'd like to ask her if I got it closer to the target this second time around. She sounds like a mom I would like to meet.

Let's review the important concepts I have put forward one more time, focusing especially on the principles calculated to produce a positive outcome in the years to come.

1. You should not blame yourself for the temperament with which your child was born. She is simply a tough kid to handle, and your task is to match her stride for stride.
2. Your strong-willed child is in greater danger because of his inclination to test the limits and scale the walls. Your utmost diligence and wisdom will be required to deal with him. You simply have to be tougher than he is, but do it without being angry and oppressive.
3. If you fail to understand his lust for power and independence, you can exhaust your resources and bog down in guilt. It will benefit no one.
4. For parents who have just begun, take charge of your baby now, hold tightly to the reins of authority, and quickly begin building into her an attitude of respect and obedience. You will need every ounce of awe you can muster in coming years. Once you have established your right to lead, begin to let go of the reins systematically, year by year.
5. Don't panic, even during the storms of adolescence. They never last forever. The sun will shine again, producing, perhaps, a beautiful rainbow over your spirit. *You're going to get through this.*
6. Don't let your child stray too far from you emotionally. Stay in touch. Don't write him off, even when your every impulse is to do just that. He needs you now more than ever before.
7. Give that kid time to find herself, even if she appears not to be searching.

8. Most importantly, I urge you to hold your children before the Lord in fervent prayer day by day by day. Begin every morning with a prayer for wisdom and guidance. I am convinced that there is no other true source of confidence in parenting. There is not enough knowledge in the books, mine or anyone else's, to counteract the evil that surrounds our kids today. We must bathe them in fervent prayer when we are in our prayer closet, saying words similar to these:

"Lord, You know my inadequacies. You know my weaknesses, not only in parenting, but in every area of my life. I'm doing the best I can to raise my kids properly, but it may not be good enough. As You provided the fish and the loaves to feed the five thousand hungry people, now take my meager effort and use it to bless my family. Make up for the things I do wrong. Satisfy the needs that I have not met. Compensate for my blunders and mistakes. Wrap Your great arms around my children, and draw them close to You. And be there when they stand at the great crossroads between right and wrong. All I can give them is my best, and I will continue to do that. I submit them to You now and rededicate myself to the task You have placed before me. The outcome rests securely in Your hands."

I've found that God is faithful, as a loving Father, to hear and answer that cry of the heart. Turn to Him for solace when you've reached the end of your rope. He will be there to comfort you and work within the soul of your beloved child.

Well, we began this discussion twelve chapters ago with the story of our dog, Siggie, and his revolutionary tendencies. Let's end with an update. Siggie is long gone now, but we still miss him. It's hard to explain how a worthless old hound could be so loved by his family, although I'm sure other dog lovers will understand our sentiment. We were somewhat prepared for Siggie's demise, after being told by the vet that he had developed a progressive heart leak, but the moment of crisis came without warning.

I was brushing my teeth early one morning when I heard Siggie's sharp cry. He could scream like a baby, and my wife rushed to his assistance.

"Jim, come quickly!" she said. "Siggie is having a heart attack!" I rushed into the family room, toothbrush still in hand. Siggie was lying just outside his bed, and he appeared to be in great pain. He was hunched down on his paws; his eyes unfocused and glassy. I bent down and petted him gently and agreed that he was probably dying. I was not sure what to do for a dog in the midst of a heart attack, since paramedics are somewhat sensitive about offering their services to animals. I certainly wasn't going to give him CPR. I picked up Siggie and laid him carefully on his bed, and he rolled on one side and remained completely motionless. His feet were rigidly held together, and it did, indeed, look as though the end had come.

I returned to my study to telephone the veterinarian, but Shirley called me again. She had taken a closer look at the immobile dog and discovered the nature of his problem. (Are you ready for this?) There are little claws or toenails on the sides of a dog's legs, and Siggie had somehow managed to get them hooked! That is why he couldn't move, and why he yelped when he tried to walk. There is not another dog anywhere in the world that could have handcuffed (pawcuffed?) himself, but with Siggie anything was possible. Shirley unhooked his toenails, and the senile old dog celebrated by running around like a puppy again.

When I am an old man thinking back on the joys of parenting—the Christmas seasons and the camping trips and the high-pitched voices of two bubbly children in our home—I will also remember a stubborn little dachshund named Sigmund Freud and his mild-mannered canine successor, Mindy, who made such important contributions to our family throughout those happy days. One of them was stubborn as a mule; the other just wanted to do everything right. But we loved them both, and so it was with our children. One of them was strong-willed and the other compliant (but sneaky at times). They are grown now, and both of them turned out to be great human beings who love their parents (especially me) and are deeply committed to Jesus Christ. It doesn't get any better than that.

*"I have no greater joy than to hear
that my children are walking in the truth."*
(3 JOHN 4)

ENDNOTES

CHAPTER 1

[1]Jon Meacham, *Franklin and Winston: An Intimate Portrait of an Epic Friendship* (New York: Random House, 2003), 15.

CHAPTER 2

[1]Henry Wadsworth Longfellow, "There Was a Little Girl," *Random Memories* (Boston: Houghton Mifflin, 1922), 15.

CHAPTER 3

[1]John Caldwell Holt, *Escape from Childhood: The Needs and Rights of Children* (New York: Penguin Books, 1974).

[2]Jim Stingley, "Advocating Children's Liberation," *Los Angeles Times* (July 28, 1974).

[3]Raymond Corsini and Genevieve Painter, "A Marvelous New Way to Make Your Child Behave," *Family Circle* (April 1975): 26.

[4]Oklahoma State Department of Health Web page, "Positive Discipline," http://www.health.state.ok.us/program/mchecd/posdisc.html.

[5]L. S. Kabada, "Discipline Debate: Parents, Parenting Experts Divided over Dealing with Children's Behavior," *Chicago Tribune* (June 27, 1999): CN 7.

[6]Stella Chess and Alexander Thomas, *Know Your Child: An Authoritative Guide for Today's Parents* (New York: Basic Books, 1987).

[7]Ibid.

[8]Ibid.

[9]Ibid.

[10]Ibid.

[11]Ibid.

[12]Ibid.

[13]T. J. Bouchard, L. L. Heston, E. D. Eckert, M. Keyes, and S. Resnick, "The Minnesota Study of Twins Reared Apart: Project Description and Sample Results in the Developmental Domain" (1981).

[14]Ibid.

[15]M. McGue and D. T. Lykken, "Genetic Influence on Risk of Divorce," *Psychological Science* 3 (1992): 368–373.

[16]Ibid.

[17]James C. Dobson, Internal Study of 35,000 Parents. First published in *Parenting Isn't for Cowards* (Dallas: Word Publishing, 1987).

[18]Dobson, *Parenting Isn't for Cowards.*

[19]As quoted in General Douglas MacArthur's farewell speech, West Point (May 12, 1962).

CHAPTER 4

[1]James C. Dobson, *The New Dare to Discipline* (Wheaton, IL: Tyndale House Publishers, 1996).
[2]B. Spock and S. J. Parker, *Dr. Spock's Baby and Child Care* (New York: Pocket Books, 1998).
[3]Lisa Whelchel, *Creative Correction* (Wheaton, IL: Tyndale House Publishers, 2000).
[4]Susanna Wesley, "The Journal of John Wesley: The Mother of the Wesleys," http://www.ccel.org/w/wesley/journal/htm/vi.iv.xx.htm.
[5]Thomas Gordon, *Parenting Effectiveness Training: The Proven Program for Raising Responsible Children* (New York: Three Rivers Press, 2000).

CHAPTER 5

[1]Ronald Kotulak, "Babies Learn to Reason Earlier than Thought, Researcher Finds," *Chicago Tribune* (January 7, 1999): N4.
[2]Martha Sherrill, "Mrs. Clinton's Two Weeks out of Time: The Vigil for Her Father, Taking a Toll Both Public and Private," *The Washington Post* (April 3, 1993): C1.
[3]James C. Dobson, *Bringing Up Boys* (Wheaton, IL: Tyndale House Publishers, 2001).

CHAPTER 6

[1]"Parents May Worsen Terrible Twos," *Fort Worth Star Telegram* (April 7, 1999): 5.
[2]Spock and Parker, *Baby and Child Care*.
[3]Benjamin Spock, "How Not to Bring Up a Bratty Child," *Redbook* (February 1974): 29–31.
[4]Ibid.
[5]Ibid.

CHAPTER 7

[1]*American Psychological Association Monitor* 7, no. 4 (1976).
[2]T. Berry Brazelton, *Toddlers and Parents: A Declaration of Independence* (New York: Delacorte Press, 1974), 101–110.
[3]Ibid.
[4]Oklahoma State Department of Health Web page, "Positive Discipline."
[5]Luther Woodward, *Your Child from Two to Five,* ed. Morton Edwards (New York: Permabooks, 1955), 95–96.
[6]Ibid.
[7]Ibid.
[8]Ibid.
[9]Dobson, *The New Dare to Discipline*.
[10]Reprinted by permission of United Press International.
[11]H. T. Harbin and D. J. Madden, "Battered Parents: A New Syndrome," *American Journal of Psychiatry* 136 (1979): 1288–1291.

CHAPTER 8

[1]Author Unknown. The poem "Behind in His Reading" was sent to me by Freda Carver, a former librarian at Focus on the Family.
[2]Patrice O'Shaughnessy with Michael S. C. Claffey, Russ Buettner, Robert Gearty, Anemona Hartocollis, and Barbara Ross, "Child's Doomed Life," *New York Daily News* (November 26, 1995): 5.
[3]Ibid.
[4]Ibid.
[5]Ibid.
[6]L. G. Russek and G. E. Schwartz, "Perceptions of Parental Caring Predict Health Status in

Midlife: A 35-Year Follow-Up of the Harvard Mastery of Stress Study," *Psychosomatic Medicine* 59, no. 2 (1997): 144–149.

[7]Ibid.

[8]Ibid.

[9]Ibid.

[10]Scott M. Montgomery, Mel J. Bartley, and Richard G. Wilkinson, "Family Conflict and Slow Growth," *Archives of Disease in Childhood* 77 (1997): 326–330.

[11]Ibid.

[12]Ibid.

[13]Dobson, *The New Dare to Discipline.*

[14]Den A. Trumbull and S. Dubose Ravenel, "To Spank or Not to Spank," *Physician.*

[15]Ibid.

[16]Ibid.

[17]Internal memo (January 28, 1982). Phone conversation with California Assemblyman John Vasconcellos, citing recommendations contained in the report from the Commission on Crime Control and Violence.

[18]Ben Sherwood, "Even Spanking Is Outlawed: Once-Stern Sweden Leads Way in Children's Rights," *Los Angeles Times* (August 11, 1985): A2.

[19]Kathleen Engman, "Corporal Punishment v. Child Abuse: Society Struggles to Define 'Reasonable Force,'" *The Ottawa Citizen* (December 30, 1996): C8.

CHAPTER 9

[1]Marguerite and Willard Beecher, *Parents on the Run: A Commonsense Book for Today's Parents* (New York: Crown Publishers, Inc., 1955), 6–8.

[2]Dobson, *Parenting Isn't for Cowards.*

[3]U.S. Census Bureau, "Census 2000 Summary," http://factfinder.census.gov/servlet/QTTable?_bm=y&-geo_id=01000US&-qr_name=DEC_2000_SF1_U_QTP10&-ds_name=DEC_2000_SF1_U&-_lang=en&-_sse=on.

CHAPTER 10

[1]Nielsen Report, 2000.

[2]MTV Media Kit (1993).

[3]*Associated Press* (February 2, 2004): "Nielsen estimates that 143.6 million people watched at least part of the game."

[4]D. Donahue, "Struggling to Raise Good Kids in Toxic Times: Is Innocence Evaporating in an Open-Door Society?" *USA Today* (October 1, 1998): D1.

[5]Ibid.

[6]Ellen Edwards, "Plugged-In Generation: More than Ever, Kids Are at Home with Media," *Washington Post* (November 18, 1999): A1.

[7]David Bauder, "Survey: It May Not Be Punishment to Send Children to Their Rooms," *Associated Press* (June 26, 1997).

[8]Dobson, *Bringing Up Boys.*

[9]Urie Bronfenbrenner, "The Social Ecology of Human Development," *Brain and Intelligence: The Ecology of Child Development*, ed. Fredrick Richardson (Hyattsville, Md.: National Educational Press, 1973).

[10]K. Bosworth, D. L. Espelage, and T. R. Simon, "Factors Associated with Bullying Behavior in Middle School Students," *Educational Research* 41, no. 2 (1999): 137–153.

[11]Maria Bartini and Anthony Pellegrini, "Dominance in Early Adolescent Boys: Affiliative and Aggressive Dimensions and Possible Functions," *Merrill-Palmer Quarterly* (2001).

[12]Shannon Brownlee, Roberta Hotinski, Bellamy Pailthorp, Erin Ragan, and Kathleen Wong, "Inside the Teen Brain," *US News & World Report* (August 9, 1999): 44.

[13]Ibid.

[14]Ibid.

[15]B. S. Bowden and J. M. Zeisz, "Supper's On! Adolescent Adjustment and Frequency of Family Mealtimes," paper presented at 105th annual meeting of the American Psychological Association, Chicago (1997).

[16]Daisy Yu, "A Consumer Underclass: Scorned Teens," *Los Angeles Times* (March 18, 2001): B13.

[17]Ibid.

[18]James Brooke, "Terror in Littleton: The Overview: 2 Students in Colorado School Said to Gun Down As Many As 23 and Kill Themselves in a Siege," *The New York Times* (April 21, 1999): A6.

[19]Patricia Hersch, *A Tribe Apart: A Journey into the Heart of American Adolescence* (New York: Ballantine Books, 1999).

[20]M. D. Resnick, P. S. Bearman, R. W. Blum, K. E. Bauman, K. M. Harris, J. Jones, J. Tabor, T. Beuhring, R. Sieving, M. Shew, M. Ireland, L. H. Bearinger, and J. R. Udry, "Protecting Adolescents from Harm: Finding from the National Longitudinal Study on Adolescent Health," *Journal of the American Medical Association* 278; "New Analyses of National Data Reveal Risk, Protective Factors for Youth Violence and Other Risks, Leading Researchers Report at Capitol Hill Briefing," PR Newswire (June 3, 1999).

[21]Andrea Billups, "The State of Our Nation's Youth: Most Teenagers Rate Parents Number 1: Poll Shows Fear of Violence, Worry over Decline of Families," *The Washington Times* (August 11, 1999): A6.

[22]Barbara Kantrowitz and Pat Wingert with Anne Underwood, "How Well Do You Know Your Kid?" *Newsweek* (May 10, 1999): 36.

[23]Michael Medved and David Wallechinsky, *What Really Happened to the Class of '65?* (New York: Random House, Inc., 1976).

[24]Ibid.

[25]Ibid.

[26]Ibid.

[27]Ibid.

[28]Domeena C. Renshaw, *The Hyperactive Child* (Chicago: Nelson-Hall Publishers, 1974).

[29]Deborah Davis Locker, "Bomb Threats Shake Hartland District: Schools Boost Security, Add Cameras after Six Warning Notes Are Left," *The Detroit News* (November 5, 2002): C5.

CHAPTER 11

[1]Dennis Swanberg, Diane Passno, and Walt Larimore, *Why A.D.H.D. Doesn't Mean Disaster* (Wheaton, IL: Tyndale House Publishers, 2004); Russell A. Barkley, "Attention Deficit Hyperactivity Disorder," online lecture, University of Massachusetts Medical Center, Worcester, Mass.

[2]Claudia Wallis, "Life in Overdrive: Doctors Say Huge Numbers of Kids and Adults Have Attention Deficit Disorder: Is It for Real?" *Time* (July 18, 1994): 42.

[3]Swanberg, Passno, and Larimore, *Why A.D.H.D. Doesn't Mean Disaster*.

[4]Ibid.

[5]Ibid.

[6]Ibid.

[7]Edward Hallowell and John Ratey, *Driven to Distraction: Recognizing and Coping with Attention Deficit Disorder from Childhood through Adulthood* (New York: Simon & Schuster, 1995), 73–76.

Endnotes

[8]Wallis, "Life in Overdrive," 42.

[9]L. Goldman, M. Genel, R. Bezman, and P. Slanetz, "Diagnosis and Treatment of Attention-Deficit/Hyperactivity Disorder in Children and Adolescents," *Journal of the American Medical Association* (April 1998): 1100–1107.

[10]J. P. Guevara and M. T. Stein, "Evidence Based Management of Attention Deficit Hyperactivity Disorder," *British Medical Journal* (November 2001): 1232–1235.

[11]G. B. LeFever, K. V. Dawson, and A. L. Morrow, "The Extent of Drug Therapy for Attention Deficit-Hyperactivity Disorder among Children in Public Schools," *American Journal of Public Health* (September 1999): 1359–1364.

[12]Centers for Disease Control and Prevention report (May 2002), http://www.cdc.gov/nchs/releases/02news/attendefic.htm.

[13]R. J. DeGrandpre, *Ritalin Nation: Rapid-Fire Culture and the Transformation of Human Consciousness* (New York: W. W. Norton & Company, 2000).

[14]D. Papolos and J. Papolos, *The Bipolar Child* (New York: Broadway Books, 1999), chapter 6.

[15]S. Pliszka, "The Use of Psychostimulants in the Pediatric Patient," *Pediatric Clinics of North America* (October 1998): 1087, citing J. Elia, B. G. Borcherding, J. L. Rapoport, and C. S. Keysor, "Methylphenidate and Dextroamphetamine Treatments of Hyperactivity: Are There True Nonresponders?" *Psychiatry Research* (February 1991): 141–155.

[16]"Medication for Children with Attentional Disorders." American Academy of Pediatrics Committee on Children with Disabilities and Committee on Drugs, *Pediatrics* (August 1996): 301–304.

[17]C. J. Musser, P. A. Ahmann, F. W. Theyer, P. Mundt, S. K. Broste, and N. Mueller-Rizner, "Stimulant Use and the Potential for Abuse in Wisconsin As Reported by School Administrators and Longitudinally Followed Children," *Journal of Developmental Behavior Pediatrics* (June 1998): 187–192.

[18]Mari Yamaguchi, "Japan Develops Gadget to Alert Bed-Wetting Children," *Associated Press* (April 20, 1999).

[19]Willard Hartup, http://www.personal.psu.edu/faculty/j/g/jgp4/research/clippings/rroom.htm.

[20]J. J. Gillis, J. W. Gilger, B. F. Pennington, and J. C. DeFries, "Attention Deficit Disorder in Reading Disabled Twins: Evidence for a Genetic Etiology," *Journal of Abnormal Child Psychology* (June 1992): 303–315.

[21]H. Gjone, J. Stevenson, and J. M. Sundet, "Genetic Influence on Parent-Reported Attention-Related Problems in a Norwegian General Population Twin Sample," *Journal of the American Academy of Child and Adolescent Psychiatry* (May 1996): 588–596.

[22]Renshaw, *The Hyperactive Child,* 118–120.

CHAPTER 12

[1]C. S. Lewis, *The Four Loves* (New York: Harvest Books, 1971).

Whether you received *The New Strong-Willed Child* as a gift, borrowed it from a friend, or purchased it yourself, we're glad you read it. Dr. James Dobson, the author of this book, founded Focus on the Family in 1977 to address the many challenges and needs facing today's family.

If this book has been helpful and you would like to receive more information on child rearing or other family issues, Focus on the Family is here to assist you.

www.family.org
(800) A-FAMILY

Visit

www.christianbookguides.com

for a discussion guide for *The New Strong-Willed Child*.